also by america's test kitchen

Vegetables Illustrated

The New Essentials Cookbook

Cook's Illustrated Revolutionary Recipes

Dinner Illustrated

Tasting Italy: A Culinary Journey

The Complete Diabetes Cookbook

The Complete Slow Cooker

The Complete Make-Ahead Cookbook

The Complete Mediterranean Cookbook

The Complete Vegetarian Cookbook

The Complete Cooking for Two Cookbook

Cooking at Home with Bridget and Julia

Just Add Sauce

How to Roast Everything

How to Braise Everything

Nutritious Delicious

What Good Cooks Know

Cook's Science

The Science of Good Cooking

The Perfect Cake

The Perfect Cookie

Bread Illustrated

Master of the Grill

Kitchen Smarts

Kitchen Hacks

100 Recipes: The Absolute Best Ways to
Make the True Essentials

The New Family Cookbook

The America's Test Kitchen Cooking School Cookbook

The Cook's Illustrated Meat Book

The Cook's Illustrated Baking Book

The Cook's Illustrated Cookbook

The America's Test Kitchen Family Baking Book

The Best of America's Test Kitchen (2007–2019 Editions)

The Complete America's Test Kitchen TV Show
Cookbook 2001–2019

Air Fryer Perfection

Cook It in Your Dutch Oven

Sous Vide for Everybody

Multicooker Perfection

Food Processor Perfection

Pressure Cooker Perfection

Vegan for Everybody

Naturally Sweet

Foolproof Preserving

Paleo Perfected

The How Can It Be Gluten-Free Cookbook: Volume 2

The How Can It Be Gluten-Free Cookbook

The Best Mexican Recipes

Slow Cooker Revolution Volume 2: The Easy-Prep Edition

Slow Cooker Revolution

The Six-Ingredient Solution

The America's Test Kitchen D.I.Y. Cookbook

THE COOK'S ILLUSTRATED ALL-TIME BEST SERIES

All-Time Best Brunch

All-Time Best Dinners for Two

All-Time Best Sunday Suppers

All-Time Best Holiday Entertaining

All-Time Best Appetizers

All-Time Best Soups

COOK'S COUNTRY TITLES

One-Pan Wonders

Cook It in Cast Iron

Cook's Country Eats Local

The Complete Cook's Country TV Show Cookbook

FOR A FULL LISTING OF ALL OUR BOOKS

CooksIllustrated.com

AmericasTestKitchen.com

praise for america's test kitchen titles

"It's all about technique and timing, and the ATK crew delivers their usual clear instructions to ensure success. . . . The thoughtful balance of practicality and imagination will inspire readers of all tastes and skill levels."

PUBLISHERS WEEKLY (STARRED REVIEW) ON *HOW TO ROAST EVERYTHING*

"This encyclopedia of meat cookery would feel completely overwhelming if it weren't so meticulously organized and artfully designed. This is Cook's Illustrated at its finest."

THE KITCHN ON *THE COOK'S ILLUSTRATED MEAT BOOK*

"*The Perfect Cookie* . . . is, in a word, perfect. This is an important and substantial cookbook. . . . If you love cookies, but have been a tad shy to bake on your own, all your fears will be dissipated. This is one book you can use for years with magnificently happy results."

THE HUFFINGTON POST ON *THE PERFECT COOKIE*

Selected as one of the 10 Best New Cookbooks of 2017

THE LA TIMES ON *THE PERFECT COOKIE*

Selected as the Cookbook Award Winner of 2017 in the Baking category

INTERNATIONAL ASSOCIATION OF CULINARY PROFESSIONALS (IACP) ON *BREAD ILLUSTRATED*

Selected as one of Amazon's Best Books of 2015 in the Cookbooks and Food Writing category

AMAZON ON *THE COMPLETE VEGETARIAN COOKBOOK*

"This book upgrades slow cooking for discriminating, 21st-century palates—that is indeed revolutionary."

THE DALLAS MORNING NEWS ON *SLOW COOKER REVOLUTION*

"A beautifully illustrated, 318-page culinary compendium showcasing an impressive variety and diversity of authentic Mexican cuisine."

MIDWEST BOOK REVIEW ON *THE BEST MEXICAN RECIPES*

"Some 2,500 photos walk readers through 600 painstakingly tested recipes, leaving little room for error."

ASSOCIATED PRESS ON *THE AMERICA'S TEST KITCHEN COOKING SCHOOL COOKBOOK*

"This book is a comprehensive, no-nonsense guide . . . a well-thought-out, clearly explained primer for every aspect of home baking."

THE WALL STREET JOURNAL ON *THE COOK'S ILLUSTRATED BAKING BOOK*

"If there's room in the budget for one multicooker/Instant Pot cookbook, make it this one."

BOOKLIST ON *MULTICOOKER PERFECTION*

"The book offers an impressive education for curious cake makers, new and experienced alike. A summation of 25 years of cake making at ATK, there are cakes for every taste."

THE WALL STREET JOURNAL ON *THE PERFECT CAKE*

"Some books impress by the sheer audacity of their ambition. Backed up by the magazine's famed mission to test every recipe relentlessly until it is the best it can be, this nearly 900-page volume lands with an authoritative wallop."

CHICAGO TRIBUNE ON *THE COOK'S ILLUSTRATED COOKBOOK*

"The 21st-century *Fannie Farmer Cookbook* or *The Joy of Cooking*. If you had to have one cookbook and that's all you could have, this one would do it."

CBS SAN FRANCISCO ON *THE NEW FAMILY COOKBOOK*

"The go-to gift book for newlyweds, small families, or empty nesters."

ORLANDO SENTINEL ON *THE COMPLETE COOKING FOR TWO COOKBOOK*

"The sum total of exhaustive experimentation . . . anyone interested in gluten-free cookery simply shouldn't be without it."

NIGELLA LAWSON ON *THE HOW CAN IT BE GLUTEN-FREE COOKBOOK*

"A one-volume kitchen seminar, addressing in one smart chapter after another the sometimes surprising whys behind a cook's best practices. . . . You get the myth, the theory, the science, and the proof, all rigorously interrogated as only America's Test Kitchen can do."

NPR ON *THE SCIENCE OF GOOD COOKING*

"This impressive installment from America's Test Kitchen equips readers with dozens of repertoire-worthy recipes. . . . This is a must-have for beginner cooks and more experienced ones who wish to sharpen their skills."

PUBLISHERS WEEKLY (STARRED REVIEW) ON *THE NEW ESSENTIALS COOKBOOK*

spiced

UNLOCK THE POWER OF SPICES TO TRANSFORM YOUR COOKING

AMERICA'S TEST KITCHEN

Library of Congress Cataloging-in-Publication Data
Names: America's Test Kitchen (Firm)
Title: Spiced : unlock the power of spices to transform your cooking / America's Test Kitchen.
Description: Boston, MA : America's Test Kitchen, [2019] | Includes index.
Identifiers: LCCN 2018053510 | ISBN 9781945256776 (hardcover)
Subjects: LCSH: Cooking (Herbs) | Spices. | LCGFT: Cookbooks.
Classification: LCC TX819.H4 S67 2019 | DDC 641.6/383--dc23
LC record available at https://lccn.loc.gov/2018053510

AMERICA'S TEST KITCHEN

AMERICA'S TEST KITCHEN
21 Drydock Avenue, Boston, MA 02210

Manufactured in the United States of America
10 9 8 7 6 5 4 3 2 1

Distributed by Penguin Random House Publisher Services
Tel: 800.733.3000

Pictured on front cover Chicken Tagine with Fennel, Chickpeas, and Apricots (page 140)

Pictured on back cover Spice-Crusted Rib-Eye Steaks (page 86), Ginger-Turmeric Frozen Yogurt (page 269), Tandoori Chicken with Raita (page 143), Spice-Infused Oils (page 204), Smoky Shishito Peppers with Espelette and Lime (page 167)

Editorial Director, Books **Elizabeth Carduff**

Executive Editor **Adam Kowit**

Executive Food Editor **Dan Zuccarello**

Deputy Food Editor **Anne Wolf**

Senior Editors **Leah Colins, Sacha Madadian**

Associate Editors **Tim Chin, Joseph Gitter**

Editorial Assistant **Brenna Donovan**

Art Director, Books **Lindsey Timko Chandler**

Deputy Art Directors **Allison Boales, Courtney Lentz, and Janet Taylor**

Associate Art Director **Katie Barranger**

Photography Director **Julie Bozzo Cote**

Photography Producer **Meredith Mulcahy**

Contributing Photography Direction **Kristen Connors, Susan Levin, Tabitha Rodrigue**

Senior Staff Photographer **Daniel J. van Ackere**

Staff Photographers **Steve Klise and Kevin White**

Additional Photography **Keller + Keller and Carl Tremblay**

Food Styling **Tara Busa, Catrine Kelty, Chantal Lambeth, Kendra McKnight, Elle Simone Scott, and Kendra Smith**

Photoshoot Kitchen Team

    Photo Team and Special Events Manager **Timothy McQuinn**

    Lead Test Cook **Jessica Rudolph**

    Assistant Test Cooks **Sarah Ewald, Jacqueline Gochenouer, and Eric Haessler**

Senior Manager, Publishing Operations **Taylor Argenzio**

Production Manager **Christine Spanger**

Imaging Manager **Lauren Robbins**

Production and Imaging Specialists **Dennis Noble, Jessica Voas, and Amanda Yong**

Copy Editor **Deri Reed**

Proofreader **Elizabeth Wray Emery**

Indexer **Elizabeth Parson**

Chief Creative Officer **Jack Bishop**

Executive Editorial Directors **Julia Collin Davison and Bridget Lancaster**

contents

welcome to america's test kitchen

This book has been tested, written, and edited by the folks at America's Test Kitchen. Located in Boston's Seaport District in the historic Innovation and Design Building, it features 15,000 square feet of kitchen space, including multiple photography and video studios. It is the home of *Cook's Illustrated* magazine and *Cook's Country* magazine and is the workday destination for more than 60 test cooks, editors, and cookware specialists. Our mission is to test recipes over and over again until we understand how and why they work and until we arrive at the best version.

We start the process of testing a recipe with a complete lack of preconceptions, which means that we accept no claim, no technique, and no recipe at face value. We simply assemble as many variations as possible, test a half-dozen of the most promising, and taste the results blind. We then construct our own recipe and continue to test it, varying ingredients, techniques, and cooking times until we reach a consensus. As we like to say in the test kitchen, "We make the mistakes so you don't have to." The result, we hope, is the best version of a particular recipe, but we realize that only you can be the final judge of our success (or failure). We use the same rigorous approach when we test equipment and taste ingredients.

All of this would not be possible without a belief that good cooking, much like good music, is based on a foundation of objective technique. Some people like spicy foods and others don't, but there is a right way to sauté, there is a best way to cook a pot roast, and there are measurable scientific principles involved in producing perfectly beaten, stable egg whites. Our ultimate goal is to investigate the fundamental principles of cooking to give you the techniques, tools, and ingredients you need to become a better cook. It is as simple as that.

To see what goes on behind the scenes at America's Test Kitchen, check out our social media channels for kitchen snapshots, exclusive content, video tips, and much more. You can watch us work (in our actual test kitchen) by tuning in to *America's Test Kitchen* or *Cook's Country* on public television or on our websites. Listen in to test kitchen experts on public radio (SplendidTable.org) to hear insights that illuminate the truth about real home cooking. Want to hone your cooking skills or finally learn how to bake—with an America's Test Kitchen test cook? Enroll in one of our online cooking classes. However you choose to visit us, we welcome you into our kitchen, where you can stand by our side as we test our way to the best recipes in America.

facebook.com/AmericasTestKitchen
twitter.com/TestKitchen
youtube.com/AmericasTestKitchen
instagram.com/TestKitchen
pinterest.com/TestKitchen

AmericasTestKitchen.com
CooksIllustrated.com
CooksCountry.com
OnlineCookingSchool.com

spice your way to flavor

introduction

You might think of spices as culinary accessories—nice additions to well-cooked food but not necessary ones. But a steak, even if rosy-red inside and buttery-tender, is something much better when salted to its middle and coated in cracked peppercorns that enhance its browned crust. Burnished roasted vegetables on your plate become more enticing with a sprinkling of an eye-catching, fragrant spice-and-nut mix. Spices are much more than accessory: They bring food to life, providing warmth and aroma to dishes; they elevate even a salad to a multidimensional masterpiece; and they introduce us to the flavor profiles of cuisines of the world. Adding spice is the simplest way to take a dish beyond basic, and we think that knowing techniques for doing so is an important part of cooking well, just like knowing how to sauté or roast.

We're here to teach you about the world of spices, yes—the spices in our arsenal (from Aleppo pepper to wasabi powder) as well as how to make your own spice blends (and why you should). But learning about different spices isn't enough to make you a better cook: What makes *Spiced*, we think, revolutionary is that it delves into the *hows* of seasoning food. We teach you that no matter the spice or blend you reach for—and to some extent no matter the cuisine—there are key techniques that will unlock the spice's flavors and aromas and make your food taste its best. That's why we've structured this cookbook so each chapter isn't about a type of spice or a type of food, but about concrete—and easy—methods for working with spices. In each, you'll learn different ways to apply spices before, during, or even after the cooking process for extraordinary, confidence-building results.

There's a whole chapter that focuses on the spice building blocks: salt and pepper. Find out why salt doesn't just flavor food but affects its texture, too. Make your own flavored salts like Fresh Herb Salt or Cumin-Sesame Salt to add a special touch to your next pork chop or fish fillet. Learn the flavor differences behind a rainbow of peppercorns, from floral to piney. Or check out a chapter about coating all kinds of foods (not just meat!) with homemade spice rubs like Jerk Rub and Classic Steak Rub, or one that teaches the importance of toasting or blooming (cooking in oil or butter) dried chiles or other spices at the start of cooking to produce chilis, curries, stews, and more boasting incredible depth of flavor. On the flip side, a chapter on finishing spices shows how a last-minute sprinkle or a drizzle of the right blend, spiced sauce, or condiment can add flavor and texture to already-cooked food. And don't forget dessert: You'll see that spices—and not just cinnamon and vanilla—have their place in baked goods and sweets.

Along the way, you'll find 139 recipes for meals, appetizers, and sides to which you can apply these techniques and 47 homemade spice blends. Or feel free to branch out on your own. Once you unlock the world of possibility hidden in your pantry, your meals will instantly improve and feature flavors from around the globe—in a sprinkle, drizzle, or dash.

how to use this book

This isn't just a book of spiced recipes, and there are many ways you can apply the spices in these pages to your food. Here's a guide to a few different ways to use this book to spice up your dishes.

get a lesson in spices

This introduction teaches you the basics: what spices we use, their flavor profiles and unique characteristics, and what kinds of blends and condiments we make from them. We'll also provide recipe suggestions for spices and blends to get you started with them. This is the first step to being confident in reaching for different spices in your cooking.

master techniques for applying spices

Each chapter presents a category of techniques for working with spices, and follows with foolproof recipes that put the technique to use. For example, in a chapter that covers blooming spices you'll learn that dumping and stirring curry powder into the pot will result in curry with a dusty flavor or texture; you must cook the curry powder in oil before introducing other ingredients to bring out its warm notes. Another chapter helps you to recreate spice rubs you see on supermarket shelves and shows how to use them on everything from roasted meats to nuts. Like to DIY? There's a chapter for that: Make infusions—like spice oils or brines for pickles—and find recipes that use them to add intrigue to food.

be your own spice blender

Spices are often best when they work in harmony. Each chapter provides recipes for multipurpose spice blends. (If you don't want to make them yourself, you can purchase premade blends from the supermarket.) You'll find recipes using all of the blends, but we also offer simple ideas for incorporating the blends in your everyday cooking. (You might be surprised how simple foods—say a dish of rice—can transcend the ordinary when spiced.)

start with the main event

Take what you brought home from the market— vegetables, grains, proteins—and then flip through the pages of this book for spicy suggestions.

chicken + spice = 5 ways to a livelier dinner

How do you perk up this go-to protein? Let's count the ways spices prevent main dish monotony.

1 sprinkle it with salt Top your salad with grilled chicken and a sprinkle of coarse finishing salt so each component sings (page 32).

2 rub it with spice Rub a spice blend on top and underneath a whole chicken's skin for flavor throughout (page 72).

3 simmer it in bloomed spices Unlock the flavor of spices by sautéing them and then build a braised chicken dish from this flavor base (page 141).

4 finish it with spice Crispy meets creamy when chicken cutlets are paired with a sauce spiked with homemade curry powder (page 189).

5 bathe it in an infusion Lavish a chicken-and-couscous one-pan supper with chili-and-spice-infused harissa paste (page 213).

what's a spice?

When you hear "spice," you might immediately think of the earthy-toned grounds sold in jars. Of course, those spices are ground from a particle bigger than themselves—whole spices, which are of different shapes and sizes as they come from various parts of plants. While there is no single definition for a spice and different resources categorize them in various ways, we're defining spices as anything from a plant that is dried and can flavor food (that includes tea!). (Note: Some sources exclude anything coming from leaves, flowers, or stems from the appellation, putting them in an exclusive herb category, but since we use these in the same way, they're welcome here.) Here are the major categories of whole spices we use—some we leave whole to infuse foods with flavor or to add texture, some we grind in blends, and some we use both ways.

salt
Salt might not be a plant, but we include this mineral because it's a primary—actually, the most essential—seasoning of food. It can come from salt mines or from evaporating sea water.

seeds
Seeds are the embryos of plant life—and many are edible, flavorful seasonings. Some are more herbal in flavor like cumin and coriander seeds; some are aromatic like the cardamom seeds that live inside its pods; some are nuttier like sesame seeds or poppy seeds.

roots and rhizomes
These are the parts of the plant that live under the soil (rhizomes are simply a large group of roots) and are dried and often ground, like ginger and turmeric.

buds and flowers
Ranging from unopened flower buds like cloves to the buds and petals of roses or lavender flowers, these can be warm and earthy or bright, perfume-y, and floral.

arils
Arils grow from a fruit's seed and cover the seed in lacy fashion. Mace, for example, is the aril that surrounds nutmeg.

stigmas
These are a flower's pollen receivers. The most expensive spice in the world—saffron—is the dried stigmas of the crocus flower; saffron is so expensive because the stigmas are painstaking to extract.

fruits and berries
After flowering, a plant bears fruit. If it can be dried for use as a seasoning, it's a spice. Chiles, allspice, star anise, true peppercorns, pink peppercorns, and vanilla beans are all examples.

dried herbs
These are the dried leaves of plants, from piney rosemary to coarser thyme and leafier oregano.

bark
Bark doesn't sound appetizing? Well one of our favorite spices—the many species of cinnamon—comes from tree bark.

how we use spices

The power of spices comes not just from their inherent intense flavors, but from the ways those flavors are released during cooking or how they're combined with other ingredients to create complex new tastes. Here are common ways in which we apply spices and spice blends in our cooking.

coarse finishing salts
Special textured salts finish dishes with pop and crunch.
Page 22

flavored salts
Salinity + spice (or herb or zest or seed) = a finishing flavor explosion that cuts through rich dishes and accents mild ones. *Page 24*

dry rubs
Complementary spices come together to coat food with flavor. *Page 73*

wet rubs
Mix a spice rub with oil or another liquid and it will spread into all the nooks and crannies of foods. *Page 80*

toasted dried chiles
Toasting a chile releases grassy, fruity, or warm aromas, which add complexity to sauces and stews. *Page 114*

blooming spice blends
When bloomed in hot oil, spice blends—from chili to curry powders—start dishes with global flavor. *Page 116*

spiced sauces

Stir spices into a sauce mixture and then dip, drip, dollop, drizzle, or douse flavor onto food. *Page 178*

finishing spice blends

Add incredible flavor (and crunch) to finished dishes with just a sprinkle. *Page 156*

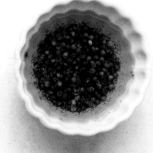

spice-infused oils

Steep spices in oil and use to dip your bread or anoint your food with style. *Page 204*

spice-infused vinegars

Oil isn't the only medium for infusion; steep chiles in vinegar and splash rich dishes with bright heat. *Page 223*

condiments

Pickles, olives, chutneys, mayonnaise (or aïoli if you're fancy) are all better with a spicy kick. *Page 223*

infusions and distillations

Get the essence of spice—without the solids—in extracts that flavor dessert. *Page 236*

spiced sugars

Cinnamon and spice make sugar nice; mix spices with sugar for blends that flavor desserts. *Page 234*

spice blends

Combine spices (and other ingredients) to create blends that give recipes flavor and flair.

recipes and their spices

This recipe list shows at a glance which spices and blends are used in which recipes.

breakfast and breads

Blueberry Streusel Muffins (238): *cinnamon, vanilla*

Everything Bagel Bread (250): *Everything Bagel Blend (159)*

Pumpkin Spice Muffins (241): *Pumpkin Pie Spice (234), vanilla*

Pumpkin Spice Sugar Doughnuts (243): *Pumpkin Pie Spice (234)*

Rose Water–Glazed Doughnuts (243): *Rose Water (237)*

Spiced Granola with Walnuts and Dried Apple (247): *Pumpkin Pie Spice (234), vanilla*

St. Lucia Buns (244): *saffron, turmeric*

Strawberry–Black Pepper Sugar Doughnuts (243): *Strawberry–Black Pepper Sugar (234)*

Tropical Granola with Dried Mango and Ginger (247): *ginger, nutmeg, vanilla*

Vanilla Sugar Doughnuts (242): *Vanilla Sugar (234)*

Za'atar Finger Bread (253): *Za'atar (156), coarse finishing salt*

appetizers and snacks

Barbecue-Spiced Roasted Chickpeas (164): *smoked paprika, garlic powder, onion powder*

Black Pepper Candied Bacon (109): *black peppercorn*

Blue Cheese Log with Pistachio Dukkah and Honey (168): *Pistachio Dukkah (158)*

Bruschetta with Ricotta, Roasted Red Peppers, and Rosemary Oil (207): *Rosemary Oil (204)*

Cheddar Cheese Log with Everything Bagel Blend (159): *Everything Bagel Blend (158)*

Chili-Lime Spiced Nuts (110): *chili powder, cumin, cayenne*

Chipotle Candied Bacon (109): *chipotle chile powder, cumin, garlic powder*

Cinnamon-Ginger Spiced Nuts (110): *cinnamon, ginger, coriander*

Feta Cheese Log with Advieh and Olive Oil (169): *Advieh (156)*

Five-Spice and Sesame Candied Bacon (109): *Five-Spice Powder (74), sesame seed*

Goat Cheese Log with Hazelnut-Nigella Dukkah (169): *Hazelnut-Nigella Dukkah (158)*

Homemade Yogurt Cheese with Hazelnut-Nigella Dukkah (161): *Hazelnut-Nigella Dukkah (158)*

Hot-and-Sweet Popcorn (163): *cinnamon, chili powder*

Marinated Green and Black Olives (209): *dried oregano, dried thyme, red pepper flake*

Marinated Cauliflower and Chickpeas with Saffron (210): *saffron, smoked paprika*

Orange-Cardamom Spiced Nuts (110): *cardamom, black peppercorn, vanilla extract*

Parmesan–Black Pepper Popcorn (163): *black peppercorn*

Polenta Fries with Saffron Aïoli (186): *coarse finishing salt, Saffron Aïoli (181)*

Radish Baguette with Chive Butter and Salt (29): *coarse finishing salt*

Shishito Peppers with Fennel Pollen, Aleppo, and Lemon (167): *aleppo, fennel pollen*

Shishito Peppers with Mint, Poppy Seeds, and Orange (167): *dried mint, poppy seeds*

Shishito Peppers with Mustard and Bonito Flakes (167): *dry mustard*

Smoky Shishito Peppers with Espelette and Lime (167): *espelette pepper, paprika*

Southern Cheese Straws (249): *paprika, cayenne*

Spanish-Spiced Roasted Chickpeas (164): *coriander, cumin, smoked paprika*

Spiced Roasted Chickpeas (164): *paprika, coriander, turmeric, allspice, cumin, cayenne*

salads

Chicken Salad with Pickled Fennel, Watercress, and Macadamia Nuts (224): *fennel, black peppercorn, mustard seed*

Fattoush (183): *sumac*

Grilled Chicken Salad (32): *coarse finishing salt*

Smashed Cucumber Salad (Pai Huang Gua) (66): *salt, sesame seed, Sichuan Chili Oil (205)*

Wasabi Tuna Salad (185): *Wasabi Mayonnaise (180)*

Wedge Salad with Creamy Black Pepper Dressing (30): *black peppercorn*

beef

Best Ground Beef Chili (122): *ancho chile, cumin, coriander, paprika, garlic powder, dried mexican oregano, black peppercorn, dried thyme, chipotle chile*

Coffee-Chipotle Top Sirloin Roast (89): *chipotle chile, coriander, paprika, dry mustard, coarse finishing salt*

Crispy Spiced Ground Beef Tacos (126): *Smoky Cocoa Chili Powder (117)*

Flank Steak Tacos with Cumin and Corn Relish (229): *cumin, coriander*

Green Peppercorn–Crusted Beef Tenderloin with Sun-Dried Tomato Hollandaise Sauce (39): *green peppercorn, nutmeg*

Hungarian Beef Stew (137): *paprika, bay leaf*

Pan-Seared Flank Steak with Sage-Shallot Compound Butter (191): *dried sage*

Pan-Seared Steaks with Brandy–Pink Peppercorn Sauce (35): *pink peppercorn*

Peppercorn-Crusted Beef Tenderloin with Hollandaise Sauce (38): *black peppercorn, nutmeg*

Pink Peppercorn–Crusted Beef Tenderloin with Cilantro-Lime Hollandaise Sauce (39): *pink peppercorn, nutmeg*

Pomegranate-Braised Beef Short Ribs with Prunes and Sesame (144): *Ras el Hanout (117), sesame seed*

Sichuan Braised Tofu with Beef (149): *sichuan peppercorn, sichuan chili powder*

Southwestern Burgers with Chipotle Ketchup (218): *Chipotle Ketchup (216)*

Spice-Crusted Rib-Eye Steaks (86): *black peppercorn, coriander, dry mustard, red pepper flake*

White Peppercorn–Crusted Beef Tenderloin with Tarragon Hollandaise Sauce (39): *white peppercorn, nutmeg*

pork

Grill-Roasted Pork Loin (48): *salt, black peppercorn*

Herbes de Provence–Rubbed Pork Tenderloins with Vegetables (91): *Herbes de Provence (73)*

Oven-Roasted Jerk Pork Ribs (94): *Jerk Rub (74)*

Pan-Roasted Pork Tenderloin with Cider-Caraway Vinaigrette (192): *Cider-Caraway Vinaigrette (178)*

South Carolina Pulled Pork (92): *dry mustard, paprika, cayenne*

Thick-Cut Pork Chops with Smoked Salt (41): *Smoked Salt (24)*

Wisconsin Brats and Beer (220): *Dijon Mustard (217), caraway*

lamb

Anise-Rubbed Rack of Lamb with Sweet Mint-Almond Relish (96): *anise*

Grilled Lamb Kofte with Za'atar Yogurt Sauce (195): *smoked hot paprika, cumin, black peppercorn, coriander, cloves, nutmeg, cinnamon, Za'atar Yogurt Sauce (180)*

Lamb Vindaloo (130): *Vindaloo Curry Powder (118)*

Roast Butterflied Leg of Lamb with Coriander, Fennel, and Black Pepper (128): *coriander seed, fennel seed, black peppercorn, bay leaf*

poultry

Barbecue Roast Chicken and Potatoes (84): *Barbecue Rub (73)*

Chicken Tagine with Fennel, Chickpeas, and Apricots (140): *paprika, turmeric, cumin, ginger, cayenne, cinnamon*

Crispy Pan-Fried Chicken Cutlets with Garlic-Curry Sauce (189): *Mild Curry Powder (118)*

Crispy-Skinned Chicken Breasts with Lemon-Rosemary Pan Sauce (58): *salt*

Cumin-Coriander Rubbed Cornish Game Hens (78): *cumin, coriander, paprika, cayenne*

Five-Spice Roast Chicken with Turnips (85): *Five-Spice Powder (74)*

Herbes de Provence Roast Chicken with Fennel (85): *Herbes de Provence (73)*

Latin-Style Fried Chicken (83): *cumin, smoked paprika, dried mexican oregano, white peppercorn*

One-Pan Chicken with Couscous, Carrots, and Harissa (213): *Harissa (205)*

Oregano-Anise Rubbed Cornish Game Hens (79): *dried oregano, anise*

Peri Peri Grilled Chicken (80): *dried arbol chile, paprika, Five-Spice Powder (74), cayenne, bay leaf*

Ras el Hanout Roast Chicken and Potatoes (85): *Ras el Hanout (117)*

Seared Duck Breasts with Green Peppercorn Sauce (37): *green peppercorn*

Tandoori Chicken with Raita (143): *Garam Masala (117), cumin, Everyday Chili Powder (116)*

seafood

Blackened Snapper with Rémoulade (99): *Cajun-Style Rub (74)*

Crab Cakes with Cajun-Spiced Dip (196): *Creamy Cajun-Spiced Dip (181)*

Crispy Salt and Pepper Shrimp (52): *salt, black peppercorn, sichuan peppercorn, cayenne*

Fluke Crudo with Furikake (170): *Furikake (159)*

Grilled Shrimp Skewers with Chipotle-Coriander Oil and Avocado-Grapefruit Salad (215): *Chipotle-Coriander Oil (204)*

Grilled Shrimp Skewers with Fennel Oil and Zucchini Ribbon Salad (215): *Fennel Oil (204)*

Grilled Shrimp Skewers with Harissa and Carrot Salad (215): *Harissa (205)*

Grilled Shrimp Skewers with Sichuan Chili Oil and Napa Cabbage Slaw (214): *Sichuan Chili Oil (205)*

Juniper and Fennel–Rubbed Roast Side of Salmon with Orange Beurre Blanc (100): *fennel, juniper*

Marinated Green and Black Olives (209): *dried thyme, dried oregano, red pepper flake*

Pan-Roasted Fish Fillets with Herb Salt (43): *Fresh Herb Salt (24)*

Pan-Seared Salmon with Cilantro-Mint Chutney (51): *salt*

Popcorn Shrimp (103): *Cajun-Style Rub (74), black peppercorn*

Salt-Baked Whole Branzino (62): *salt*

Seared Scallops with Mango Chutney and Mint (230): *coriander, dry mustard, turmeric, cayenne*

Spanish Shellfish Stew (138): *paprika, saffron, red pepper flake*

Thai Panang Curry with Shrimp (133): *Thai Panang Curry Paste (119)*

pasta and noodles

Rigatoni with Spiced Beef Ragu (147): *Five-Spice Powder (74)*

Soba Noodles with Pork, Scallions, and Shichimi Togarashi (172): *Shichimi Togarashi (158)*

Spaghetti with Pecorino Romano and Black Pepper (44): *black peppercorn*

vegetarian entrées

Black Bean Chili (121): *mustard seed, cumin, Everyday Chili Powder (116), chipotle chile*

Classic Vegetable Curry with Potatoes and Cauliflower (134): *Mild Curry Powder (118)*

Panang Vegetable Curry with Eggplant and Red Bell Peppers (135): *Thai Panang Curry Paste (119)*

Shakshuka (153): *cumin, turmeric*

Tex-Mex Cheese Enchiladas (125): *ancho chile, cumin, black peppercorn, dried mexican oregano, garlic powder*

Vadouvan Vegetable Curry with Sweet Potatoes and Green Beans (135): *Vadouvan Curry Powder (118)*

Vindaloo Vegetable Curry with Okra and Tomatoes (135): *Vindaloo Curry Powder (118)*

side dishes and condiments

Grilled Brined Asparagus with Cilantro-Yogurt Sauce (55): *salt*

Grilled Brined Carrots with Cilantro-Yogurt Sauce (54): *salt*

Grilled Brined Zucchini with Cilantro-Yogurt Sauce (55): *salt*

Grilled Eggplant With Chermoula (198): *Chermoula (180)*

Quick Collard Greens with Hot Pepper Vinegar (227): *Hot Pepper Vinegar (223)*

Roasted Fennel with Rye Crumble (176): *dried thyme, caraway*

Preserved Lemons (68): *salt*

Salt-Crusted Fingerling Potatoes (65): *salt*

Sautéed Radishes with Vadouvan Curry And Almonds (150): *Vadouvan Curry Powder (118)*

Sautéed Spinach with Yogurt and Pistachio Dukkah (175): *Pistachio Dukkah (158)*

Spice-Roasted Butternut Squash with Honey-Lemon Butter (106): *cumin, cinnamon, cayenne*

Spice-Roasted Butternut Squash with Honey-Lime Butter (106): *cumin, allspice, cayenne*

Spice-Roasted Butternut Squash with Honey-Orange Butter (106): *cumin, coriander, cayenne*

Thick-Cut Steakhouse Oven Fries (105): *Classic Steak Rub (73), coarse finishing salt*

desserts

Anise Biscotti (257): *anise*

Chocolate Chai Masala Truffles (270): *chai tea, cinnamon*

Crème Brûlée (266): *vanilla bean*

Gingerbread Layer Cake (262): *ginger, cinnamon, white peppercorn, cayenne*

Ginger-Turmeric Frozen Yogurt (269): *ginger, turmeric*

Lavender Tea Cakes (260): *lavender, vanilla*

Mexican Chocolate Truffles (271): *cinnamon, cayenne*

Molasses Spice Cookies (254): *cinnamon, ginger, clove, allspice, black peppercorn, Vanilla Sugar (234)*

Orange Blossom Crème Brûlée (267): *orange blossom water*

Pistachio Baklava with Cardamom and Rose Water (258): *cardamom, Rose Water (237)*

Pink Peppercorn–Pomegranate Panna Cotta (265): *pink peppercorn*

Tea-Infused Crème Brûlée (267): *Irish breakfast tea*

spices a–z

Learn about the overall flavor, origin, and typical uses of spices we commonly use in the recipes as well as the spice blends in this book.

aleppo pepper

Made from dried, crushed Aleppo peppers (a name that comes from the northern Syrian city), these flakes are widely used in Syria and nearby regions. Aleppo has a complex, raisin-like sweetness, tang, and slow-to-build heat with roasty notes. It's sometimes used to add finishing heat—shaken onto food such as avocado toast—like conventional red pepper flake.

allspice

Allspice is a pea-size berry from the evergreen pimento tree that grows in tropical climates, such as Jamaica's. While allspice is often included in savory Caribbean seasonings such as Jerk Rub (page 74), it's better known in the United States as a baking spice as it tastes like a blend of cinnamon, nutmeg, and clove, and we often include it in molasses-sweetened desserts.

anise

Anise seeds are a close cousin to fennel seeds, which are larger and more savory. Both contain the essential oil anethol, which gives them licorice flavor. Anise seeds flavor sweets such as Anise Biscotti (page 257) and liqueurs such as Pernod, pastis, sambuca, and ouzo. Their sweetness is also a boon when paired with delicate fish or used to tame the gamey flavor of lamb (see Anise-Rubbed Rack of Lamb with Sweet Mint-Almond Relish on page 96). In the test kitchen, we've found that fennel seed can usually be substituted for anise seed, although we prefer to bake with anise.

bay leaves

You will read more about dried herbs on page 13, but bay leaves are unique: Most recipes add bay leaves to the pot early on and leave them in for the duration of cooking so they infuse dishes with their flavor. There are two types: common Turkish bay leaves that come from bay or laurel trees, and more aromatic California bay leaves that come from a shrubby evergreen. California bay leaves have a potent, eucalyptus-like flavor, whereas Turkish bay leaves have a tea-like profile.

caraway

The ancient Greeks used caraway seeds as a cure for an upset stomach, and the seeds are still often paired with heavier foods like cabbage and cream sauces. They're pungent and herbaceous, with a slightly bitter finish, making them a natural with robust meats—and, as many people know them, in rye bread.

cardamom

Cardamom is the complex, flavorful seeds that come from mostly flavorless pods. They have a delicate, earthy, floral flavor with light sweetness and are used most often in Scandinavia (in sweets), India, and the Middle East. Green cardamom is the most commonly found variety in the United States. White cardamom is simply green cardamom that's been bleached so as not to discolor light-colored baked goods and other foods. Black cardamom (also called large cardamom) is not true cardamom but a relative. We've found that green cardamom is the most vibrant and balanced. Not surprisingly, the flavor of the bleached pods pales in comparison to the green—and they cost almost twice as much. Black cardamom offers hints of eucalyptus, and as it is generally dried over fire, it boasts smoky nuances; we appreciated these flavors in savory applications. But for an all-purpose choice, we turn to green cardamom. The flavor doesn't stick around, so buy whole pods and then remove and grind the seeds.

cayenne pepper

Craving kick? Even a pinch of the powder made from long, tapered cayenne peppers will pack heat. It's the go-to for heat in Louisiana cooking; but we use it anywhere we need clear, clean spiciness. While they're grown in a multitude of tropical and subtropical areas, the peppers' name comes from what is often cited as their place of origin, the Cayenne region of French Guiana.

celery seed

These tiny brown seeds are harvested from a variety of wild celery called lovage. But don't let their diminutive size fool you—their flavor is potent. The seeds pack a strong punch of slightly bitter, warm celery flavor and should be used sparingly. They can also be used to add a distinctive kick to potato salads or pickled vegetables.

Celery salt is a flavored salt made from salt and ground celery seed. On its own, celery salt normally seasons rims of Bloody Marys, but it has a big place as a core ingredient of Cajun-style spice blends such as Old Bay (see page 74).

chili powder

Although traditional chili powder is a blend (you'll find homemade blend recipes throughout this book) of dried, ground chiles and spices—typically cumin, oregano, garlic, paprika, and salt—its uses are as abundant as those of singular spices. Depending on the chiles used, it can range from mild to hot and is labeled accordingly. We have a homemade recipe for an Everyday Chili Powder (page 116) that, while a touch spicy, has a milder, sweeter flavor; it can be used in any application that calls for chili powder, as can the more specialized Smoky Cocoa Chili Powder (page 117) that packs more depth and heat. The spelling—"chili" with an "i"—comes from it being the core flavoring in that namesake dish. Our favorite all-purpose chili powder is from **Morton & Bassett**.

cinnamon

Few spices feel as familiar as ground cinnamon: We swirl it into oatmeal; sprinkle it on top of lattes; bake it into pies, cakes, and cookies; and even add it to savory dishes. Most cinnamon sold in this country is rolled tree bark of the cassia tree, not Ceylon cinnamon, which is known as "true" cinnamon. "Cinnamon" is actually an umbrella term for several different species of evergreen trees in the genus *Cinnamomum*. Moreover, different countries grow different species of trees, which is why different varieties are often named by country and have different flavors. Vietnamese growers, for example, cultivate *Cinnamomum loureiroi*, which is naturally higher in the volatile oils that provide heat and carry cinnamon's trademark flavors than the *Cinnamomum burmannii* grown in Indonesia. And Ceylon cinnamon is grown primarily in Sri Lanka; we've found that Ceylon cinnamon is milder and subtler than other varieties.

So what should you use? If you like big, spicy flavor and frequently use cinnamon in unbaked applications (as the volatile oils quickly dissipate), we recommend springing for **Penzey's Vietnamese Cinnamon, Ground**. But if you use cinnamon mostly for baking or you prefer a milder all-purpose cinnamon, go with the cheaper **Morton & Bassett Ground Cinnamon**.

cloves

Pungent, peppery cloves are the dried, unopened buds of an Indonesian tree. They resemble nails—in fact, the word "clove" comes from the Latin word for nail, *clavus*. Ground cloves are quite pungent, potent, and peppery, so we more frequently call for whole cloves for grinding into blends of other spices or infusing broths and condiments; however, jars of the assertive ground stuff make a statement in baked goods like our spicy Molasses Spice Cookies (page 254).

coriander

When you buy whole coriander "seeds" rather than ground coriander, you're actually buying the fruit of the coriander plant (which also gives us the herb cilantro). Coriander provides a sweet, almost fruity or citrusy flavor that enhances spice rubs for meat and fish, like the one for Cumin-Coriander Rubbed Cornish Game Hens (page 78); brings brightness to Middle Eastern and Indian spice blends like Garam Masala (page 117); and lends aroma to all manner of pickles, relishes, chutneys, and infused oils.

cumin

Cumin seeds are harvested from the annual plant *Cuminum cyminum*, which is a member of the parsley family. India is the main producer of cumin, but other sources include Turkey and Iran, and cumin is used in cuisines around the world, playing a role in both curry blends and chili powders. In America, we often use cumin in its ground form in chili, barbecue sauces, and rubs. Cumin seeds, which resemble caraway, can also add toastiness, crunch, and a distinctive "woodsy aroma" to dishes. Our favorite ground cumin is **Simply Organic Cumin**.

curry powder

While not a single spice, curry powder is an important everyday addition to cooking. We use it to flavor curries, but the conventional blend we know as curry powder is actually a Western invention (unlike the traditional Indian spice blend, **garam masala**—another must-have (see page 117); in South Asia cooks will combine a stunning multitude of chiles and spices to flavor dishes. Nonetheless, these spice blends that are inspired by Indian flavors have been embraced everywhere South Asian–style gravy-based dishes are made as fast ways to develop complex flavors. Different curry powders offer a large spectrum of aromatic qualities and heat levels. We can break it down into two basic styles: mild (or sweet) and a hotter version called Madras. Madras curry powder takes its name from the southern Indian city of Madras (now Chennai)—and it's too spicy to be substituted for sweet or mild. We also provide recipes for Vindaloo Curry Powder (page 118) to flavor the Goan curry, French Vadouvan Curry Powder (page 118), and a Thai red curry paste called Thai Panang Curry Paste (page 119). Our favorite store-bought mild curry powder is **Penzeys Sweet Curry Powder**.

dried herbs

Bay leaves, which are removed from dishes after giving up their flavor, aren't the only leaf or herb in dried form that we consider to be a spice. Dried herbs of the crushed variety—such as dried oregano (Mexican and regular), dried dill, dried thyme, dried marjoram, dried rosemary, dried mint, and dried sage—aren't subpar storage-safe versions of fresh. In fact, they sometimes can be even more complex and flavorful than their fresh counterparts and have a noteworthy place in our recipes. You can add them earlier than fresh in the cooking process without losing flavor; their hardiness allows them to infuse oils; and they can meld seamlessly into spice rubs, crusts, and finishing seasonings. Classic Steak Rub (page 73), Herbes de Provence (page 73), and Za'atar (page 156) are examples of spice blends made largely from dried herbs. We don't work with dried versions of delicate leafy herbs such as basil, cilantro, and parsley; these become bland and musty when dried. If you're using dried herbs to substitute for fresh, use only half as much dried herbs as fresh, and add them at the same time as you would add fresh.

espelette pepper

This chile powder is worth seeking out. Often used as a condiment in the Basque region where it's grown, the spicy, fruity dried pepper contributes both warm heat and paprika-like sweetness to dishes.

fennel

Dried fennel seeds have an herbal, piney flavor that pairs well with rich meats. The popular sausage flavoring is stronger in taste than similar licorice-y anise seeds and tastes great in very savory dishes. It is the only non-herb spice in Herbes de Provence (page 73), and one of the main flavors in Chinese Five-Spice Powder (page 74). As every part of the fennel plant is edible, dried fennel seeds can point up the flavor of fresh fennel as it does in our Chicken Salad with Pickled Fennel, Watercress, and Macadamia Nuts (page 224). Additionally, the most prized part of the fennel plant, fennel pollen, has a beautifully delicate flavor that we like to use as a finisher for blistered shishito peppers (see page 167).

fenugreek

Fenugreek is a nutty seed with a unique maple-like flavor that is used in India and the Middle East. Fenugreek isn't used all that commonly on its own, but it's quite often a component of spice blends. It has an allium aroma with a burnt-sugar sweetness and is even a bit starchy—making it able to thicken blends and dishes a bit, too.

garlic powder

Garlic powder seamlessly mixes into spice rubs, letting you add subtle garlic flavor with no distinguishable garlic texture (or moisture, or propensity for burning). Made from dehydrated, ground garlic cloves, it's easy to keep on hand as a pantry staple. Our favorite is **Spice Islands Garlic Powder**.

ginger

Ground ginger adds a warm, spicy flavor and aroma to baked goods and many Asian and Indian dishes. Dried ginger is sharper and less floral than fresh and can supplement fresh for a spicy bite; because of profound differences in moisture, pungency, and flavor, they aren't interchangeable in recipes. For reasons similar to garlic powder, dried ginger (instead of fresh) is a nice addition to spice blends. Our favorite is **Spice Islands Ground Ginger**.

juniper berries

Piney juniper berries come from the berry-like seed cones of the wide-spreading juniper shrub, a member of the cypress family. Known for their place in gin, juniper berries also are common in European cuisines; they're particularly nice with pork or game meats or fruity savory dishes, but we even rub salmon with them (see page 100).

lavender

Don't relegate lavender to soaps and perfumes. It's actually a relative of mint, and the dried flower buds give sweets an exotic floral quality. You can infuse the buds into ice cream, custards, and syrups or bake them into desserts like our Lavender Tea Cakes (page 260). A little lavender goes a long way.

mustard

Mustard seeds are, of course, the base of the condiment mustard (we make homemade Dijon on page 217), but they're also used in long-cooked dishes of India, punchy pickle brines, and even cheese sauces to bring interest, pungency, and heat. All that is needed is water or oil and some heat to bring them to life. Depending on where the mustard plant is grown, it can produce black, brown, yellow, or white seeds. Black (not very common) and brown mustard seeds are more pungent than yellow and white mustard. They are available whole or ground.

nigella seeds

Nigella seeds (also called *charnushka*) are common in India and the Middle East. The seeds have an oniony bite and a slightly astringent, piney taste. You can sprinkle them on rolls in place of poppy or sesame seeds or stir them into chutneys. Note: They're often mislabeled as black cumin or caraway. The seeds are prominent in Hazelnut-Nigella Dukkah (page 158).

nutmeg

Heady and powerful, nutmeg is a hard, brown seed from a tropical tree. It's often used in dairy-based savory dishes like quiche and creamed spinach, or in sweets such as Tropical Granola with Dried Mango and Ginger (page 247). A little nutmeg goes a long way, so measure it carefully. You can grate a small amount from a whole nutmeg in almost the same time it'd take you to measure ground nutmeg—and the flavor will shine.

Mace is another warm spice from the same plant as nutmeg. And it tastes a lot like nutmeg, too—but more pungent (and that's saying something). That's because it's made from the lacy membrane, or aril, that surrounds the nutmeg seed inside the fruit. Dried, whole mace comes in "blades," but the ground form is more common. We pitted mace against nutmeg and found that you can substitute one for the other by using half as much of the more potent mace as you would nutmeg, or twice as much nutmeg in recipes that call for mace.

paprika

Paprika is a generic term for a spice made from grinding dried red chile pods (and sometimes the seeds and stems as well) to a fine powder. Whether paprika is labeled sweet, smoked, or hot is determined by the variety (or varieties) of pepper used and how the pepper is manipulated. Sweet paprika is the most common. Typically made from a combination of mild red peppers, it is prized for its deep scarlet hue. Smoked paprika is produced by drying peppers (either sweet or hot) over smoldering embers.

Hungarian paprika has a dark, deep crimson hue and is produced in six different grades, from very mild to pungent and hot (the most commonly exported is *édesnemes*, or noble sweet).

Spanish paprika has a lighter, slightly orange tint. *Pimentón*, as it is also known, is available in its sweet form as well as in two smoked varieties: sweet and hot. The smoked paprika is created by drying ripe red chile peppers slowly, according to tradition, over smoldering oak fires for upwards of two weeks. (Regular paprika is air-dried in the sun or by machine.) In their two simplest categories, sweet and smoked paprika both have their place, with smoked hot being more of a specialty product. Our favorite sweet paprika is **The Spice House Hungarian Sweet Paprika**. We like it in traditional Hungarian Beef Stew (page 137) and as a sweet backnote in a number of other dishes. Our favorite smoked paprika is **Simply Organic Smoked Paprika**.

peppercorns

We provide a complete primer on peppercorns on pages 26–27; these berries come in a rainbow of colors and have different levels of spiciness and effects. While we teach how to employ all kinds of peppercorns, black pepper graces almost every dish we cook; our favorite black peppercorn is to **Tone's Whole Black Peppercorns**. We like to buy our peppercorns whole and grind them; once the shell of peppercorns are cracked open, the aroma and flavor immediately start to fade.

poppy seeds

They come from the same plant that produces opium, but we're interested in poppy seeds for their peppery, smoky-sweet flavor. Eastern Europeans love them in pastries; in the United States, we know them from baked treats that have emigrated from that same neck of the woods: bagels, challah, and pretzels. We also like them in coleslaw, egg noodles, salad dressing, and our Everything Bagel Blend (page 159), and they add crunch to lemon–poppy seed muffins.

red pepper flakes

Red pepper flakes are just dried and crushed red chile peppers, and they add heat—to a nose-clearing degree if used in abundance—to dishes, but also some depth since that heat comes from chiles. They add another layer of flavor to pasta sauces or roasted vegetables.

rose

Rose is more than just a pretty flower. When we use floral rose as a spice in the test kitchen, we use it in the form of dried rose buds, not the petals; food grade buds are much easier to find at spice shops and specialty markets. In addition to being distilled to make Rose Water (page 237) for flavoring sweets and drinks, rose buds are used in savory dishes and spice blends of the Middle East like Advieh (page 156). Another flower distillate is orange blossom water (we use it in Orange Blossom Crème Brûlée (page 267)) made from harder-to-source orange flower petals.

saffron

Saffron is made from the dried stigmas of *Crocus sativus* flowers; the stigmas are so delicate they must be harvested by hand in a painstaking process. (It takes about 200 hours to pick enough stigmas to produce just 1 pound of saffron, which typically sells for thousands of dollars.) Luckily, a little saffron goes a long way, adding a distinct reddish-gold color, notes of honey and grass, and a slight hint of bitterness to dishes like paella, risotto, and Spanish Shellfish Stew (page 138). Though the bulk of commercially produced saffron comes from Spain and Iran, it is also harvested on a small scale in India, Greece, France, and—closer to home—Lancaster County, Pennsylvania. Our favorite saffron is **Morton & Bassett Saffron Threads**.

salt

Before exploring the fun finishing salts you can experiment with on pages 22–25, it's important to understand where and how we use the different kinds, including workaday table and kosher salts. Whether mined from underground salt deposits or obtained by evaporating seawater, salt in its most basic form is the same: sodium chloride. What distinguishes one salt from another is texture, shape, and mineral content. These qualities can affect how a salt tastes as well as how it interacts with food.

Table salt, also known as common salt, consists of tiny, uniformly shaped crystals created during rapid vacuum evaporation. It usually includes anti-caking agents that help it pour smoothly. Fine-grain table salt dissolves easily; use it for most applications, both sweet and savory, and in brines.

Coarser-grain kosher salt is raked during the evaporation process to yield the larger crystals that were originally used for koshering meat. Unlike table salt, kosher salt doesn't contain any additives. Kosher salt is tops for seasoning meat in advance of cooking to promote tenderness. The large grains are easy to distribute evenly over meat's surface. Mix it with spices or condiments for a flavorful seasoning salt.

salt measure conversions

We develop our recipes with **Diamond Crystal Kosher Salt**; if you're using Morton Kosher Salt, which is denser than Diamond Crystal, note that 3 teaspoons Diamond Crystal kosher salt = 2¼ teaspoons Morton kosher salt = 1½ teaspoons table salt.

Sea salt is the product of seawater evaporation—a time-consuming, expensive process that yields irregularly shaped, mineral-rich flakes that vary in color but only slightly in flavor. Note that not all flaky/coarse salts are sea salt—a common misconception. For us, texture—not exotic provenance—is the main consideration given that flavor differences are slight. Look for brands boasting large, flaky crystals. And keep in mind that mixed into food, pricier sea salt doesn't taste any different than table salt. Instead use flaky sea salt, such as Maldon (see page 22), as a finishing salt, where its delicate crunch stands out.

sesame seeds

Look for these seeds on bagels, in a stir-fry, ground into tahini, or in a host of nutty finishing spice blends like North African Pistachio Dukkah (page 158) and Japanese Shichimi Togarashi (page 158). These oily seeds from a sesame plant can be grayish ivory, brown, red, or black and are used in both savory and sweet recipes. Their nutty, subtle honey quality suits candies, granola, bread, and sweets like the classic Southern benne wafers (they were originally known in the United States as benne seeds). They're even sprinkled on our Five-Spice and Sesame Candied Bacon (page 109).

star anise

As the name suggests, these pods are eight-pointed star-shaped fruits from an evergreen tree native to East and Southeast Asia, and they taste like anise. The warm, licorice-like flavor of star anise works well in foods both sweet and savory (such as custards or Asian marinades). It's an essential element of Five-Spice Powder (page 74). Try flavoring sugar syrup with whole pods and drizzling the syrup over citrus fruits.

sumac

Ground sumac is made from dried berries that are harvested from a shrub grown in southern Europe and in the Middle East. It is an essential component in the Middle Eastern spice blend Za'atar (page 156), but it can also be used as an ingredient in spice rubs or sprinkled over foods as a finishing touch like in Fattoush (page 183). It's bright, with a clean, citrusy flavor and a slight raisiny sweetness—both more balanced and more complex-tasting than lemon juice. While ground sumac can liven up dry rubs and dressings, we like it best sprinkled over vegetables, grilled meats, stews, eggs, hummus, and even popcorn so as not to mute its bright flavor. You can find both ground sumac and sumac berries, which you can grind yourself.

turmeric

Most of the world's turmeric is grown in India, where it has been cultivated for centuries. The portion of the plant that's above ground is green and leafy. The edible part is the underground stem, or rhizome. It's small and knobby, with dark orange flesh and a thin brown peel. It looks similar to ginger, another rhizome in the same family. It's possible to find the fresh stuff in some markets, but it's not as widely available as ground turmeric. A key ingredient in curry powders (see page 118), we often combine warm, slightly bitter turmeric with strong spices such as cinnamon, cumin, ginger, and coriander, and we use it as much for its striking golden color (as in our St. Lucia Buns (page 224)) as we do for its flavor. Our favorite ground turmeric is **Frontier Co-op Ground Turmeric Root**.

vanilla

Vanilla, from the seeds and pod of the vanilla orchid, is the most commonly used flavoring in desserts. In extract form, it's sold in pure and imitation varieties. Our top choice is a real extract—real vanilla has around 250 flavor compounds compared to imitation vanilla's one, giving it a complexity we appreciate in cooked applications and in cold and creamy desserts. Our favorite pure vanilla is **McCormick Pure Vanilla Extract**, but you can also make your own (see page 236).

When you're really going to taste and see the vanilla, like in Vanilla Sugar (page 234) or the elegant topping on our Lavender Tea Cakes (page 260), we've found that beans impart deeper flavor than extract. We recommend splurging on **McCormick Madagascar Vanilla Beans** ($15.99 for two) for their plump, seed-filled pods and complex caramel-like flavor.

wasabi

Spicy, pungent wasabi is a relative of horseradish that grows in Japan. Beware: A lot of American products are green-colored sushi-accompanying imposters—you'll have to seek out powders and pastes at specialty markets or online.

from grinding to storing: a spice practical

Once you've stocked your spice rack, made your own blends, and even gotten comfortable using spices in your cooking, you'll want to understand these key spice techniques.

how to choose ground or whole

Nearly every spice you find ground in jars at the supermarket can be purchased whole as well—and we generally recommend purchasing whole spices when you can. Yes, it's easy to simply stick a teaspoon measure into a jar of ground spices and go, but you'll get more flavor if you buy whole spices and grind them just before using, as grinding releases the volatile compounds that give the spice its flavor and aroma. The longer a ground spice is stored, the more compounds disappear. Fresh-ground spices improve dishes with their superior aroma, vibrancy, and roundness of flavor.

how to store spices

Jarred whole spices are typically at their best for two years while ground spices stay fresh for about one year. Keep spices away from heat, light, and moisture, all of which shorten shelf life. To check the freshness of your spices, crumble a small amount of the dried powder or herb between your fingers and take a whiff. If it releases a lively aroma, it's still good. If the aroma and color of the spice have faded, it's time to restock.

how to clean a spice grinder

Generally, you can use a damp cloth to wipe out the interior of a spice grinder. But sometimes your spice grinder requires more heavy-duty cleansing to remove oils and spice granules in its nooks, especially after grinding items like dried chiles. (You don't want your ground anise seeds to be mysteriously spicy.) Naturally you can't submerge the unit in water, so we've developed a "dry-cleaning" method: Add several tablespoons of raw white rice to the spice grinder and pulverize to a fine powder, about 1 minute; the rice powder will absorb the residue and oils left behind by previously ground spices. Dump out the rice flour and then wipe out the grinder with a damp cloth as normal. This prevents the muddling of flavors that can occur when oils and spice granules build up in your grinder. A good rule of thumb is to use this method weekly, but you can simply do it every time it looks like your grinder needs a good cleaning.

spice equipment

salt storage container

Salt containers placed near the stove make it easy to season a steak or a pot of boiling water on the fly. There are two basic kinds: "Salt pigs" are open-mouthed cylindrical vessels, while salt boxes have lids and tend to be slightly smaller. Not surprisingly, the lidded salt boxes did a superior job of protecting their salt from messes. We like the flip-top **Bee House Salt Box ($20.80)**.

pepper mill

Pepper is one of the most fundamental spices and there are few dishes we don't add a grind of peppercorns to. The **Cole & Mason Derwent Gourmet Precision Pepper Mill ($30)** is tops. It makes grind selection a snap, with clear markings corresponding to grind size, and every one of its six fixed settings performed well. Its transparent acrylic body proved easy to load and grasp.

spice grinder

The test kitchen standard for grinding spices is an inexpensive blade-type electric coffee grinder. We use this for spices only, and we recommend reserving a separate unit to grind coffee. The **Krups Fast-Touch Coffee Mill ($19.99)** creates an exceptionally fine grind of all spices.

---

do you need a mortar and pestle?

No, but this alternative to an electric grinder can be pretty cool. Mortars that hold at least 3 cups are the most versatile, and you want one with a rough interior to help grip and grind ingredients and a long, heavy pestle that keeps knuckles from scraping the mortar's edge. Our winner, the **Frieling "Goliath" Mortar and Pestle Set ($58)**, made of heavy, stable granite has these qualities, is comfortable to hold and somewhat surprisingly makes grinding by hand a breeze. In addition to grinding whole spices to powder it can be used to crack whole spices like peppercorns for chunky, textured spice crusts.

First, you need to season your mortar and pestle. Do this by grinding 3 tablespoons of raw rice (yes, rice again!) until it's reduced to a fine powder. Repeat the process two more times. To use the mortar and pestle efficiently, use a circular grinding motion, maintaining downward pressure at all times, instead of up-and-down pounding motions, until the spices are ground.

---

rasp grater

In addition to being useful for a number of tasks, such as grating hard cheese or chocolate, a rasp grater is especially good for grating whole nutmeg and cinnamon. Our favorite is a standard: The **Microplane Premium Classic Zester/Grater ($13)** breezes through all of these tasks with minimal effort and stays sharp.

nutmeg grinder

While we love our rasp grater and it's certainly good for grating nutmeg, it does make us a bit nervous; one slip of the seed and you can grate your fingers. The **Microplane Spice Grinder ($15)** is a twist on a regular grater. It has a comfortable handle, and a slender, tightly curled, 5-inch-long grating surface that provides a good margin of safety for your fingertips. It can produce mounds of nutmeg in no time flat.

---

fine-mesh strainer

We use a fine-mesh strainer in the spice kitchen to separate out solids from infusions and to sift out unusable powdery spice from cracked spices. The **Rösle Fine Mesh Strainer, Round Handle, 7.9 inches, 20 cm ($34)** is perfect for these tasks as it has a roomy, medium-depth basket of very fine, tight, stiff mesh.

---

skillet

A skillet is our go-to vessel for blooming or toasting spices. We also use the bottom to crush peppercorns for recipes that rely on crunch and flavor from them. The best skillet (that is also a general kitchen workhorse) is the **All-Clad d3 Stainless Steel 12" Fry Pan with Lid ($120)**.

other tools to have

- Cheesecloth for infusions.
- Small airtight containers and jars (glass is ideal as it's nonporous and spices have lots of oils, but plastic is acceptable) for storing spices.
- Squeeze bottles for sauces and condiments.
- Mason jars for infusions.
- A splatter screen to prevent spices you toast from hopping out of the skillet.

season smarter

getting more out of salt and pepper

You simply can't cook without salt and pepper. These two most basic spices are the keys to making food taste like its best self. Salt isn't just the fine table stuff in the shaker (although that's certainly an important staple used throughout our recipes), and peppercorns aren't just the bitey jet-black ones. No, there's a world of salt and pepper—a variety of salt grain sizes, a rainbow of peppercorn colors—to add to food before cooking, or to sprinkle onto finished dishes before serving for a flavorful tough. And in addition to flavor, salt with large flakes or crushed peppercorns can add appealing texture and crunch you don't get from fine-grain table spices. Broaden your salt and pepper horizons.

SEASON IT

Salt and pepper are so elemental to our cooking (we go through the basics on pages 16–17) that you probably don't think too much about them beyond routine. Their addition is part prescribed (by the amount listed on a recipe's ingredient list) and part instinctive (we season to taste). Try expanding your collection beyond the white and black, and learn how to intensify the flavor and textures of your food in ways beyond the obvious.

› finishing salts

We season with salt at different times during the cooking process so it blends in properly: Applying kosher salt to meat in advance of cooking (see pages 56–57) can improve flavor and texture; seasoning a salad dressing to taste with fine-grain table salt ensures the salt dissolves; sprinkling carrots with salt before roasting gives it time to penetrate the vegetables' rigid cell walls; salting stews before braising ensures even, well-rounded seasoning as salt's rate of diffusion increases with heat (and seasoning fattier foods like richly marbled meat more aggressively than lean foods is smart because fat has a dulling effect on taste).

Finishing salts, on the contrary, aren't meant to blend in or provide even seasoning. These colorful coarse salts heighten the flavor of just about anything—fresh garden vegetables, a just-seared rich strip steak, or maybe buttery chocolate chip cookies—and bring out dimension, stimulating the appetite. And their crunch provides surprising textural contrast that makes food pop. Here you'll find the accessible options you can use in our recipes that call for "coarse finishing salt."

scale of saltiness

The varying crystal structures of finishing salts yield different types of crunch. Their larger granules also make a given measure less shockingly salty than that of kosher or table salt because they pack less densely; that is, fewer granules fit into that measure. This allows you to more ably detect the flavor notes of the salt. Shape matters, too: The large, flat flakes of Maldon take up more surface area across your tongue, meaning fewer granules per area and slower dissolving. Higher-moisture salts are less aggressively salty because of their dissolution rate as well; they stick to each other and so will not dissolve quickly on the tongue. Let this guide your choice in different applications.

maldon sea salt

Maldon, the southeastern town in England, has been producing salt since at least as far back as 1086. Seawater is collected at high tide, filtered, left to settle in tanks, and then carefully heated until Maldon's characteristic large flake pyramids form. Thanks to its availability and affordable price, it's one of the most common finishing salts.

tasting notes Clean with a mild brininess and round mineral flavor. Large, light, airy, thin flakes and pyramids have a delicate and shattering texture and soft crunch that dissolves easily.

› **try on** Most anything except wet foods as its pristine, delicate flakes dissolve quickly.

hawaiian black lava salt

This salt is typically manufactured by evaporating sea waters that have filtered through volcanic soils. However, it derives its color wholly through the addition of finely ground activated charcoal, which gives earthiness and the perception of a milder salinity.

tasting notes Mildly salty, tastes of the sea, slightly vegetal, and reminiscent of seaweed. Pebbly, coral-like texture.

> **try on** Cocktail rims or other places you don't want a wallop of saltiness; wetter foods as it maintains crunch; light-colored foods for striking color contrast.

himalayan pink salt

Mined from the vast deposits in the Punjab in Pakistan (near but not in the Himalayas), this rock salt gains its pink hue from multiple trace minerals present. It's sold in its rock state, which is too hard to bite so we like to grind it, not too fine, for ideal texture.

tasting notes Pure, pungent salt flavor.

> **try on** Popcorn, pretzels, or anywhere you want a clean salt flavor but also some textural interest. Otherwise use for its lovely color.

fleur de sel

This is traditionally manufactured in the coastal regions of France, Italy, and Spain. As water evaporates from salt-saturated pools, the salt will fall out of solution and either sink to the bottom or, if the conditions are just right, form the delicate white crystals of fleur de sel.

tasting notes Clean, briny seawater with hints of clay, slate, and rock. Yielding crunch and uneven grind size, moderate moisture, maintains structure even when slightly wet.

> **try on** Anything! We find it the most majestic of the finishing salts.

› flavored salts

Another way to finish food with salt is even more playful: flavoring your salts so they provide both salinity and spice. Buying flavored salts at a specialty store can be expensive. Here are simple recipes for our favorites, as well as serving suggestions. All of these flavored salts make about ½ cup and can be stored in an airtight container for up to 1 month.

fresh herb salt

½ cup kosher salt
1 cup minced fresh chives, dill, or tarragon

Using your hands, rub salt and chives in large bowl until well combined. Spread mixture into even layer on parchment paper–lined rimmed baking sheet. Let sit at room temperature, away from direct sunlight, until completely dry, 36 to 48 hours, stirring every 12 hours to break up any clumps.

› **how to use** Sprinkle on tomato salad, seared chicken breasts, bean dips, fried eggs.

chili-lime salt

¼ cup kosher salt
2 tablespoons plus 2 teaspoons chili powder
1½ teaspoons grated lime zest

Combine all ingredients in bowl, then spread onto large plate. Microwave, stirring occasionally, until zest is dry and no longer clumps, about 2 minutes. Let cool to room temperature, about 15 minutes.

› **how to use** Sprinkle on grilled fish, seared scallops, grilled corn, fresh fruit such as pineapple, mango, or watermelon.

cumin-sesame salt

2 tablespoons cumin seeds
2 tablespoons sesame seeds
2 tablespoons kosher salt

Toast cumin seeds and sesame seeds in 8-inch skillet over medium heat, stirring occasionally, until fragrant and sesame seeds are golden brown, 3 to 4 minutes. Transfer to spice grinder and let cool for 10 minutes. Pulse seeds until coarsely ground, about 6 pulses. Transfer to bowl and stir in salt.

› **how to use** Sprinkle on baked winter squash, grilled steak, sautéed mushrooms, roasted cauliflower, steamed white rice.

smoked salt

½ cup kosher salt
1 teaspoon liquid smoke

Combine salt and liquid smoke in bowl, then spread onto large plate. Microwave, stirring occasionally, until only slightly damp, about 2 minutes. Let sit until completely dry and cool, about 10 minutes.

› **how to use** Sprinkle on grilled meats and vegetables, roasted asparagus, caramels.

sriracha salt

½ cup kosher salt
⅓ cup Sriracha sauce

Combine salt and Sriracha in bowl, then spread on large plate. Microwave, stirring occasionally, until only slightly damp, 6 to 8 minutes. Let sit until completely dry and cool, about 10 minutes.

› **how to use** Sprinkle on French fries or baked potato, avocado toast, fresh noodles; coat rim of Bloody Mary glass.

› peppercorns

Nearly every ingredient list calls for pepper next to salt. Pepper rouses our palates for the meal before us, which is why a grind at the table is still offered in some restaurants. Grinding peppercorns releases their aroma and volatile oils. Do it yourself for the freshest flavor; preground pepper tastes as dusty as it looks. Sometimes we crack peppercorns so they maintain crunch for coating foods or swirling into a sauce. Just like salt, there are benefits to adding pepper at different points in a recipe. At the start, it's easy to distribute. It can also be adjusted to taste along the way, or simmered in a pan sauce to unlock its full flavor. For braises that cook for a very long time, its floral aroma can dissipate as its volatile compounds are fleeting. That said, there are other notes that come through so early additions can infuse a dish with earthy, meaty, or even tea-like flavors.

black peppercorns
Beyond its heat and sharp bite, black pepper enhances our ability to taste food, stimulating our salivary glands so we experience flavors more fully. It has complexity and depth from sun-drying.

tasting notes Spicy, pungent, floral, smoky, and/or citrus-y—depends on varietal.

› **try with** Red meat, smoked fish, citrus salads, caramel desserts, Parmesan or Manchego cheese; use as your everyday pepper.

green peppercorns
Green peppercorns, which resemble capers, are simply unripe black peppercorns and are usually soft. They're sold dried or packed in brine or vinegar.

tasting notes Pine and juniper notes. Flavor is tart and bright when compared with black.

› **try with** Stuffings, sauces for fish or pork loin, hearty green vegetables, cauliflower, salad dressings, oyster mignonette; add whole or lightly crushed.

how to crack peppercorns
Cracked peppercorns should be about half the size of whole ones. In some elegant applications, when the texture of the pepper is of supreme importance, we'll sift the inevitable dusty matter through a fine-mesh strainer and discard.

To crack, rock bottom edge of skillet over 2 tablespoons peppercorns on cutting board until they crack; repeat.

white peppercorns

White peppercorns are fully ripened black peppercorns that have been soaked in water to ferment, and their outer skin is removed before the berries are dried. Although stripping the skin away removes much of the volatile oils and aroma compounds (most notably piperine, which is responsible for pepper's pungent heat), allowing the berries to ripen longer lets them develop complex flavor, while fermenting adds a layer of funky, earthy flavor.

tasting notes Sharp, floral, citrus and licorice flavors.

> **try with** Light-colored cream sauces and soups, flaky white fish and shellfish, clam chowder, mashed potatoes, stir-fries.

sichuan peppercorns

These small, reddish brown husks aren't peppercorns; they're the dried fruit rinds from a small Chinese citrus tree called the prickly ash. They don't add heat per se; instead, they contribute a unique tingling or buzzing sensation, much like carbonation, that can even trigger salivation in some. This is due to a pungent compound called *sanshool* that acts on receptors that usually respond to touch.

tasting notes Lively, lemony, menthol-like, numbing.

> **try with** Bloody Marys, sweet potatoes, buttered popcorn, cucumber salads with rice vinegar and sesame oil.

pink peppercorns

Also not peppercorns, striking pink peppercorns are a berry from a tropical evergreen. They do carry some heat like true peppercorns, however.

tasting notes Mild, fruity, floral.

> **try with** Creamy custard desserts, game meat, fatty fish, roasted shallots, Camembert, fruit such as raw watermelon or grilled peaches.

radish baguette with chive butter and salt

serves 8 to 12

10 tablespoons cultured European-style unsalted butter, softened

6 tablespoons minced fresh chives

Salt and pepper

1 teaspoon lemon juice

1 teaspoon extra-virgin olive oil

1 cup coarsely chopped fresh parsley

1 (18-inch) baguette, halved lengthwise

8 ounces radishes, trimmed and sliced thin

Coarse finishing salt

why this recipe works Radishes, butter, and salt are a time-tested combination: Creamy butter adds a richness that both complements the radish and tempers its bite, and the salt brings out the flavors, providing the only necessary seasoning. The French (of course) make the trio a rustic-chic snack, spreading a generous amount of butter on a fresh baguette and layering on radishes. For our version, we left the baguette whole, which allowed us to shingle lots of radish slices on top in a pretty fish scale pattern for radish flavor in every bite. We created a simple compound butter with chives and rich and tangy cultured European-style butter that was an ultraflavorful adhesive. We liked topping off the radishes with an additional component: a parsley salad, which provided brightness and visual contrast. But while the simple freshness of all these ingredients made our tartine special, the component that brought it all together was, actually, the most granular: the finishing sprinkle of coarse salt. The salinity of a sprinkling is necessary, but it's also the crunch that makes the dish—a crunch that's different from the fresh snap of radish and is instead a shattering bite of flaky grains against the frilly herb salad. You can use your preferred coarse finishing salt in this recipe; for information on finishing salts, see pages 22–23.

1 Combine butter, ¼ cup chives, ¼ teaspoon salt, and ¼ teaspoon pepper in bowl. Whisk remaining 2 tablespoons chives, lemon juice, and oil together in second bowl. Add parsley and toss to coat. Season with pepper to taste.

2 Spread butter mixture over cut sides of baguette. Shingle radishes evenly over butter and top with parsley salad. Cut baguette crosswise into 12 pieces and sprinkle with finishing salt to taste. Serve.

wedge salad with creamy black pepper dressing

serves 6

- 4 slices bacon, chopped
- Salt and coarsely ground pepper
- ¼ cup extra-virgin olive oil
- ¼ cup sour cream
- ¼ cup mayonnaise
- 2 tablespoons buttermilk
- 2 teaspoons Dijon mustard
- 2 teaspoons red wine vinegar
- 1 garlic clove, minced
- 1 head iceberg lettuce (2 pounds), cored and cut into 6 wedges
- 12 ounces cherry tomatoes, halved

why this recipe works Ranch might be the most popular salad bar dressing, but we think similarly creamy peppercorn dressing is an unsung hero, adding unique intrigue and heat to salads, and we particularly like it on a classic wedge. Typically, though, it either tastes nothing like pepper, or it makes your eyes burn with too much spice—a common conundrum when working with raw black pepper. We certainly wanted to taste the black pepper and feel some fire, but adding a ton of freshly cracked stuff left us with a mouthful of chewy, acerbic pepper bits. To tame the intensity, we turned on the stove: We simmered coarsely ground peppercorns in the fat left from cooking some bacon for our wedge. Gently cooking peppercorns in fat tames their heat by pulling out the fat-soluble compound piperine, which packs that heat, leaving a more mellow pepper flavor but plenty of presence. We drained the mellowed peppercorns before adding them to a creamy and tangy—but not gloppy—base of olive oil, sour cream, mayo, buttermilk, Dijon mustard, and red wine vinegar. If you don't have buttermilk, substitute 2 tablespoons milk and increase the vinegar to 2½ teaspoons.

1 Cook bacon in 10-inch skillet over medium heat until crispy, 5 to 7 minutes. Using slotted spoon, transfer bacon to paper towel–lined plate; set aside.

2 Add 1 tablespoon pepper to fat in skillet and cook over low heat until faint bubbles appear. Continue to cook, swirling skillet occasionally, until pepper is fragrant, 7 to 10 minutes. Drain pepper in fine-mesh strainer over bowl. Discard fat and wipe bowl clean. Whisk drained pepper, oil, sour cream, mayonnaise, buttermilk, mustard, vinegar, and garlic together in now-empty bowl. Season dressing with salt to taste.

3 Arrange lettuce wedges on individual plates and top evenly with dressing, bacon, and tomatoes. Season with pepper to taste and serve.

grilled chicken salad

serves 4

- 4 (6- to 8-ounce) boneless, skinless chicken breasts, trimmed

  Salt and pepper

- 6 tablespoons extra-virgin olive oil

- 2 tablespoons red wine vinegar

- 1 garlic clove, minced

- 8 ounces (8 cups) baby arugula

- 8 ounces fresh whole-milk mozzarella cheese, torn into bite-size pieces (2 cups)

- 8 ounces cherry tomatoes, halved

- ½ cup pitted kalamata olives, chopped

  Coarse finishing salt

why this recipe works We typically add salt to salads by seasoning the dressing or adding a briny ingredient to the bowl. But seasoning salad more directly, by sprinkling the mix with a coarse salt just before serving, is an appealing way to heighten the impact of the constituent ingredients and add unique texture. For example, just a few perfectly flavorful ingredients and some salt elevate this vibrant summer week-night arugula and grilled chicken salad. Cherry tomatoes, kalamata olives, and bite-size pieces of fresh mozzarella—all dressed with a sharp red wine vinaigrette—contribute garden freshness, brininess, and richness, respectively. Then we sprinkle on the salt, and the crystals offer textural contrast to and enhance the flavors of the soft milky mozzarella, sweet juicy tomatoes, and moist charred chicken. To keep the salt level in check, use a gentle hand when seasoning the chicken before cooking. You can use your preferred coarse finishing salt in this recipe; for information on finishing salts, see pages 22–23.

1A for a charcoal grill Open bottom vent completely. Light large chimney starter filled with charcoal briquettes (6 quarts). When top coals are partially covered with ash, pour evenly over grill. Set cooking grate in place, cover, and open lid vent completely. Heat grill until hot, about 5 minutes.

1B for a gas grill Turn all burners to high, cover, and heat grill until hot, about 15 minutes. Leave all burners on high.

2 Pat chicken breasts dry with paper towels and lightly season with salt and pepper. Clean and oil cooking grate. Place breasts on grill and cook until chicken registers 160 degrees, about 6 minutes per side. Transfer breasts to cutting board, tent with aluminum foil, and let rest for 5 minutes.

3 Slice breasts ½ inch thick. Whisk oil, vinegar, garlic, ⅛ teaspoon salt, and pinch pepper together in large bowl. Add arugula, mozzarella, tomatoes, and olives and toss to combine. Divide salad among individual plates, top with chicken, and sprinkle with finishing salt to taste. Serve.

pan-seared steaks with brandy–pink peppercorn sauce

serves 4

2 (1-pound) boneless strip or rib-eye steaks, 1 to 1½ inches thick, trimmed and halved crosswise

Salt and pepper

1 tablespoon vegetable oil, plus extra as needed

1 large shallot, minced

¼ cup brandy

¾ cup chicken broth

2 tablespoons pink peppercorns, cracked

3 tablespoons unsalted butter, cut into 3 pieces and chilled

¼ teaspoon red wine vinegar

why this recipe works On its own, a simple well-cooked steak, with an appealing browned crust and rosy interior, is immensely satisfying; pair it with a flavorful sauce and it's the perfect special occasion dinner: elegant and impressive but quick and simple to execute. We found we could cook flavorful boneless strip steaks or rib-eyes to our medium-rare liking in just about 10 minutes. Peppercorn sauce is a classic pairing with steak. We love how the peppery bite sharpens the rich meat, but the combination is adaptable. With a rainbow of peppercorns now in our cabinet, we wondered if something different might give the dish a new dimension. While the steaks rested, we browned some shallot in the beef drippings and deglazed the pan with brandy. It was at this point that we incorporated cracked pink peppercorns along with some chicken broth and reduced the sauce. Simmered with the broth, the peppercorns added waves of complexity and softened to a pleasantly chewy texture. Their fruity pepperiness both lightened and complemented the rich brandy sauce. We prefer these steaks cooked to medium-rare, but if you prefer them more or less done, see our guidelines on page 280.

1 Pat steaks dry with paper towels and season with salt. Heat oil in 12-inch skillet over medium-high heat until just smoking. Place steaks in skillet and cook, without moving, until well browned on first side, about 4 minutes. Flip steaks and continue to cook, without moving, until well browned on second side and meat registers 120 to 125 degrees (for medium-rare), 3 to 7 minutes. Transfer steaks to plate, tent with aluminum foil, and let rest while preparing sauce.

2 Pour off all but 1 tablespoon fat from skillet. (If necessary, add extra oil to equal 1 tablespoon.) Add shallot and cook over medium heat until softened, 1 to 2 minutes. Off heat, carefully add brandy, scraping up any browned bits.

3 Stir in broth and peppercorns and return skillet to medium heat. Bring to simmer and cook until reduced to ⅓ cup, 4 to 6 minutes. Off heat, whisk in butter, 1 piece at a time, until melted and sauce is thickened and glossy. Whisk in vinegar and any accumulated steak juices. Season with salt to taste. Serve steaks with sauce.

seared duck breasts with green peppercorn sauce

serves 4

4 (6-ounce) boneless duck breasts, skin and fat cap trimmed to ¼ inch

Salt and pepper

2 shallots, minced

¾ cup ruby port

2 tablespoons dried green peppercorns, cracked

1 cup chicken broth

½ cup heavy cream

1 teaspoon lemon juice

why this recipe works Duck breasts are a study in contrast: They have rich, meaty flavor and the texture of beef, but under their cap of fat, the flesh itself is as lean as chicken breast. That's why the French pair them with a light port-cream sauce speckled with green peppercorns: The slightly gamy flavor of duck stands up to the bright, vegetal notes and tames the pungency of green peppercorns, and the meat's leanness allows for a lick of cream. Even with their contrasts, duck breasts are simple to cook. We wanted to render the fat for browned, crispy skin. First, we scored the skin in a crosshatch pattern before cooking to render fat more efficiently. We preheated a skillet over medium heat, added the duck breasts skin side down, and reduced the heat to medium-low. We cooked the breasts skin side down for 25 minutes, flipping them to cook only a few minutes on the flesh side. As the duck breasts cooked, the fat insulated the meat while it slowly rendered, and the meat finished tender and medium-rare—perfect. Adjust the burner as needed to maintain a constant but gentle simmer during the skin-down cooking time. We prefer dried green peppercorns here, but green peppercorns packed in brine also work; rinse and coarsely chop them before using.

1   Using sharp knife, cut slits ½ inch apart in crosshatch pattern in duck skin and fat cap, being careful not to cut into meat. Pat breasts dry with paper towels and season with salt and pepper. Heat 12-inch skillet over medium heat for 3 minutes. Reduce heat to medium-low, place breasts skin side down in skillet, and cook until fat begins to render, about 5 minutes. Continue to cook, adjusting heat as needed for fat to maintain constant but gentle simmer, until most of fat has rendered and skin is deep golden and crisp, 20 to 25 minutes.

2   Flip breasts and continue to cook until duck registers 120 to 125 degrees (for medium-rare), 2 to 5 minutes. Transfer breasts to cutting board, tent with aluminum foil, and let rest while making sauce.

3   Pour off all but 1 tablespoon fat from skillet. Add shallots and cook over medium-high heat until softened, about 2 minutes. Stir in port and peppercorns and cook, scraping up any browned bits, until liquid has reduced to syrupy consistency, about 4 minutes. Stir in broth and cream and cook until sauce has thickened and reduced to about 1 cup, about 5 minutes. Off heat, stir in lemon juice and season with salt and pepper to taste. Slice breasts ½ inch thick and serve with sauce.

peppercorn-crusted beef tenderloin with hollandaise sauce

serves 4 to 6

Each peppercorn crust adds a different dimension—not just heat—to the beef. Center-cut tenderloin roasts are also sold as Châteaubriand. Sift the cracked peppercorns through a fine-mesh strainer. Make sure the butter for the hollandaise is hot. We prefer this roast cooked to medium-rare, but if you prefer it more or less done, see our guidelines on page 280.

tenderloin

- ¼ cup black peppercorns, cracked and sifted
- ¼ cup extra-virgin olive oil
- 1½ teaspoons grated orange zest
- ¼ teaspoon ground nutmeg
- 2 teaspoons kosher salt
- ¾ teaspoon sugar
- ¼ teaspoon baking soda
- 1 (2-pound) center-cut beef tenderloin roast, trimmed

hollandaise sauce

- 3 large egg yolks
- 2 tablespoons lemon juice
- Salt
- Pinch cayenne pepper, plus extra for seasoning
- 16 tablespoons unsalted butter, melted and still hot (180 degrees)

1 for the tenderloin Heat peppercorns and 3 tablespoons oil in small saucepan over low heat until faint bubbles appear. Continue to cook, swirling saucepan occasionally, until fragrant, 7 to 10 minutes. Strain mixture through fine-mesh strainer over small bowl. Discard oil and wipe bowl clean. Combine peppercorns, orange zest, nutmeg, and remaining 1 tablespoon oil in now-empty bowl.

2 Adjust oven rack to middle position and heat oven to 300 degrees. Set wire rack in rimmed baking sheet. Combine salt, sugar, and baking soda, then rub mixture evenly over tenderloin until surface is tacky. Coat top and sides of tenderloin with peppercorn mixture, pressing firmly to adhere. Transfer tenderloin to prepared rack and roast until meat registers 120 to 125 degrees (for medium-rare), 45 to 55 minutes. Transfer tenderloin to carving board, tent with aluminum foil, and let rest for 20 minutes.

3 for the hollandaise sauce Meanwhile, process egg yolks, lemon juice, ¼ teaspoon salt, and cayenne in blender until frothy, about 10 seconds, scraping down sides and bottom of blender jar as needed. With blender running, slowly add hot butter and process until hollandaise is thickened and emulsified, about 2 minutes. Adjust consistency with hot water as needed. (Hollandaise should slowly drip from spoon.) Season with salt and extra cayenne to taste. Slice tenderloin ½ inch thick and serve with hollandaise.

white peppercorn–crusted beef tenderloin with tarragon hollandaise sauce

Substitute white peppercorns for black peppercorns. Stir 1 tablespoon minced fresh tarragon into sauce before serving.

pink peppercorn–crusted beef tenderloin with cilantro-lime hollandaise sauce

Substitute pink peppercorns for black peppercorns; reduce cooking time to 3 to 5 minutes in step 1. Substitute lime juice for lemon juice. Stir 2 teaspoons minced fresh cilantro and ½ teaspoon grated lime zest into sauce before serving.

green peppercorn–crusted beef tenderloin with sun-dried tomato hollandaise sauce

Substitute dried green peppercorns for black peppercorns. Add 3 tablespoons chopped oil-packed sun-dried tomatoes and 2 tablespoons water to blender with egg yolks.

thick-cut pork chops with smoked salt

serves 4

4 (12-ounce) bone-in pork rib chops, 1½ inches thick, trimmed

Kosher salt and pepper

1–2 tablespoons vegetable oil

Smoked Salt (page 24)

why this recipe works If cooked properly, a simple rib pork chop on the bone, large and impressive at 12 ounces, is appealing: a brown sear on succulent meat that's tender with just enough bite. But go a step further by finishing with a flavored salt you make yourself and you call attention to the browned sear, enhance the perception of the meat's richness, and introduce some extra flavor without covering up any of the sweetness of the pork as a sauce might do. Smoke and pork work well together so we picked our Smoked Salt (page 24) from the pantry. For a seared pork chop that lived up to our ideal, we turned the conventional method upside down, first cooking chops (that we salted and rested before cooking; for more information on salting, see pages 56–57) in a low oven and then searing them. Slowly cooking the meat first rather than starting in the smoking pan allowed enzymes to break down protein, tenderizing the thick chops. The surface gently dried out in the oven and then became beautifully caramelized in the pan. If the pork is enhanced (injected with a salt solution), do not salt in step 1. You can substitute any of the flavored salts on page 24 for the Smoked Salt.

1 Cut 2 slits, about 2 inches apart, through outer layer of fat and silverskin on each pork chop. Sprinkle entire surface of each chop with ½ teaspoon kosher salt and place on wire rack set in rimmed baking sheet. Let sit at room temperature for 45 minutes.

2 Adjust oven rack to middle position and heat oven to 275 degrees. Pat chops dry with paper towels and season with pepper. Transfer sheet to oven and cook until pork registers 120 to 125 degrees, 30 to 45 minutes.

3 Heat 1 tablespoon oil in 12-inch skillet over high heat until just smoking. Place 2 chops in skillet and sear until well browned and crusty, 2 to 3 minutes, lifting once halfway through cooking to redistribute fat underneath. Flip chops and cook until well browned on second side, 2 to 3 minutes. Transfer chops to plate and repeat with remaining 2 chops, adding 1 tablespoon oil if skillet is dry.

4 Reduce heat to medium. Use tongs to stand 2 pork chops on their sides. Holding chops together with tongs, return to skillet and sear sides of chops (with exception of bone side) until browned and pork registers 145 degrees, about 2 minutes; transfer to clean plate. Repeat with remaining 2 chops; transfer to plate, tent with aluminum foil, and rest for 10 minutes. Sprinkle chops with smoked salt to taste. Serve.

pan-roasted fish fillets with herb salt

serves 4

4 (6- to 8-ounce) skinless cod fillets, 1 to 1½ inches thick

Salt and pepper

½ teaspoon sugar

1 tablespoon vegetable oil

Fresh Herb Salt (page 24)

why this recipe works Flaky white fish tastes clean and fresh, but its mild manner could benefit from a boost of finishing flavor to enhance interest. We don't always want to splash it with a rich sauce or coat it and fry it to do this. To honor the delicate flavor of pristine white fish fillets, we sometimes like just a sprinkle. This is the perfect place to utilize a flavored salt: The salinity brings to mind the taste of the sea and the herb, citrus, or spice is a subtle enhancement. Our simple pan-roasted method delivers moist fillets with an appealing chestnut-brown crust (which also enhances flavor) every time: We began by browning just one side of thick fillets in a hot nonstick skillet before roasting the fillets in the oven. Sprinkling the fillets with sugar that caramelizes guaranteed browning in the short cook time. Halibut, sea bass, and red snapper are good substitutes for cod. Because most fish fillets differ in thickness, some pieces may finish cooking before others—be sure to immediately remove any fillet that reaches 140 degrees. You will need a 12-inch ovensafe nonstick skillet for this recipe. You can substitute any of the flavored salts on page 24 for the Fresh Herb Salt.

1 Adjust oven rack to middle position and heat oven to 425 degrees. Pat cod fillets dry with paper towels, season with salt and pepper, and sprinkle sugar lightly over 1 side of each fillet.

2 Heat oil in 12-inch ovensafe nonstick skillet over high heat until just smoking. Lay fillets sugared side down in skillet and press lightly to ensure even contact with skillet. Cook until browned on first side, 1 to 1½ minutes.

3 Turn fillets over using 2 spatulas and transfer skillet to oven. Roast until fish flakes apart when gently prodded with paring knife and registers 140 degrees, 7 to 10 minutes. Sprinkle with herb salt to taste. Serve.

spaghetti with pecorino romano and black pepper

serves 4 to 6

- 6 ounces Pecorino Romano cheese, 4 ounces finely grated (2 cups) and 2 ounces coarsely grated (1 cup)
- 1 pound spaghetti
- 1½ teaspoons salt
- 2 tablespoons heavy cream
- 2 teaspoons extra-virgin olive oil
- 1½ teaspoons pepper

why this recipe works Pepper isn't just a flavor enhancer, and the famed simple Roman pasta dish *cacio e pepe* is probably one of the best examples of how black pepper can be the star flavoring in a dish: The clean spice notes shine, cutting through the richness and saltiness of a light Pecorino Romano sauce that naps thin strands of spaghetti. In theory, the sauce forms itself when cheese and some cooking water are stirred with the pasta, as the cooking water provides starch that keeps the cheese's proteins from clumping together. We found in practice, however, that the cheese still clumped. For an ultrasmooth sauce, we cut the amount of cooking water in half when boiling the pasta; this upped the starch level in the water, providing more of a safeguard. A couple spoonfuls of heavy cream further ensured a fluid sauce since the cream contains molecules called lipoproteins that act as a sort of liaison between protein and fat, keeping them emulsified. Do not adjust the amount of water for cooking the pasta; the amount used is critical to the success of the recipe. Make sure to stir the pasta frequently while cooking so that it doesn't stick to the pot. Draining the pasta water into the serving bowl warms the bowl and helps keep the dish hot until it is served. Letting the dish rest briefly before serving allows the flavors to develop and the sauce to thicken to the right consistency.

1 Place finely grated Pecorino in medium bowl. Set colander in large serving bowl.

2 Bring 2 quarts water to boil in large pot. Add pasta and salt and cook, stirring often, until al dente. Drain pasta in prepared colander, reserving cooking water. Pour 1½ cups cooking water into 2-cup liquid measuring cup and discard remainder. Transfer drained pasta to now-empty bowl.

3 Slowly whisk 1 cup reserved cooking water into finely grated Pecorino until smooth, then whisk in cream, oil, and pepper until combined. Gradually pour cheese mixture over pasta and toss to combine. Let pasta rest for 1 to 2 minutes, tossing frequently and adjusting consistency with remaining reserved cooking water as needed. Serve, passing coarsely grated Pecorino separately.

BRINE IT

Salt is the most elemental and important seasoning; but look below the surface, and salt can do much more. Brining—soaking food in a solution of salt and water—is an important example. It makes lean foods (and not just meat!) juicy, tender, and flavorful throughout. It's not magic; it's basic science.

what's happening?

During brining, salt moves from the area of greater concentration (the surrounding liquid brine) to the area of lesser concentration (the interior of the food being brined), bringing the liquid with it in a process called osmosis. Meanwhile, the salt changes the structure of the proteins, so they're better able to hold onto the moisture received in osmosis, even after cooking. Through this, there's also a compromising of structural integrity, which reduces toughness and results in a more tender product. And, of course, the method seasons food to the very center.

brining lean meat

Lean meats—chicken, turkey, and some cuts of pork—are the traditional brining candidates. By the time these cuts cook to the proper internal temperature, much of their moisture has been expelled. And without much flavorful fat, they become leathery and tough. Additionally, for whole chickens or turkeys, there's both light and dark meat. The dark meat contains more fat and connective tissue, and it needs to be cooked to 175 degrees for them to melt and for the meat to become tender. However, if cooked to this temperature, the lean white meat would be incredibly dry (its doneness temperature is 160 degrees). Brining, in effect, negates some of the effects of uneven cooking, adding moisture to and protecting the white breast meat so it won't be dry even if overcooked a bit. Use the chart below to brine whatever lean cut you bring home from the market before cooking via pan-searing, roasting, or grilling.

brining formulas for poultry and pork

MEAT	COLD WATER	TABLE SALT	TIME
Chicken			
1 (3- to 8-pound) Whole Chicken	2 quarts	½ cup	1 hour
2 (3- to 8-pound) Whole Chickens	3 quarts	¾ cup	1 hour
4 pounds Bone-In Chicken Pieces	2 quarts	½ cup	½ to 1 hour
Boneless, Skinless Chicken Breasts (up to 6 breasts)	1½ quarts	3 tablespoons	½ to 1 hour
Turkey			
1 (12- to 17-pound) Whole Turkey	2 gallons	1 cup	6 to 12 hours
1 (18- to 24-pound) Whole Turkey	3 gallons	1½ cups	6 to 12 hours
Bone-In Turkey Breasts	1 gallon	½ cup	3 to 6 hours
Pork			
Bone-In Pork Chops (up to 6)	1½ quarts	3 tablespoons	½ to 1 hour
Boneless Pork Chops (up to 6)	1½ quarts	3 tablespoons	½ to 1 hour
1 (2½- to 6-pound) Boneless Roast	2 quarts	¼ cup	1 to 1½ hours

Note: Do not brine longer than recommended.

setting up for brining

You don't need much to brine, just your protein, table salt (the tiny grains dissolve in water more quickly than kosher salt), and a container. Zipper-lock bags work well for chicken breasts and chops. For whole roasts and birds, we use large heavy-duty plastic containers in the test kitchen. And for really big jobs, like a turkey, you might need a cooler. In that case, keep the brine cold with ice packs.

sweeten the pot

Sometimes we'll add sugar to our brines. The sugar encourages browning, which can be slowed down by brining, and helps the skin on poultry to brown.

what about beef?

In general, beef has a higher fat content than poultry and pork, so it doesn't need a brine to remain juicy. The cuts that are on the leaner side (think: tender cuts such as strip steaks or tenderloin roasts) should ideally be cooked only to about 125 degrees (for medium-rare). In comparison, pork and chicken require a higher doneness temperature (140 to 145 for pork, 160 for white-meat poultry, and 175 for dark-meat poultry) and are, therefore, in greater danger of drying out. Tougher cuts of beef, such as chuck roast or brisket, are cooked longer, to more than 195 degrees, but their extensive marbling of fat and collagen melts and acts as a natural moisturizer. Added water would merely dilute the rich, beefy flavor.

what else to brine?

The salty secret doesn't stop with pork and poultry. We also brine seafood and even vegetables in the following pages.

fish and shellfish

Fish (and shrimp) is generally pretty lean and even fattier salmon can benefit from some extra moisture during the pan-searing process. Fillets, especially of salmon, often have a thicker and a thinner end, and fish that is perfectly cooked at its thickest point can be overcooked and dry at the thinner end. Brining prevents this drying. We've found that you can brine any species of fish, and quickly—a weekday boon. That's because the structure of muscle is different than in meat: Instead of long, thin fibers (as long as 10 centimeters in meat), fish is constructed of very short (up to 10 times shorter) bundles of fibers, so the brine penetrates and does its job at a faster clip. Additionally, brining helps reduce the presence of albumin, a protein that can congeal into an unappealing white mass on the surface of fish when heated.

Fish For up to six 1-inch-thick fish steaks or fillets, use ¼ tablespoons of salt dissolved in 2 quarts of water and brine for 15 minutes.

Shrimp For up to 2 pounds of shell-on shrimp, use 2 tablespoons salt dissolved in 1 quart of water and brine for 15 minutes.

vegetables

Salt makes its way into vegetables as they cook. But when you season vegetables that cook quickly via dry heat, the salt flavor remains only superficial. When we cook vegetables in a way to preserve their crunch, like during grilling, the salt doesn't have enough time to penetrate as it does during roasting. But if you brine your vegetables, the salt diffuses into them, so instead of a layer of intense salt surrounding a bland interior, the vegetables taste more like themselves, not salty.

For up to 2 pounds of vegetables, use ¼ cup salt dissolved in 4 cups water and brine for 1 hour.

grill-roasted pork loin

serves 6

Salt and coarsely ground pepper

1 (2½- to 3-pound) boneless blade-end pork loin roast, trimmed and tied at 1½-inch intervals

2 tablespoons extra-virgin olive oil

2 cups wood chips

why this recipe works Succulent pork roast with a peppered crust and smoke-flavored meat is an impressive dinner. But in the dry heat, the lean loin loses much of its moisture before it's done on the grill. Brining keeps the meat juicy (and even more flavorful). We used a two-step grilling process, searing the roast directly over hot coals for a nice crust and finishing it gently over indirect heat. We prefer to brine our own meat; however, if your pork is enhanced (injected with a salt solution), do not brine in step 1 and add 1 tablespoon salt to the pepper. If you'd like to use wood chunks instead of wood chips when using a charcoal grill, substitute two medium wood chunks, soaked in water for 1 hour, for the wood chip packet.

1 Dissolve ¼ cup salt in 2 quarts cold water in large container. Submerge roast in brine, cover, and refrigerate for 1 to 1½ hours. Remove roast from brine and pat dry with paper towels. Rub roast with oil, then sprinkle with 1 tablespoon pepper. Let sit at room temperature for 1 hour.

2 Just before grilling, soak wood chips in water for 15 minutes, then drain. Using large piece of heavy-duty aluminum foil, wrap soaked chips in 8 by 4½-inch foil packet. (Make sure chips do not poke holes in sides or bottom of packet.) Cut 2 evenly spaced 2-inch slits in top of packet.

3A **for a charcoal grill** Open bottom vent halfway. Light large chimney starter three-quarters filled with charcoal briquettes (4½ quarts). When top coals are partially covered with ash, pour evenly over half of grill. Place wood chip packet on coals. Set cooking grate in place, cover, and open lid vent halfway. Heat grill until hot and wood chips are smoking, about 5 minutes.

3B **for a gas grill** Remove cooking grate and place wood chip packet directly on primary burner. Set grate in place, turn all burners to high, cover, and heat grill until hot and wood chips are smoking, about 15 minutes. Leave primary burner on high and turn off other burner(s). (Adjust primary burner as needed to maintain grill temperature of 300 to 325 degrees.)

4 Clean and oil cooking grate. Place roast fat side up on hotter side of grill and cook (covered if using gas) until well browned, 10 to 12 minutes, turning as needed. Slide roast to cooler side of grill, parallel with and as close as possible to heat. Cover (position lid vent over roast if using charcoal) and cook for 20 minutes. Rotate roast 180 degrees, cover, and cook until pork registers 140 degrees, 10 to 30 minutes. Transfer roast to carving board, tent with foil, and let rest for 20 minutes. Remove twine and slice ½ inch thick. Serve.

pan-seared salmon with cilantro-mint chutney

serves 4

chutney

2 cups fresh cilantro leaves

1 cup fresh mint leaves

½ cup water

¼ cup sesame seeds, lightly toasted

1 (2-inch) piece ginger, peeled and sliced into ⅛-inch-thick rounds

1 jalapeño chile, stemmed, seeded, and sliced into 1-inch pieces

2 tablespoons vegetable oil

2 tablespoons fresh lime juice

1½ teaspoons sugar

½ teaspoon salt

salmon

1 (2-pound) center-cut skin-on salmon fillet, 1 to 1½ inches thick

Salt and pepper

why this recipe works Pan-searing salmon sounds straightforward: Simply cook fillets in oil in a hot pan on both sides until nicely browned on the exterior but still pink on the interior. But there's a flaw: While inevitably rosy at the thickest point, a fillet becomes a bit overcooked and dry at the thinner end. We brine meat all the time and found that the technique applies just as well to fish. Brining took just 15 minutes for the salmon—not much time at all—and it both seasoned the fish deeply and kept every centimeter moist. Leaving the skin on the fillets further protected them during cooking. Additionally, the skin releases fat into the pan, which is then used to sear the second side until crisp. This salmon was excellent with just a squirt of lemon, but a cilantro-mint chutney was easy to make, and its bright, herbal flavors balanced the salmon's richness. To ensure uniform pieces of fish that cooked at the same rate, we found it best to buy a whole center-cut fillet and cut it into four pieces ourselves. Using skin-on salmon is important here; the skin can be peeled off before serving. If using wild salmon, cook it until it registers 120 degrees. For a spicier chutney, reserve and add the jalapeño ribs and seeds.

1 **for the chutney** Process all ingredients in blender until smooth, about 30 seconds, scraping down sides of jar with spatula after 10 seconds.

2 **for the salmon** Cut salmon crosswise into 4 fillets. Dissolve ¼ cup salt in 2 quarts cold water in large container. Submerge salmon in brine and let sit at room temperature for 15 minutes.

3 Remove salmon from brine and pat dry with paper towels. Sprinkle bottom of 12-inch nonstick skillet evenly with ½ teaspoon salt and ½ teaspoon pepper. Place salmon skin side down in skillet and sprinkle tops of fillets with ¼ teaspoon salt and ¼ teaspoon pepper. Heat skillet over medium-high heat and cook fillets without moving them until fat begins to render, skin begins to brown, and bottom ¼ inch of fillets turn opaque, 6 to 8 minutes.

4 Using 2 spatulas, flip fillets and continue to cook without moving them until centers are still translucent when checked with tip of paring knife and register 125 degrees, 6 to 8 minutes. Transfer fillets skin side down to serving platter and let rest for 5 minutes. Serve with chutney.

crispy salt and pepper shrimp

serves 4 to 6

1½ pounds shell-on medium-large shrimp (31 to 40 per pound)

2 tablespoons Chinese rice wine or dry sherry

Kosher salt

2½ teaspoons black peppercorns, coarsely ground

2 teaspoons Sichuan peppercorns, coarsely ground

2 teaspoons sugar

¼ teaspoon cayenne pepper

4 cups vegetable oil

5 tablespoons cornstarch

2 jalapeño chiles, stemmed, seeded, and sliced into ⅛-inch-thick rings

3 garlic cloves, minced

1 tablespoon grated fresh ginger

2 scallions, sliced thin on bias

Shredded iceberg lettuce

why this recipe works There's probably no recipe that better showcases salt and pepper working in multiple ways and together than Chinese salt and pepper shrimp, an enticing dish of plump, moist fried shrimp with shells as shatteringly crispy—and appealing to eat—as fried chicken skin, and a killer savory-spicy flavor profile. A quick salt–rice wine soak improved the shrimp's texture, plumping them, as well as contributing flavor; the Sichuan peppercorns gave the dish sparkling spice and aromatic piquancy, while black peppercorns provided a straightforward hit of heat. We added the black peppercorns and Sichuan peppercorns along with cayenne and sugar to the coating and then fried more of the same with ginger and garlic to make a flavorful paste that we tossed the fried shrimp in for great depth. For an extra jolt of spiciness, we also fried a couple of thinly sliced jalapeños. We like to use frozen shrimp; thaw them overnight in the fridge or under running cold water and blot them dry. Use a Dutch oven that holds 6 quarts or more for this recipe. Serve with steamed white rice.

1 Adjust oven rack to upper-middle position and heat oven to 225 degrees. Set wire rack in rimmed baking sheet and line large plate with triple layer of paper towels. Toss shrimp with rice wine and 1 teaspoon salt in large bowl and let sit at room temperature for 15 minutes. Combine black peppercorns, Sichuan peppercorns, sugar, and cayenne in small bowl.

2 Heat oil in large Dutch oven over medium heat until oil registers 385 degrees. Meanwhile, drain shrimp and pat dry with paper towels; wipe bowl dry with paper towels. Transfer shrimp to now-empty bowl, add 3 tablespoons cornstarch and 1 tablespoon peppercorn mixture, and toss until well coated.

3 Carefully add one-third of shrimp to hot oil and fry, stirring occasionally to keep shrimp from sticking together, until light brown, 2 to 3 minutes. Adjust burner, if necessary, to maintain oil temperature between 375 and 385 degrees. Using wire skimmer or slotted spoon, transfer shrimp to prepared plate and let drain briefly. Transfer shrimp to prepared rack and keep warm in oven. Return oil to 385 degrees and repeat frying shrimp in 2 more batches, retossing each batch thoroughly with coating mixture before frying. Line plate with clean paper towels as needed.

4 Return oil to 385 degrees. Toss jalapeño rings with remaining 2 tablespoons cornstarch in separate bowl. Shake off excess cornstarch, then carefully add jalapeño rings to oil and fry until crisp, 1 to 2 minutes. Transfer jalapeño rings to prepared plate. After frying, reserve 2 tablespoons frying oil.

5 Heat reserved oil in 12-inch skillet over medium-high heat until shimmering. Add garlic, ginger, and remaining peppercorn mixture and cook, stirring occasionally, until mixture is fragrant and just beginning to brown, about 45 seconds. Add shrimp, scallions, and ½ teaspoon salt and toss to coat. Line serving platter with shredded lettuce. Arrange shrimp on platter and sprinkle with jalapeño rings. Serve immediately.

grilled brined carrots with cilantro-yogurt sauce

serves 4

Salt

1½ pounds young carrots with greens attached, carrots unpeeled, greens chopped (1¼ cups)

1¼ cups coarsely chopped fresh cilantro leaves and stems

½ cup plain Greek yogurt

¼ cup dry-roasted peanuts, chopped

1 jalapeño chile, stemmed, seeded, and minced

1 teaspoon grated fresh ginger

1 garlic clove, minced

¼ teaspoon ground coriander

1 ice cube

why this recipe works We love grilling whole young carrots, but they're really tricky to season evenly. If you dust raw carrots with salt, it bounces right off. You can rub carrots with fat to give the salt something to stick to, but that seasoning will be only skin deep with little time to penetrate the carrots during their brief stay on the grill. Enter: brining. Soaking in salt water flavored the carrots deeply. We grilled the brined carrots quickly over a hot fire to develop char without sacrificing crunch. Drizzled with cilantro-yogurt sauce and sprinkled with peanuts, these carrots might just become your new favorite side dish. Young carrots (not to be confused with baby-cut carrots) are immature carrots. Look for carrots that are 3 to 5 inches long and ½ to 1 inch in diameter, with the leafy green tops still attached. Do not peel the carrots. If you can't find young carrots, mature carrots can be substituted: Halve the carrots lengthwise if thicker in diameter. Additional cilantro can be substituted for the carrot tops. The ice cube added to the sauce ensures it stays bright green. For a spicier dish, reserve and add the jalapeño ribs and seeds to the sauce before processing.

1 Dissolve ¼ cup salt in 4 cups water in large bowl. Submerge carrots in brine and let sit at room temperature for 1 hour. Remove carrots from brine and pat dry with paper towels.

2 Meanwhile, process 1 cup carrot tops, 1 cup cilantro, yogurt, 3 tablespoons peanuts, jalapeño, ginger, garlic, coriander, and ice cube in blender until smooth and creamy, about 2 minutes, scraping down sides of blender jar as needed. Transfer yogurt sauce to small bowl and season with salt to taste. Cover and refrigerate until ready to serve.

3A for a charcoal grill Open bottom vent completely. Light large chimney starter filled with charcoal briquettes (6 quarts). When top coals are partially covered with ash, pour evenly over half of grill. Set cooking grate in place, cover, and open lid vent completely. Heat grill until hot, about 5 minutes.

3B for a gas grill Turn all burners to high, cover, and heat grill until hot, about 15 minutes. Leave all burners on high.

4 Clean and oil cooking grate. Place carrots on grill (directly over coals if using charcoal) and cook, turning occasionally, until carrots are well charred on all sides and exteriors are just beginning to soften, 3 to 7 minutes. Transfer carrots to serving platter. Drizzle with yogurt sauce and sprinkle with remaining ¼ cup carrot tops, remaining ¼ cup cilantro, and remaining 1 tablespoon peanuts. Serve.

grilled brined asparagus with cilantro-yogurt sauce

Look for asparagus that is at least ½ inch thick at base.

Substitute 2 pounds thick asparagus, trimmed, for carrots and additional 1¼ cups chopped cilantro for carrot tops. Cook asparagus, turning occasionally, until spears are charred on all sides and just beginning to soften on exteriors, 2 to 4 minutes.

grilled brined zucchini with cilantro-yogurt sauce

Substitute 3 large zucchini, halved lengthwise, for carrots and additional 1¼ cups chopped cilantro for carrot tops. Increase salt in brine to 5 tablespoons. Place zucchini cut side down on grill and cook until well charred on bottom and flesh just begins to soften, 3 to 4 minutes. Flip zucchini and continue to cook until skin side is charred, about 2 minutes.

SALT IT

Brining is an excellent technique to prevent chalky, dried-out meat. But it's not always the best option: All the added moisture of a brine makes it difficult to get the bronzed, crispy poultry skin that we love, for example. And meats that are relatively well-marbled seem juicy after cooking without help; they could benefit just from some enhanced seasoning or tenderizing. In these cases, we lose the water and turn straight to salt.

what's happening?

Proteins naturally contain some salt and lots of water, which normally coexist in a happy balance. But when salt is applied directly to meat, it first draws the moisture out to the surface through osmosis, where the liquid dissolves that applied salt. You'd think drawing out moisture would make the meat, well, less moist. It doesn't—as long as you give it some time. Once the salt dissolves in the surface moisture, it creates a super-concentrated brine, which moves into the meat. This migration causes muscle fibers to swell to make room for the liquid and dissolves other proteins, which then act like a sponge so that the meat soaks up and holds onto moisture during cooking. And the surface of the meat is left much drier, meaning it can more easily brown, and in the case of skin, crisp.

season from on high

Ever notice that some chefs season food by sprinkling it from a good foot above the counter? Is this just kitchen theatrics or is there a reason for the practice? We sprinkled chicken breasts with salt and pepper (so we could see the seasoning) from different heights—4 inches, 8 inches, and 12 inches—and found the higher the starting point, the more evenly distributed the salt and pepper, which means better-tasting food. So go ahead and put on a seasoning show.

SALTED SKIN
The skin of a salted bird is crisp and bronze.

BRINED SKIN
The skin of a brined bird is softer and paler.

salting formulas for proteins

CUTS	TIME	KOSHER SALT	METHOD
Steaks, Lamb Chops, Pork Chops	1 hour	¾ teaspoon per 8-ounce chop or steak	Apply salt evenly over surface and let rest at room temperature, uncovered, on wire rack set in rimmed baking sheet.
Beef, Lamb, and Pork Roasts	At least 6 hours or up to 24	1 teaspoon per pound	Apply salt evenly over surface, wrap tightly with plastic wrap, and let rest in refrigerator.
Whole Chicken	At least 6 hours or up to 24	1 teaspoon per pound	Apply salt evenly inside cavity and under skin of breasts and legs and let rest in refrigerator on wire rack set in rimmed baking sheet. (Wrap with plastic wrap if salting for longer than 12 hours.)
Bone-In Chicken Pieces; Boneless or Bone-In Turkey Breast	At least 6 hours or up to 24	¾ teaspoon per pound	Apply salt evenly between skin and meat, leaving skin attached, and let rest in refrigerator on wire rack set in rimmed baking sheet. (Wrap with plastic wrap if salting for longer than 12 hours.)
Whole Turkey	24 to 48 hours	1 teaspoon per pound	Apply salt evenly inside cavity and under skin of breasts and legs, wrap tightly with plastic wrap, and let rest in refrigerator.

what else to salt?

We salt proteins knowing we'll let them sit so the moisture that's drawn out enters the meat again. We presalt vegetables, however, for a different reason. Sure, salting seasons them, but for ultrawatery vegetables like cabbage, cucumbers, and tomatoes, we often want to get rid of that moisture for good so it doesn't lead to soggy salads and slaws or diluted dressings. Since it's so abundant, all that released water can just drain away or be blotted off. (We often salt the vegetables, give them a toss, and then let them drain in a fine-mesh strainer or colander.)

For eggplant, we often salt it before cooking. Eggplant is chock-full of air pockets and water; when you cook it in oil without removing some of that water beforehand, the air sacs absorb the oil, which can turn the eggplant unpleasantly greasy. Tossing eggplant with salt pulls water out from inside the eggplant via osmosis, which in turn collapses some of the eggplant's cells, reducing the amount of air pockets so the eggplant absorbs less oil.

crispy-skinned chicken breasts with lemon-rosemary pan sauce

serves 2

chicken

2 (10- to 12-ounce) bone-in split chicken breasts

Kosher salt and pepper

2 tablespoons vegetable oil

pan sauce

1 shallot, minced

1 teaspoon all-purpose flour

¾ cup chicken broth

2 tablespoons lemon juice

1 tablespoon unsalted butter, chilled

1 teaspoon minced fresh rosemary

Salt and pepper

why this recipe works The ultimate chicken breasts boast skin that's paper-thin, deep golden brown, and so well crisped it crackles when you take a bite. To get there, we started by deboning, pounding, and salting our chicken breasts. The salting not only helped the lean meat retain moisture, but it also dried out the skin so it could crisp readily. Poking holes in both the skin and the meat with a sharp knife prior to salting further encouraged these results. We wanted the chicken to come in direct contact with the hot pan from edge to edge for crisping across the skin's entire surface area. So we started the breasts skin side down in a cold pan and weighed them down briefly to anchor the skin to the pan so the skin didn't contract and could brown evenly. Partway through cooking, we removed the weight to promote evaporation and let the skin continue to crisp. Two 10- to 12-ounce chicken breasts are ideal, but three smaller ones can fit in the same pan; the skin will be slightly less crispy. A boning knife or sharp paring knife works best to remove the bones from the breasts. You must salt the chicken for at least 1 hour or up to 8 hours for this recipe. To maintain the crispy skin, spoon the sauce around the chicken.

---

1 for the chicken Place 1 chicken breast skin side down on cutting board with ribs facing away from knife hand. Run tip of knife between breastbone and meat, working from thick end of breast toward thin end. Angling blade slightly and following rib cage, repeat cutting motion several times to remove ribs and breastbone from breast. Find short remnant of wishbone along top edge of breast and run tip of knife along both sides of bone to separate it from meat. Remove tenderloin (reserve for another use) and trim excess fat, taking care not to cut into skin. Repeat with second breast.

2 Using tip of paring knife, poke skin on each breast evenly 30 to 40 times. Turn breasts over and poke thickest half of each breast 5 to 6 times. Cover breasts with plastic wrap and pound thick ends gently with meat pounder until ½ inch thick. Sprinkle each breast with ½ teaspoon salt. Place breasts skin side up on wire rack set in rimmed baking sheet, cover loosely with plastic, and refrigerate for at least 1 hour or up to 8 hours.

3 Pat chicken dry with paper towels and sprinkle each breast with ¼ teaspoon pepper. Add oil to 12-inch skillet and swirl to coat. Place breasts skin side down in oil and place skillet over medium heat. Place heavy skillet or Dutch oven on top of breasts. Cook breasts until skin is beginning to brown and meat is beginning to turn opaque along edges, 7 to 9 minutes.

4 Remove weight and continue to cook until skin is well browned and very crispy, 6 to 8 minutes. Flip breasts, reduce heat to medium-low, and cook until second side is lightly browned and chicken registers 160 degrees, 2 to 3 minutes. Transfer breasts to individual plates and let rest while preparing pan sauce.

5 for the pan sauce Pour off all but 2 teaspoons fat from skillet, add shallot, and cook over medium heat until softened, about 2 minutes. Add flour and cook, stirring constantly, for 30 seconds. Slowly whisk in broth and lemon juice, scraping up any browned bits and smoothing out any lumps. Bring to simmer and cook until thickened, 2 to 3 minutes. Off heat, whisk in butter and rosemary. Stir in any accumulated chicken juices and season with salt and pepper to taste. Spoon sauce around breasts and serve.

preparing crispy-skinned chicken breasts

1 Run tip of knife between breast-bone and meat, working from thick end of breast toward thin end.

2 Following rib cage, repeat cutting motion several times to remove ribs and breastbone.

3 Find short remnant of wishbone along top edge of breast and run tip of knife along both sides to remove.

Crispy-Skinned Chicken Breasts with Lemon-Rosemary Pan Sauce

Salt-Baked Whole Branzino

salt-baked whole branzino

serves 4

8 cups (3 pounds) kosher salt

⅔ cup water, plus extra as needed

4 large egg whites

2 (1½- to 2-pound) whole branzino, about 16 inches long, scaled, gutted, fins snipped off with scissors

3 garlic cloves, minced

1 lemon, sliced thin, plus lemon wedges for serving

why this recipe works The tradition of baking whole fish in a thick salt crust goes back at least as far as fourth-century-BC Sicily. Why (beyond presentation) would we do this? We found that baking branzino in a salt crust not only seasoned the fish throughout—and perfectly— but it also cooked the entire body evenly for some of the most succulent fish we've tasted. In fact, when we compared a salt-crusted fish to a whole fish baked directly on a baking sheet, the fillet touching the sheet was overcooked by 30 degrees by the time the top fillet was just done; the insulated salt-encased fish cooked evenly. Traditionally sea salt is used but we found that affordable kosher salt worked just fine. We combined the salt with a mixture of egg whites and water to create a workable paste. Avoid fish weighing more than 2 pounds. Red snapper and sea bass are good substitutes for branzino. We developed this recipe using Diamond Crystal kosher salt. If using Morton kosher salt, the weight equivalence for 8 cups is 4½ pounds. To take the temperature, insert the thermometer into the fillets through the opening by the gills.

1 Adjust oven rack to upper-middle position and heat oven to 325 degrees. Line rimmed baking sheet with parchment paper. Stir salt, water, and egg whites in large bowl until well combined. (Mixture should hold together when squeezed; if necessary, continue to stir, adding extra water, 1 tablespoon at a time, until mixture holds.)

2 Rinse branzino under cold running water and pat dry inside and out with paper towels. Working with 1 branzino at a time, open cavity, spread half of garlic on flesh, and stuff with half of lemon slices.

3 Divide 3 cups of salt mixture into two even mounds on prepared sheet. Pat mounds into 10 by 4-inch rectangles, spaced about 1 inch apart. Lay 1 branzino lengthwise across each mound. Gently pack remaining salt mixture evenly around each branzino, leaving heads and tails exposed. Roast until branzino registers 135 degrees, 40 to 45 minutes, rotating sheet halfway through roasting. Transfer sheet to wire rack and let branzino rest for 5 minutes.

4 Using back of serving spoon, gently tap top and sides of salt crusts to crack into large pieces and discard. Using spatula, transfer branzino to cutting board and brush away excess salt. Fillet each branzino by making vertical cut just behind head from top of fish to belly. Make another cut along top of branzino from head to tail. Starting at head and working toward tail, gently slide spatula between top fillet and bones to separate; transfer fillet to serving platter skin side up. Gently lift tail and peel skeleton and head from bottom fillet; discard head, skeleton, and lemon slices. Transfer second fillet skin side up to platter; discard skin. Serve with lemon wedges.

preparing salt-baked whole branzino

1 Divide 3 cups of salt mixture into two even mounds on prepared sheet. Pat mounds into 10 by 4-inch rectangles.

2 Lay 1 branzino lengthwise across each mound.

3 Gently pack remaining salt mixture around each, leaving heads and tails exposed.

serving branzino

1 Using back of serving spoon, gently tap top and sides of salt crusts to crack into large pieces.

2 Make vertical cut just behind head from top of branzino to belly. Make another cut along top of branzino from head to tail.

3 Starting at head and working toward tail, gently slide spatula between top fillet and bones to separate.

salt-crusted fingerling potatoes

serves 4 to 6

- 4 cups water
- 1 teaspoon salt
- 2 pounds fingerling potatoes, unpeeled
- 2 sprigs fresh rosemary

why this recipe works In the United States, salt-crusted potatoes first became famous in Syracuse, New York, where potatoes coated in a crystallized sheath of salt were a cheap snack for thirsty barflies, many of whom worked in the local salt-producing industry. But cooks from Colombia to the Canary Islands have been cooking potatoes this way since at least the early 17th century. Traditionally, the potatoes are cooked in a small amount of ocean water until the liquid evaporates, leaving behind softened, salty spuds with a unique mineral-y flavor. The high concentration of salt in the water boils the potatoes at a higher temperature than unsalted water, so the spuds' starch cooks gently but more completely, resulting in creamier, less-grainy flesh. The salt doesn't easily penetrate the skin, which is why the interior of the potato doesn't become overly salty as it cooks. To re-create the experience without having to trek to the beach, we boiled fingerlings in a skillet with 1 teaspoon of salt and enough water to mostly cover them. Covering the skillet for the first 15 minutes of cooking ensured that the potatoes cooked through and were fluffy and tender. Removing the lid for the second half of the cooking time allowed the water to evaporate, giving the potatoes a crackly, salty sheen. Use potatoes of similar size to ensure consistent cooking. Serve with melted butter, if desired.

1 Whisk water and salt in 12-inch skillet until salt is dissolved, about 15 seconds. Add potatoes and rosemary sprigs (potatoes may not be fully submerged) and bring to simmer over medium-high heat. Reduce heat to medium-low, cover, and cook until potatoes are nearly tender, about 15 minutes.

2 Uncover and increase heat to medium-high. Simmer vigorously until all water has evaporated and potatoes are fully tender, 15 to 20 minutes. Discard rosemary sprigs. Serve.

smashed cucumber salad (pai huang gua)

serves 4

2 (14-ounce) English cucumbers

1½ teaspoons kosher salt

4 teaspoons Chinese black vinegar

1 teaspoon garlic minced to paste

1 tablespoon soy sauce

2 teaspoons toasted sesame oil

1 teaspoon sugar

1 teaspoon sesame seeds, toasted

why this recipes works Smashed cucumbers, or *pai huang gua*, is a Sichuan dish that is typically served with rich, spicy food. We started with English cucumbers, which are nearly seedless and have thin, crisp skins. Placing them in a zipper-lock bag and smashing them into large, irregular pieces sped up the salting step that helped expel excess water that would dilute the dressing and result in a watery dish. The craggy pieces also did a better job of holding on to the dressing. Using black vinegar, an aged rice-based vinegar, added a mellow complexity to the soy and sesame dressing. We recommend using Chinese *Chinkiang* (or *Zhenjiang*) black vinegar in this dish for its complex flavor. If you can't find it, substitute 2 teaspoons rice vinegar plus 1 teaspoon balsamic vinegar. Toast the sesame seeds in a dry skillet over medium heat until fragrant (about 1 minute) and then remove the pan from the heat so the seeds won't scorch. We like to drizzle the cucumbers with homemade Sichuan Chili Oil (page 205) when serving them with milder dishes such as grilled fish or chicken.

1   Trim and discard ends from cucumbers. Cut each cucumber crosswise into three equal lengths. Place pieces in large zipper-lock bag and seal bag. Using small skillet or rolling pin, firmly but gently smash cucumbers until flattened and split lengthwise into 3 to 4 spears each. Tear spears into rough 1- to 1½-inch pieces and transfer to colander set in large bowl. Toss cucumbers with salt and let stand for at least 15 minutes or up to 30 minutes.

2   While cucumbers sit, whisk vinegar and garlic together in small bowl; let stand for at least 5 minutes or up to 15 minutes.

3   Whisk soy sauce, oil, and sugar into vinegar mixture until sugar has dissolved. Transfer cucumbers to medium bowl; discard any extracted liquid. Add dressing and sesame seeds to cucumbers and toss to combine. Serve immediately.

preserved lemons

makes 4 preserved lemons

12 lemons, preferably Meyer

½ cup kosher salt

why this recipe works Moroccan preserved lemons show how transformative salt can be. Once preserved in salt, lemon becomes an almost completely different ingredient, an incredible, versatile condiment: The lemon rinds become soft and aromatic and can be sliced thin or minced before adding to a dish. Their bright, ultralemony flavor, balanced by brininess and sourness, adds great interest to stews, salad dressings, cooked grains, sautéed vegetables, and more. Some recipes we found called for packing the lemons in a jar with a copious amount of salt. However, we found that creating a cavity in each lemon and filling it with 2 tablespoons of kosher salt was enough to cure the lemons without making them overly salty. We used kosher salt because its large grains were easy to work with. We placed the salted lemons in a 1-quart glass jar and poured lemon juice over the top before storing them in the refrigerator for six to eight weeks, shaking the jar once a day for the first few days to ensure even distribution. When the lemons were fully preserved, they appeared softened and a bit deflated. Rinsing the preserved lemons before using gives them a slightly cleaner flavor but isn't absolutely necessary. Tasters preferred removing the flesh and pith and using just the rind, but you can use all parts. Look for Meyer lemons from August through March; regular lemons can be substituted. Wash, scrub, and dry the lemons well before preserving them. You will need a 1-quart glass jar with a tight-fitting lid for this recipe.

1 Wash and dry 4 lemons. Cut lengthwise into quarters, stopping 1 inch from bottom so lemons stay intact at base. Juice remaining 8 lemons to yield 1½ cups juice; set aside any extra juice.

2 Gently stretch 1 cut lemon open and pour 2 tablespoons salt into center. Working over bowl, gently rub cut surfaces of lemon together, then place lemon in 1-quart jar. Repeat with remaining cut lemons and remaining salt. Add any accumulated salt and juice in bowl to jar.

3 Pour 1½ cups lemon juice into jar and press gently to submerge lemons. (Add reserved extra juice to jar as needed to cover lemons completely.) Cover jar tightly with lid and shake. Refrigerate lemons, shaking jar once per day for first 4 days to redistribute salt and juice. Let lemons cure in refrigerator until glossy and softened, 6 to 8 weeks. (Preserved lemons can be refrigerated for at least 6 months.)

4 To use, cut off desired amount of preserved lemon. If desired, use knife to remove pulp and white pith from rind before using.

preparing preserved lemons

1 Cut lengthwise into quarters, stopping 1 inch from bottom so lemons stay intact at base.

2 Gently stretch 1 cut lemon open. Pour 2 tablespoons salt into center. Gently rub cut surfaces together.

3 Add lemons and accumulated salt and juice to 1-quart jar. Pour over 1½ cups lemon juice.

give it a rub

robust coatings for meat and more

Grill chicken parts and the fire will kiss them with flavor; but rub the chicken with a zesty spice blend before it hits the grate, and it'll form an irresistible crust on the rich, crisp skin and elevate the flavor of the juicy meat. Don't just rely on condiments to punch up crispy steak fries; instead, flavor the fries themselves by tossing hot potatoes with a lively mix of spices in addition to the salt—and then try to eat just a few. Spice rubs and coatings are one of the simplest ways to add spice as they're applied superficially—just coat and cook. And when you make your own rubs from the freshest spices, you're in control of flavor.

MIX AND COAT

Spice rubs are combinations of spices that work together to create a complex, aromatic mix that you can apply to proteins, vegetables, or other everyday foods before cooking to add unexpected dimension. When the spiced food hits heat—of the oven, pan, grill, or hot oil—the spices' flavors come alive. Best of all, you can make all of these flavor-boosting mixes yourself.

tips for using spice rubs

In the pages that follow, we'll give you recipes for spice rubs and suggested applications. But before you grab your spice grinder, here are some hows and whys of homemade rubs.

grind whole spices

Sure, you could create a spice rub by mixing together the required ground spices from supermarket jars. But when it's an option, we prefer to grind whole spices before mixing them into blends. Why? Grinding releases the volatile compounds that give a spice its flavor and aroma. And the longer the ground spice sits around, the more those compounds dissipate. In fact, whole spices have a shelf life about twice that of preground spices. Grinding spices yourself, then, before using them alone or before including them in a blend ensures a fresher result, and freshly ground spices have a hands-down superior aroma and flavor.

turn away from toasting

In chapter three, we'll tout toasting whole spices to develop flavor when they're dropped directly into a dish. But we usually don't toast the spices in our rub and blend recipes before grinding. Why not? Since cooking "toasts" the spice rubs—at least it adds heat that unlocks flavor—we found that pretoasting was often superfluous and we liked the multipurpose nature of blends made from raw spices.

season spice rubs

Taste a bit of a store-bought spice blend and it will likely include salt: It might even briefly taste better than homemade versions if you're tasting it raw because salt enhances the flavor of everything. But we intentionally leave salt out of our rubs. Why? We like to be able to add either table or kosher salt in different amounts, depending on the application. Using a measured amount of salt in our rubs would eliminate this flexibility and could result in one dish tasting overseasoned and another one using the same rub underseasoned. So since we leave salt out of our homemade rubs, be sure to adjust the seasoning of our recipes if you substitute a store-bought version so you don't end up with a supersalty dish.

sugar and spice

Brown sugar, which contributes rich molasses flavor, nicely complements some spice rubs, especially those that pack heat. But there are a couple other reasons for sweetening your spice rubs. First, when a rub includes brown sugar, the sugar's moisture gives the spices superior clinging ability. Second, the sugar boosts browning of the rubbed food during cooking; this is especially attractive in rubs that are classically associated with barbecued foods and contribute to a nice crust—or bark, as it's known in the world of barbecue.

keep it crisp

Spice rubs give food big flavor, but there's another benefit. Unlike wet sauces and mops for proteins and vegetables, a spice rub can add deep flavor to foods—skin-on poultry or potato wedges, say— without turning the skin soggy or preventing the exteriors from crisping as would happen with barbecue sauces and the like. Also, drippy marinades tend to cause flare-ups on the grill; a spice rub is much easier to manage.

› spice rubs

Walk into most supermarkets, and you'll find any of these rubs. But you can make many rubs from staple spices you might already have, saving you from buying yet another jar. And you should. Spice blends from home-ground spices are fresher and more aromatic, keep longer, and can be made in just the right quantities. Below find the rubs we love to stock in our spice cabinet because they're so versatile, along with our ideas on how to put them to work. All of these rubs make about ½ cup and can be stored in an airtight container at room temperature for up to one month. Use them to coat proteins (pages 76–77), in our recipes, or according to the suggestions below.

| classic steak rub | herbes de provence | barbecue rub |

classic steak rub

This earthy, herbal, bitey rub is a popular steakhouse seasoning— for more than just steak.

- **2 tablespoons peppercorns**
- **3 tablespoons coriander seeds**
- **4 teaspoons dried dill**
- **2 teaspoons red pepper flakes**

Process peppercorns and coriander seeds in spice grinder until finely ground, about 30 seconds; transfer to small bowl. Stir in dill and pepper flakes.

› **how to use** Sprinkle on a loaded baked potato, rub on swordfish steaks or hot smoked salmon before grilling, mix into ground beef for burgers, toss with mushrooms before roasting.

herbes de provence

This delicate, aromatic blend of dried herbs from southern France can freshen up all kinds of foods.

- **2 tablespoons dried thyme**
- **2 tablespoons dried marjoram**
- **2 tablespoons dried rosemary**
- **2 teaspoons fennel seeds**

Combine all ingredients in bowl.

› **how to use** Season shallots before roasting, top delicate fish such as trout before baking, add to vegetable stews, sprinkle over goat cheese drizzled with honey, mix into homemade breakfast sausage, stir into homemade savory jams.

barbecue rub

Barbecue can mean a lot of different things depending on the region of the country, but this spicy-sweet all-purpose rub is immediately recognizable as "barbecue."

- **3 tablespoons chili powder**
- **3 tablespoons packed brown sugar**
- **2 teaspoons pepper**
- **¾ teaspoon cayenne pepper**

Combine all ingredients in bowl.

› **how to use** Sprinkle over watermelon, rub on ribs before grilling, rub on chicken before smoking, sprinkle on avocado halves before searing, toss with cauliflower before roasting.

› spice rubs

cajun-style rub

You can substitute 2 tablespoons ground celery seeds plus 2 tablespoons salt for the celery salt.

- 2 tablespoons coriander seeds
- ¼ cup celery salt
- 2 tablespoons paprika
- 1 teaspoon cayenne pepper
- ½ teaspoon ground cinnamon

Process coriander seeds in spice grinder until finely ground, about 30 seconds; transfer to small bowl. Stir in celery salt, paprika, cayenne, and cinnamon.

› **how to use** Stir into ranch dressing or onion dip, toss with homemade Chex mix, sprinkle over deviled eggs or grilled corn, mix into crab cakes.

five-spice powder

Chinese five-spice powder has a kick that offsets richness in both sweet and savory recipes. In traditional Chinese cooking, the five elements of the cosmos—earth, fire, metal, water, and wood—are represented by five-spice powder.

- 5 teaspoons fennel seeds
- 4 teaspoons white peppercorns or 8 teaspoons Sichuan peppercorns
- 1 tablespoon whole cloves
- 8 star anise pods
- 1 (3-inch) cinnamon stick, broken into pieces

Process fennel seeds, peppercorns, and cloves in spice grinder until finely ground, about 30 seconds; transfer to small bowl. Process star anise and cinnamon in now-empty spice grinder until finely ground, about 30 seconds; transfer to bowl with other spices and stir to combine.

› **how to use** Rub on duck or chicken breasts before searing, shake into a whiskey sour, sauté with kale, stir into batters, use in mulled cider.

jerk rub

Fiery yet fruity Caribbean-style jerk rub is possible with pantry staples and a little brown sugar.

- 5 teaspoons allspice berries
- 5 teaspoons black peppercorns
- 2 teaspoons dried thyme
- 3 tablespoons packed brown sugar
- 1 tablespoon garlic powder
- 2 teaspoons dry mustard
- 1 teaspoon cayenne pepper

Process allspice, peppercorns, and thyme in spice grinder until coarsely ground, about 30 seconds; transfer to small bowl. Stir in sugar, garlic powder, mustard, and cayenne.

› **how to use** Mix into scrambled eggs, stir into guacamole, rub onto chicken parts before roasting, sprinkle on grilled pineapple.

southwestern rub

The flavors of the Southwest are classically bold and fiery but also warm and round, and this spice blend hits all the right notes.

- 3 tablespoons cumin seeds
- 2 tablespoons coriander seeds
- ¾ teaspoon ground cinnamon
- 3 tablespoons chili powder
- ¾ teaspoon red pepper flakes

Process cumin seeds, coriander seeds, and cinnamon in spice grinder until finely ground, about 30 seconds; transfer to small bowl. Stir in chili powder and pepper flakes.

› **how to use** Sprinkle on avocado toast, rub on halibut before grilling, rub onto pork shoulder before slow-roasting, rub on meat and vegetables for fajitas, stir into mayonnaise for a sandwich spread.

SPICE UP PROTEINS

Ever buy your meat for the week—and then not know what to do with it? Our spice rubs are the solution when you don't have a plan. Pick a rub, follow our recipe for applying it to a protein, and every meal can be special. We prefer to use one of our homemade rubs (pages 73–75) for these recipes, but you can substitute your favorite store-bought. Depending on its level of salt, you may need to reduce the amount of salt in the recipe.

spice-rubbed pan-seared salmon
serves 4
To ensure uniform cooking, buy a 1½- to 2-pound center-cut salmon fillet and cut it into four pieces. If using wild salmon, cook it until it registers 120 degrees.

- **3 tablespoons spice rub (pages 73–75)**
  Salt
- **4 (6- to 8-ounce) skin-on salmon fillets**
- **1 teaspoon vegetable oil**

1 Combine spice rub and ½ teaspoon salt in bowl. Using sharp knife, make 3 or 4 shallow slashes about 1 inch apart on skin side of each fillet, being careful not to cut into flesh. Pat salmon dry with paper towels and rub flesh side evenly with spice rub; season skin side with salt.

2 Heat oil in 12-inch nonstick skillet over medium heat until shimmering. Place salmon flesh side down in skillet and cook until dark brown, 3 to 5 minutes. Gently flip salmon, reduce heat to medium-low, and continue to cook until center is still translucent when checked with tip of paring knife and registers 125 degrees (for medium-rare), 9 to 12 minutes. Serve.

spice-rubbed roasted chicken parts

serves 4

- ⅓ cup extra–virgin olive oil
- ¼ cup spice rub (pages 73–75)
- 1 tablespoon salt
- 3 pounds bone-in chicken pieces (split breasts cut in half, drumsticks, and/or thighs), trimmed

1 Adjust oven rack to lowest position and heat oven to 450 degrees. Line rimmed baking sheet with aluminum foil. Whisk oil, spice rub, and salt together in large bowl. Add chicken and toss to coat.

2 Arrange chicken skin side up on prepared sheet. Roast until well browned and breasts register 160 degrees and drumsticks/ thighs register 175 degrees, about 25 minutes, rotating sheet halfway through roasting. Transfer chicken to serving platter, tent with foil, and let rest for 10 minutes. Serve.

spice-rubbed steaks

serves 4 to 6

We prefer these steaks cooked to medium-rare, but if you prefer them more or less done, see our guidelines on page 280.

- 1½ teaspoons salt
- 2 tablespoons spice rub (pages 73–75)
- 2 (1-pound) strip, rib-eye, or whole shell sirloin steaks, 1 to 1½ inches thick, trimmed and halved crosswise
- 1 tablespoon vegetable oil

1 Combine salt and spice rub in bowl. Pat steaks dry with paper towels and rub evenly with spice rub.

2 Heat oil in 12-inch skillet over medium-high heat until just smoking. Place steaks in skillet and cook, without moving steaks, until well browned on first side, about 4 minutes. Flip steaks and cook, without moving steaks, until well browned on second side and meat registers 120 to 125 degrees (for medium-rare), 3 to 7 minutes. Transfer steaks to plate, tent with aluminum foil, and let rest for 10 minutes. Serve.

spice-rubbed roasted pork loin

serves 6

- ¼ cup spice rub (pages 73–75)
- 1 tablespoon kosher salt
- 1 (2½- to 3-pound) boneless pork loin roast, trimmed

1 Combine spice rub and salt in bowl. Rub roast with spice rub, wrap tightly in plastic wrap, and refrigerate for at least 1 hour or up to 24 hours.

2 Adjust oven rack to upper-middle position and heat oven to 450 degrees. Set wire rack in rimmed baking sheet lined with aluminum foil. Pat pork dry with paper towels, arrange on prepared rack, and roast for 15 minutes. Reduce oven temperature to 375 degrees and continue to roast until pork registers 140 degrees, about 50 minutes. Transfer pork to carving board, tent with foil, and let rest for 20 minutes. Slice pork and serve.

cumin-coriander rubbed cornish game hens

serves 4

- 4 (1¼- to 1½-pound) whole Cornish game hens, giblets discarded
- Kosher salt and pepper
- 2 teaspoons ground cumin
- 2 teaspoons ground coriander
- 1 teaspoon paprika
- ¼ teaspoon cayenne pepper
- ¼ teaspoon vegetable oil
- 1 teaspoon baking powder
- Vegetable oil spray

why this recipe works Spice rubs are a great surface flavoring because they can liven up a dish without compromising texture—in this case the ultracrispy skin on Cornish game hens. Using a rub is particularly important for the hens: Given their small size, the meat finishes cooking long before the skin crisps so flavorings that decelerate crisping—say, wet sauces or pastes—are nonstarters. To successfully roast these little birds, we split them in half. Poking holes in the skin allowed the fat to drain during cooking and therefore aided crisping. A dry rub of potent and earthy cumin and coriander, some sweet paprika, and spicy cayenne paired nicely with the richness of burnished crispy skin and significantly boosted the hens' interest. Beyond the spices, we rubbed the birds with salt and baking powder (and the slightest amount of oil to help them stick) and then chilled them. Salt helped pull moisture to the skin's surface so that it could evaporate more quickly, and baking powder further promoted crisping and browning. If your hens weigh 1½ to 2 pounds, cook three instead of four and extend the cooking time in step 5 to 15 minutes. If your hens are frozen, be sure to thaw them in the refrigerator for 24 to 36 hours before salting.

1 Working with 1 hen at a time, use kitchen shears to cut along both sides of backbone to remove it. Flatten hens and lay breast side up on counter. Using sharp chef's knife, cut through center of breast to make 2 halves.

2 Using your fingers, gently separate skin from breast and thighs. Using metal skewer or tip of paring knife, poke 10 to 15 holes in fat deposits on top of breast halves and thighs. Tuck wingtips behind back. Pat hens dry with paper towels.

3 Combine 2 tablespoons salt, cumin, coriander, paprika, and cayenne in bowl. Sprinkle half of salt mixture on underside (bone side) of hens. Stir oil into remaining salt mixture until salt is evenly coated with oil. Stir in baking powder until well combined. Turn hens skin side up and rub salt mixture evenly over surface. Transfer hens, skin side up, to wire rack set in rimmed baking sheet and refrigerate, uncovered, for at least 4 hours or up to 24 hours.

4 Adjust oven racks to upper-middle and lower-middle positions, place second rimmed baking sheet on lower rack, and heat oven to 500 degrees. Once oven is fully heated, spray skin side of hens with oil spray and season with pepper. Carefully transfer hens, skin side down, to baking sheet and cook for 10 minutes.

5   Remove hens from oven and heat broiler. Flip hens skin side up. Transfer baking sheet with hens to upper rack and broil until well browned and breasts register 160 degrees and thighs register 175 degrees, about 5 minutes, rotating as necessary to promote even browning. Serve.

oregano-anise rubbed cornish game hens

Substitute 1 teaspoon dried oregano and ½ teaspoon anise seeds for cumin and coriander.

peri peri grilled chicken

serves 6 to 8

 3 tablespoons extra-virgin olive oil

 8 garlic cloves, peeled

 2 tablespoons salt

 2 tablespoons tomato paste

4–10 dried arbol chiles, stemmed

 1 shallot, chopped

 1 tablespoon sugar

 1 tablespoon paprika

 1 tablespoon Five-Spice Powder
    (page 74)

 2 teaspoons grated lemon zest plus
    ¼ cup juice (2 lemons)

 1 teaspoon pepper

 ½ teaspoon cayenne pepper

 3 bay leaves, crushed

 6 pounds bone-in chicken pieces
    (split breasts, thighs, and/or
    drumsticks), trimmed

 ½ cup unsalted dry-roasted peanuts,
    chopped fine

 1 (13 by 9-inch) disposable aluminum
    pan (if using charcoal) or 2 (9-inch)
    disposable aluminum pie plates
    (if using gas)

    Lemon wedges

why this recipe works While many of our spice rubs are applied dry or in combination with a little oil, we also turn to pastes to coat foods— sometimes the bite of fresh garlic, the sting of dried chiles, or the umami depth of tomato paste brings dry ground spices together. Our version of the spicy grilled dish known as *peri peri* chicken includes all three of these. The chicken has old African roots and a meandering history, but the basic idea is this: Chicken parts are marinated overnight in a paste of garlic, herbs, spices, lemon juice, and peri peri chiles—fiery local peppers whose name means "pepper pepper" in Swahili—and then grilled over a hot fire until the meat is tender and the skin is charred. Since we were resting the chicken overnight anyway, we added plenty of salt to the rub to season the meat throughout and help it stay moist when cooked over the hot fire. A complex five-spice rub as well as chopped peanuts gave our dish depth and richness. Finally, we used more commonly available—and just as fruity-tasting— arbol chiles, along with some cayenne pepper, in place of hard-to-find peri peri peppers. We prefer to use our homemade Five-Spice Powder (page 74), but you can substitute store-bought five-spice powder. When browning the chicken, move it away from the direct heat if any flare-ups occur. Serve with rice.

1 Process oil, garlic, salt, tomato paste, 4 arbols, shallot, sugar, paprika, five-spice powder, lemon zest and juice, pepper, cayenne, and bay leaves in blender until smooth, 10 to 20 seconds. Taste paste and add up to 6 additional arbols, depending on desired level of heat (spice paste should be slightly hotter than desired heat level of cooked chicken). Process until smooth. Using metal skewer or tip of paring knife, poke skin side of each chicken piece 8 to 10 times. Place chicken parts, peanuts, and spice paste in large bowl and toss until chicken is evenly coated with spice paste. Cover and refrigerate for at least 6 hours or up to 24 hours.

2A for a charcoal grill Open bottom vent halfway. Place disposable pan on 1 side of grill and add 3 cups water to pan. Light large chimney starter filled with charcoal briquettes (6 quarts). When top coals are partially covered with ash, pour evenly over other side of grill. Set cooking grate in place, cover, and open lid vent halfway. Heat grill until hot, about 5 minutes.

2B for a gas grill Remove cooking grate, place 2 disposable pie plates directly on 1 burner (opposite primary burner), and add 1½ cups water to each. Set grate in place, turn all burners to high, cover, and heat grill until hot, about 15 minutes. Turn primary burner to medium-high and turn off other burner(s). (Adjust primary burner as needed to maintain grill temperature between 325 and 350 degrees.)

3   Clean and oil cooking grate. Place chicken skin side down on hotter side of grill and cook until browned and blistered in spots, about 5 minutes per side. Move chicken to cooler side and arrange skin side up with drumsticks/thighs closest to fire and breasts farthest away. Cover (positioning lid vent over chicken if using charcoal) and cook until breasts register 160 degrees and drumsticks/thighs register 175 degrees, 50 minutes to 1 hour.

4   Transfer chicken to serving platter, tent with aluminum foil, and let rest for 10 minutes. Serve with lemon wedges.

latin-style fried chicken

serves 4

marinade and chicken

- 6 garlic cloves, chopped coarse
- 1 tablespoon salt
- 1 tablespoon pepper
- 1 tablespoon ground cumin
- 2 teaspoons smoked paprika
- 2 teaspoons dried Mexican oregano
- 2 teaspoons grated lime zest plus ¼ cup juice (2 limes)
- 3 pounds bone-in chicken pieces (split breasts cut in half crosswise, drumsticks, thighs, and/or wings), trimmed

coating

- 1¼ cups all-purpose flour
- ¾ cup cornstarch
- 1 tablespoon pepper
- 1 tablespoon garlic powder
- 1 teaspoon baking powder
- 1 teaspoon white pepper
- 1 teaspoon ground cumin
- ½ teaspoon salt
- ¼ teaspoon cayenne pepper
- 3 large egg whites, lightly beaten
- 3 quarts peanut or vegetable oil

why this recipe works While each cuisine puts its own spin on the dish, Latin-style fried chicken is set apart by its garlicky-lime marinade and an extra-crunchy coating seasoned with lots of spice. Classic Latin-style fried chicken has a thin and crispy crust; we used a combination of flour cut with cornstarch for a nice, light coating and a little baking powder made it extra crisp. To spice up this mix, we stirred in garlic powder, cumin, cayenne, salt, and two types of pepper—black for clean pepper heat and white for its pronounced citrus flavor. We discovered that lightly beaten egg whites made the best "glue" to adhere the seasoned flour coating to the chicken. Refrigerating the marinated and dredged chicken before frying ensured the coating set up nicely and thus stayed on the chicken. We prefer the robust flavor of Mexican oregano, but you can substitute any dried oregano. Don't let the chicken marinate any longer than 2 hours or it will toughen from the lime juice. Use a Dutch oven that holds 6 quarts or more for this recipe. Serve with lime wedges, if desired.

---

1 **for the marinade and chicken** Combine garlic, salt, pepper, cumin, paprika, oregano, and lime zest and juice in large bowl. Add chicken and toss to coat. Cover and refrigerate for at least 1 hour or up to 2 hours.

2 **for the coating** Whisk flour, cornstarch, pepper, garlic powder, baking powder, white pepper, cumin, salt, and cayenne together in bowl. Place egg whites in shallow dish.

3 Set wire rack in rimmed baking sheet. Remove chicken from marinade and scrape off solids. Pat chicken dry with paper towels. Working with 1 piece at a time, dip chicken into egg whites, letting excess drip back into dish, then dredge in flour mixture, pressing to adhere. Transfer chicken to prepared rack and refrigerate for at least 30 minutes or up to 2 hours.

4 Adjust oven rack to middle position and heat oven to 200 degrees. Set second wire rack in second rimmed baking sheet. Add oil to large Dutch oven until it measures about 2 inches deep and heat over medium-high heat to 325 degrees. Carefully add half of chicken to hot oil and fry until breasts register 160 degrees and drumsticks/thighs register 175 degrees, 13 to 16 minutes. Adjust burner, if necessary, to maintain oil temperature between 300 and 325 degrees. Transfer chicken to clean rack and keep warm in oven. Return oil to 325 degrees and repeat with remaining chicken. Serve.

barbecue roast chicken with potatoes

serves 4

- 2 tablespoons Barbecue Rub (page 73)
- 2 tablespoons vegetable oil
-   Salt and pepper
- 1 (3½- to 4-pound) whole chicken, giblets discarded
- 1½ pounds small red potatoes, unpeeled, halved
- 1 tablespoon minced fresh chives
- 1 teaspoon cider vinegar

A weeknight roast chicken is a blank canvas for highlighting homemade rubs and pairing with different dressed sides. You'll need a 12-inch ovensafe skillet for this recipe. Use potatoes that are 1 to 2 inches in diameter.

1   Adjust oven rack to lower-middle position and heat oven to 450 degrees. Combine rub, 1 tablespoon oil, and 1 teaspoon salt in bowl. With chicken breast side down on cutting board, use kitchen shears to cut through bones on either side of backbone. Discard backbone and trim away excess fat and skin around neck. Flip chicken, press firmly on breastbone to flatten, then pound breast to be same thickness as legs and thighs.

2   Pat chicken dry with paper towels. Gently loosen skin covering breast and thighs. Rub 2 teaspoons spice mixture underneath skin, then rub remaining spice mixture all over chicken. Tuck wingtips underneath.

3   Toss potatoes with remaining 1 tablespoon oil and ½ teaspoon salt and arrange cut side up in 12-inch ovensafe skillet. Place chicken skin side up on top of potatoes. Transfer skillet to oven and roast chicken until breast registers 160 degrees and drumsticks/thighs register 175 degrees, 45 to 60 minutes. (If chicken begins to get too dark, cover loosely with aluminum foil.)

4   Using potholders, carefully remove skillet from oven. Transfer chicken to carving board and let rest while finishing potatoes. Being careful of hot skillet handle, return skillet to oven and roast potatoes until softened, 12 to 16 minutes. Using slotted spoon, transfer potatoes to serving bowl. Add 1 tablespoon fat from skillet, chives, and vinegar and gently toss to coat. Season with salt and pepper to taste. Carve chicken and serve with potatoes.

ras el hanout roast chicken with carrots

Substitute Ras el Hanout (page 117) for barbecue rub; carrots, peeled, halved lengthwise, cut into 2-inch lengths, for potatoes; cilantro for chives; and lemon juice for cider vinegar.

five-spice roast chicken with turnips

Substitute 1 tablespoon Five-Spice Powder (page 74) for barbecue rub; 1½ pounds turnips, peeled and cut into 1½-inch pieces, for potatoes; 2 scallions, sliced thin on bias for chives; and rice vinegar for cider vinegar.

herbes de provence roast chicken with fennel

Substitute 4 teaspoons Herbes de Provence (page 73) and ¼ teaspoon pepper for barbecue rub; 3 fennel bulbs, halved, cored, and sliced ½ inch thick, for potatoes; parsley for chives; and sherry vinegar for cider vinegar.

spice-crusted rib-eye steaks

serves 4

- 2 tablespoons chopped fresh rosemary
- 1 tablespoon black peppercorns, cracked (see page 26)
- 1½ teaspoons salt
- 2 teaspoons ground coriander
- 2 teaspoons grated lemon zest
- 1½ teaspoons dry mustard
- 1 teaspoon red pepper flakes
- 2 (1-pound) boneless rib-eye steaks, 1½ inches thick, trimmed
- 1 tablespoon vegetable oil

why this recipe works What's better than a perfectly seared rib-eye? One where a generous spiced crust encases the rich, rosy meat. We tout the versatility of spice rubs, but there are cases when they require attention: They can burn if they're in contact with smoking heat for a while, or they can fall off during cooking. We wanted a nice sear on our spice-crusted steaks, but that requires pan-searing; we got around the burning issue by continually flipping the steaks, thus ensuring that each side was exposed to the heat in short intervals. We found that this technique had another advantage: It resulted in incredible steaks that were evenly cooked from top to bottom without an obnoxious gray band of meat—win-win. We didn't pat the steaks dry before applying the seasoning blend (as most recipes say to do), so the moisture from the meat acted as a glue to help the spices stick. For even more insurance, we cooked in a slick nonstick skillet, and we used a fork to flip the steaks, rather than tongs or a spatula, which could dislodge the spice coating. The coating on these rich steaks was firmly in place, but it had to taste good, too. Aromatic rosemary, coriander, and lemon zest combined with pungent dry mustard, peppercorns, and pepper flakes for a fragrant rub that also packed a punch. We prefer these steaks cooked to medium-rare, but if you prefer them more or less done, see our guidelines on page 280.

---

1 Combine rosemary, peppercorns, salt, coriander, lemon zest, mustard, and pepper flakes in bowl. Sprinkle steaks on all sides with spice mixture, pressing to adhere. (Use all of spice mixture.)

2 Set wire rack in rimmed baking sheet. Heat oil in 12-inch nonstick skillet over medium heat until just smoking. Add steaks and cook, flipping steaks with fork every 2 minutes, until well browned and meat registers 120 to 125 degrees (for medium-rare), 10 to 13 minutes. Transfer steaks to prepared rack and let rest for 5 minutes. Slice thin and serve.

coffee-chipotle top sirloin roast

serves 10 to 12

- 1 (5- to 6-pound) center-cut boneless top sirloin roast, trimmed
- 2 tablespoons kosher salt
- 4 teaspoons plus ¼ cup extra-virgin olive oil
- 4 garlic cloves, minced
- 6 anchovy fillets, rinsed and patted dry
- 1 tablespoon ground coffee
- 1 tablespoon minced canned chipotle chile in adobo sauce
- 2 teaspoons ground coriander
- 2 teaspoons paprika
- 1 teaspoon unsweetened cocoa powder
- 1 teaspoon dry mustard
- 1 teaspoon pepper
- Coarse finishing salt

why this recipe works When enhanced with a robust spice rub, an extraordinary top sirloin roast becomes an even better centerpiece dish. To keep it manageable, we cut the large, oddly shaped roast in half and then tied each along its length to create two attractive cylinders that cooked through at a gentle 225 degrees in 2 hours. This cut down on the oven time and created more surface area for our bold, complex rub made from garlic, anchovy, coffee, chipotle, and spices. The mix of subtle heat, tanginess, and a bit of bitterness was a bold complement to the beefy cut. We took a three-step approach to creating a flavorful, attractive exterior: We seared the roasts, rubbed them (so the paste wouldn't burn during searing and the beef itself had a chance to brown), and then finished them with a brief stint in a 500-degree oven that deepened the paste's color and flavor and helped crisp up the crust. A sprinkle of finishing salt after slicing brings the flavors to life. Do not omit the anchovies; they provide depth of flavor. This recipe requires refrigerating the salted beef before cooking for at least 24 hours or up to four days (a longer time is preferable). We prefer this roast cooked to medium-rare, but if you prefer it more or less done, see our guidelines on page 280. You can use your preferred coarse finishing salt in this recipe; for information on finishing salts, see pages 22–23.

1 Cut roast lengthwise along grain into 2 equal pieces. Rub 1 tablespoon salt over each piece and tie securely with kitchen twine at 1½-inch intervals. Transfer roasts to plate and refrigerate, uncovered, for at least 24 hours or up to 3 days.

2 Adjust oven rack to middle position and heat oven to 225 degrees. Pat roasts dry with paper towels. Heat 2 teaspoons oil in 12-inch skillet over high heat until just smoking. Brown 1 roast on all sides, 6 to 8 minutes; transfer to clean plate. Repeat with 2 teaspoons oil and remaining roast; transfer to plate. Let cool for 10 minutes.

3 Meanwhile, process garlic, anchovies, coffee, chipotle, coriander, paprika, cocoa, mustard, pepper, and remaining ¼ cup oil in food processor until smooth paste forms, about 30 seconds, scraping down sides of bowl as needed. Transfer roasts, fat side up, to wire rack set in rimmed baking sheet and rub evenly with paste. Roast until beef registers 120 to 125 degrees (for medium-rare), 2 to 2¼ hours. Remove roasts from oven, tent with aluminum foil, and let rest on rack for 30 minutes.

4 Heat oven to 500 degrees. Discard foil and twine. Return roasts to oven and cook until exteriors are well browned, 6 to 8 minutes. Transfer roasts to carving board and slice ¼ inch thick. Sprinkle with finishing salt to taste. Serve.

herbes de provence–rubbed pork tenderloin with vegetables

serves 4

2 large fennel bulbs, stalks discarded, bulbs halved, cored, and sliced ½ inch thick

2 cups jarred whole baby artichokes packed in water, quartered, rinsed, and patted dry

½ cup pitted kalamata olives, halved

3 tablespoons extra-virgin olive oil

2 (12- to 16-ounce) pork tenderloins, trimmed

Salt and pepper

2 teaspoons Herbes de Provence (page 73)

1 pound cherry tomatoes, halved

1 tablespoon grated lemon zest

2 tablespoons minced fresh parsley

why this recipe works Properly cooked pork tenderloin has a fine grain and buttery-smooth texture, with a mild flavor that lends itself well to bold seasonings. We found that rubbing the tenderloins with herbes de Provence not only delivered that seasoning but also allowed us to skip a browning step; with its coarse texture, a colorful crust formed itself just through roasting. Herbes de Provence provide a distinct flavor profile; a little of this blend goes a long way, so just 2 teaspoons were sufficient to flavor and coat two tenderloins without overwhelming the pork. For a vegetable that would complement both the rub and the pork, we chose sweet, mild fennel and supplemented it with artichokes, kalamata olives, and cherry tomatoes. After jump-starting the fennel in the microwave, we cooked the tenderloins on top of the vegetables in a roasting pan. In less than an hour, we were transported to Provence with a dinner that was low on fuss but high on flavor. We prefer to use our homemade Herbes de Provence (page 73), but you can substitute store-bought herbes de Provence. While we prefer the flavor and texture of jarred whole baby artichokes, you can substitute 12 ounces of frozen artichoke hearts, thawed and patted dry.

1 Adjust oven rack to lower-middle position and heat oven to 450 degrees. Combine fennel and 2 tablespoons water in bowl and microwave, covered, until softened, about 5 minutes. Drain fennel well, then toss with artichokes, olives, and oil.

2 Pat tenderloins dry with paper towels, season with salt and pepper, and sprinkle with herbes de Provence. Spread vegetables in large roasting pan, then place tenderloins on top. Roast tenderloins and vegetables until pork registers 145 degrees, 25 to 30 minutes, turning tenderloins over halfway through roasting.

3 Transfer tenderloins to cutting board, tent with aluminum foil, and let rest for 10 minutes. Meanwhile, stir tomatoes and lemon zest into vegetables and continue to roast until fennel is tender and tomatoes have softened, about 10 minutes. Stir in parsley and season with salt and pepper to taste. Slice pork ½ inch thick and serve with vegetables.

south carolina pulled pork

serves 8

pork

- 3 tablespoons dry mustard
- 2 tablespoons salt
- 1½ tablespoons packed light brown sugar
- 2 teaspoons pepper
- 2 teaspoons paprika
- ¼ teaspoon cayenne pepper
- 1 (4- to 5-pound) boneless pork butt roast, trimmed
- 4 cups wood chips

barbecue sauce

- ½ cup yellow mustard
- ½ cup packed light brown sugar
- ¼ cup distilled white vinegar
- 2 tablespoons Worcestershire sauce
- 1 tablespoon hot sauce
- 1 teaspoon salt
- 1 teaspoon pepper

why this recipe works In South Carolina, pit masters dress pulled pork in a savory mustard-based sauce nicknamed "Carolina gold." We found that a combination of grill-smoking and oven-roasting reduced the cooking time from all day to 4 or 5 hours. We rubbed a boneless pork butt with a spice rub that included dry mustard to highlight the mustard in the sauce; the rub also helped the meat develop a flavorful crust. Most South Carolina barbecue sauce recipes use yellow mustard, which our tasters praised for its bright tang. Brushing the pork with the sauce before it went, covered, into the low oven produced a second hit of mustard flavor; then, tossing the shredded pork with the remaining sauce gave the meat a final layer of flavor. Pork butt roast is often labeled Boston butt in the supermarket. If you'd like to use wood chunks instead of wood chips when using a charcoal grill, substitute four medium wood chunks, soaked in water for 1 hour, for the wood chip packets.

1 **for the pork** Combine mustard, salt, sugar, pepper, paprika, and cayenne in bowl. Pat pork dry with paper towels and rub with spice mixture. Wrap meat in plastic wrap and let sit at room temperature for at least 1 hour, or refrigerate for up to 24 hours. (If refrigerated, let sit at room temperature for 1 hour before grilling.)

2 Just before grilling, soak wood chips in water for 15 minutes, then drain. Using large piece of heavy-duty aluminum foil, wrap 2 cups soaked chips in 8 by 4½-inch foil packet. (Make sure chips do not poke holes in sides or bottom of packet.) Repeat with remaining 2 cups chips. Cut 2 evenly spaced 2-inch slits in top of each packet.

3A **for a charcoal grill** Open bottom vent halfway. Light large chimney starter half filled with charcoal briquettes (3 quarts). When top coals are partially covered with ash, pour into steeply banked pile against 1 side of grill. Place wood chip packets on coals. Set cooking grate in place, cover, and open lid vent halfway. Heat grill until hot and wood chips are smoking, about 5 minutes.

3B **for a gas grill** Remove cooking grate and place wood chip packets directly on primary burner. Set cooking grate in place, turn all burners to high, cover, and heat grill until hot and wood chips are smoking, about 15 minutes. Turn primary burner to medium-high and turn other burner(s) off. (Adjust primary burner as needed to maintain grill temperature around 325 degrees.)

4   Clean and oil cooking grate. Place roast on cooler side of grill. Cover (positioning lid vent over roast if using charcoal) and cook until pork has dark, rosy crust, about 2 hours. During final 20 minutes of grilling, adjust oven rack to lower-middle position and heat oven to 325 degrees.

5   **for the barbecue sauce** Whisk all ingredients in bowl until smooth. Measure out ½ cup sauce and reserve for cooking; set aside remaining sauce for tossing with pork.

6   Transfer pork to large roasting pan and brush evenly with the ½ cup sauce for cooking. Cover pan tightly with foil and transfer to oven. Roast until fork slips easily in and out of meat, 2 to 3 hours.

7   Remove pork from oven and let rest, still covered with foil, for 1 hour. When cool enough to handle, unwrap pork and pull meat into thin shreds, discarding excess fat and gristle. Toss pork with reserved sauce and serve.

oven-roasted jerk pork ribs

serves 4 to 6

½ cup Jerk Rub (page 74)

8 scallions, chopped coarse

¼ cup vegetable oil

¼ cup molasses

1 tablespoon salt

2 (2½- to 3-pound) racks St. Louis—style spareribs, trimmed

3 tablespoons cider vinegar

Lime wedges

why this recipe works Although many American cooks employ jerk seasoning as a spicy coating for grilled chicken, it was originally used in Jamaican cooking to season pork. As a nod to this, we developed a recipe for boldly seasoned jerk pork ribs. We started with our own take on jerk rub that, among other ingredients, includes plenty of allspice (an essential), pepper, thyme, and a hint of cayenne for heat. For coating our ribs, we blended this rub with scallions for body and pungency and some molasses for tangy sweetness and to help make a paste. We chose St. Louis—style spareribs for their uniform shape, a quality that helps them cook evenly. Letting the ribs marinate in our jerk paste for at least 1 hour infused them with spicy yet fruity flavor. Roasting them in a low 275-degree oven for 4 hours turned them meltingly tender. And brushing them with another coat of jerk paste mixed with tangy cider vinegar gave them a bright, fresh crust. We prefer to use our homemade Jerk Rub (page 74), but you can substitute store-bought jerk seasoning. Depending on the level of salt in your store-bought blend, you may need to reduce the amount of salt in this recipe. It's not necessary to remove the membrane on the bone side of the ribs.

1 Process jerk rub, scallions, oil, 3 tablespoons molasses, and salt in blender until smooth, about 2 minutes, scraping down sides of blender jar as needed. Transfer ¼ cup jerk paste to bowl, cover, and refrigerate until needed. Line rimmed baking sheet with aluminum foil and set wire rack in sheet. Place ribs meat side up on prepared rack and brush all over with remaining paste. Cover tightly with plastic wrap and refrigerate for at least 1 hour or up to 24 hours.

2 Adjust oven rack to middle position and heat oven to 275 degrees. Discard plastic and roast ribs until tender and fork inserted into meat meets no resistance, 4 to 4½ hours.

3 Stir vinegar and remaining 1 tablespoon molasses into reserved jerk paste. Brush meat side of racks with vinegar mixture. Return ribs to oven and roast until sauce sets, about 10 minutes. Transfer ribs to carving board, tent with foil, and let rest for 20 minutes. Slice racks between ribs. Serve with lime wedges.

anise-rubbed rack of lamb with sweet mint-almond relish

serves 4 to 6

relish

- ½ cup minced fresh mint
- ¼ cup sliced almonds, toasted and chopped fine
- ¼ cup extra-virgin olive oil
- 2 tablespoons red currant jelly
- 4 teaspoons red wine vinegar
- 2 teaspoons Dijon mustard

  Salt and pepper

lamb

- 2 tablespoons kosher salt
- 1 teaspoon ground anise
- ½ teaspoon pepper
- 2 (1¾- to 2-pound) racks of lamb, fat trimmed to ⅛ to ¼ inch and rib bones frenched
- 1 teaspoon vegetable oil

why this recipe works A roasted rack of lamb is a relatively simple proposition, so we sought spot-on seasoning and juicy meat. A blend of salt and an underutilized spice—floral, aromatic anise—was a magical pairing for the bold-flavored meat and dressed up our lamb for a fête. Carving a shallow crosshatch into the fat cap and rubbing the racks' surfaces with the spices loaded the lamb with flavor and ensured that the spices stuck. Cooking the meat was as simple as arranging the lamb on a wire rack set in a baking sheet and slowly roasting until the interior was uniformly rosy and reached our serving temperature. Then, to give the racks a browned crust, we seared them in a skillet before serving. The fat cap warms up in the oven so it browns quickly without the meat overcooking. A simple relish—with fresh mint, not the classic cloying mint jelly—dressed up the roast. We prefer the milder taste and bigger size of domestic lamb, but you may substitute imported lamb from New Zealand and Australia. Since imported racks are generally smaller, in step 3 season the racks with 1 teaspoon of the salt mixture and reduce the cooking time to 50 minutes to 1 hour 10 minutes. We prefer the lamb cooked to medium-rare, but if you prefer it more or less done, see our guidelines on page 280.

1 **for the relish** Combine all ingredients in bowl, seasoning with salt and pepper to taste. Let sit at room temperature for at least 1 hour before serving.

2 **for the lamb** Adjust oven rack to middle position and heat oven to 250 degrees. Combine salt, anise, and pepper in bowl. Measure out 1½ teaspoons salt mixture and reserve for seasoning; set aside remaining salt mixture until needed. Using sharp knife, cut slits ½ inch apart in crosshatch pattern in fat cap on racks, being careful not to cut into flesh.

3 Pat racks dry with paper towels and sprinkle with reserved 1½ teaspoons salt mixture. Place racks bone side down on wire rack set in rimmed baking sheet and roast until meat registers 120 to 125 degrees (for medium-rare), 1 to 1½ hours.

4 Heat oil in 12-inch skillet over high heat until just smoking. Place 1 rack bone side up in skillet and cook until well browned, 1 to 2 minutes. Transfer to carving board. Pour off all but 1 teaspoon fat from skillet and repeat browning with second rack. Tent racks with aluminum foil and let rest for 20 minutes. Cut between ribs to separate chops and sprinkle cut side of chops with ½ teaspoon salt mixture. Serve, passing relish and remaining salt mixture separately.

trimming and frenching a rack of lamb

1 If rack has fat cap, peel back thick layer of fat, along with thin flap of meat underneath it, cutting any tissue connecting cap to rack.

2 Trim remaining thin layer of fat that covers loin, leaving strip of fat that separates the loin and small eye of meat directly above it.

3 Make cut along bones, 1 inch up from eye of meat. Remove fat above cut and scrape remaining meat or fat from exposed bones.

blackened snapper with rémoulade

serves 4

½ cup mayonnaise

1½ teaspoons sweet pickle relish

1 teaspoon capers, rinsed and minced

1 teaspoon lemon juice, plus lemon wedges for serving

½ teaspoon Dijon mustard

4 (6- to 8-ounce) skin-on red snapper fillets, ¾ inch thick

5 teaspoons Cajun-Style Rub (page 74)

2 tablespoons vegetable oil

why this recipe works Snapper blackened with pungent, smoky Cajun-style spices is a New Orleans classic. Healthy amounts of paprika and cayenne provide heat and depth to our homemade Cajun rub, but the real MVP of our blend is celery salt, which adds the perfect amount of savory earthiness (and allowed us to skip seasoning the fish with salt). A cast-iron skillet was the ideal vessel for getting perfectly blackened fish. The pan can be heated until it's white-hot, and since it retains the heat beautifully, it created the dark brown, crusty, sweet-smoky, toasted-spice exterior that is hallmark. To bloom the spices on the fish adequately, and because the snapper itself is lean, we made sure we added enough oil to the pan. To complement the smoky, spicy snapper, we made a tangy, cooling rémoulade sauce with creamy mayonnaise, briny capers, spicy Dijon mustard, sweet pickle relish, and bright lemon juice. We prefer to use our homemade Cajun-Style Rub (page 74), but you can substitute store-bought Cajun seasoning or Old Bay seasoning. If your knife isn't sharp enough to cut through the skin easily, try a serrated knife. It is important to keep the skin on during cooking; remove it afterward if you choose not to serve it. If necessary, you can use a traditional 12-inch skillet; however, the fish will not be as dark in color.

1 Adjust oven rack to middle position, place 12-inch cast-iron skillet on rack, and heat oven to 500 degrees. Meanwhile, whisk mayonnaise, relish, capers, lemon juice, and mustard together in bowl; set aside rémoulade until serving.

2 Using sharp knife, make 3 or 4 shallow slashes about 1 inch apart on skin side of each fillet, being careful not to cut into flesh. Pat snapper dry with paper towels and rub with Cajun rub.

3 When oven reaches 500 degrees, carefully remove skillet from oven using potholders and place over medium-high heat; turn off oven. Being careful of hot skillet handle, add oil and heat until just smoking. Place snapper flesh side down in skillet and cook until very dark brown, about 2 minutes.

4 Gently flip snapper and continue to cook until very dark brown on second side, fillets flake apart when gently prodded with tip of paring knife, and fish registers 140 degrees, about 2 minutes. Serve with rémoulade and lemon wedges.

juniper and fennel–rubbed roast side of salmon with orange beurre blanc

serves 4 to 6

salmon

- 15 juniper berries, toasted
- ¾ teaspoon fennel seeds, toasted
- 1 teaspoon grated orange zest
- ½ teaspoon sugar
- ½ teaspoon salt
- ½ teaspoon pepper
- 1 (1¾- to 2-pound) center-cut skin-on side of salmon, pin bones removed
- 1 tablespoon vegetable oil

beurre blanc

- 3 tablespoons dry white wine
- 2 tablespoons white wine vinegar
- 1 small shallot, minced
-    Salt
- 1 tablespoon heavy cream
- 8 tablespoons unsalted butter, cut into 8 pieces and chilled
- ⅛ teaspoon sugar
- ⅛ teaspoon grated orange zest

why this recipe works Roasting a side of salmon makes serving rich, silky fish a foolproof, almost hands-off affair, and this recipe's fragrant, unique rub and elegant sauce make it dinner party perfection. While the oven and a baking sheet heated to 500 degrees, we prepared an aromatic rub, grinding floral yet bitter toasted juniper berries and fennel seeds. A touch of sugar balanced out the bitterness and promoted browning while orange zest added brightness. We slashed the skin to encourage the fat to render, applied the rub, dropped the oven temperature to 275 degrees, and transferred the salmon to the hot pan in a foil sling. The salmon roasted in the gradually cooling oven while the heat further toasted the rub. An orange beurre blanc sauce offered a sophisticated accompaniment to the fish; we prepared it while the salmon roasted by reducing white wine and vinegar on the stovetop, enriching it with cream and butter, and finishing it with orange zest. If your knife is not sharp enough to cut through the skin easily, try a serrated knife. Heavy-duty aluminum foil measuring 18 inches wide is essential for creating a sling that aids in transferring the cooked fish to a cutting board or serving platter.

---

1 **for the salmon** Adjust oven rack to lowest position, place rimmed baking sheet on rack, and heat oven to 500 degrees. Grind juniper berries and fennel seeds in spice grinder until coarsely ground, about 30 seconds. Transfer spices to bowl and stir in orange zest, sugar, salt, and pepper.

2 Cut piece of heavy-duty aluminum foil to be 12 inches longer than side of salmon and fold lengthwise into thirds. Make 8 shallow slashes, about 3 inches long and 1 inch apart, on skin side of salmon, being careful not to cut into flesh. Pat salmon dry with paper towels and lay skin side down on foil. Rub flesh side of salmon with oil, then rub with spice mixture.

3 Reduce oven temperature to 275 degrees. Using foil sling, lay salmon on preheated sheet and roast until center is still translucent when checked with tip of paring knife and registers 125 degrees (for medium-rare), 14 to 18 minutes.

4 for the beurre blanc Meanwhile, bring wine, vinegar, shallot, and pinch salt to simmer in small saucepan over medium heat and cook until about 2 scant tablespoons of liquid remain, 3 to 5 minutes. Reduce heat to medium-low and whisk in cream. Add butter, 1 piece at a time, whisking vigorously after each addition, until butter is incorporated and forms thick, pale yellow sauce, 30 to 60 seconds. Off heat, whisk in sugar. Strain sauce through fine mesh strainer into bowl. Stir in orange zest and season with salt to taste.

5 Using foil sling, transfer salmon to cutting board (or platter). Run thin metal spatula between salmon skin and salmon to loosen. Using spatula to hold salmon in place on cutting board or platter, gently pull foil out from underneath salmon. Serve with beurre blanc.

popcorn shrimp

serves 4

1½ pounds medium-large shrimp (31 to 40 per pound), peeled, deveined, and tails removed

3 quarts peanut or vegetable oil

1½ tablespoons Cajun-Style Rub (page 74)

1 teaspoon grated lemon zest, plus lemon wedges for serving

1 garlic clove, minced

1½ cups all-purpose flour

½ cup cornstarch

2 teaspoons pepper

1 teaspoon baking powder

1½ cups bottled clam juice

why this recipe works When properly fried, popcorn shrimp are just as crunchy, salty, and irresistible as their namesake. Sadly, most recipes produce greasy, gummy shrimp, often coated in too much bland batter. We wanted shrimp coated in a light, flavorful batter and fried until just golden brown. For a crisp coating, we replaced some of the flour with cornstarch. A little baking powder increased browning and provided a bit of lift to the batter. Our Cajun-style rub added flavor to the batter in a dash, giving popcorn shrimp a serious upgrade. To impart a brininess that complemented the shrimp, we replaced the water in the batter with clam juice but reduced the liquid amount so that the coating clung to the shrimp. We also wanted to boost the flavor of the shrimp themselves, so we marinated them in a little oil, lemon zest, garlic, and more Cajun rub before coating. We prefer to use our homemade Cajun-Style Rub (page 74), but you can substitute store-bought Cajun seasoning or Old Bay seasoning. Use a Dutch oven that holds 6 quarts or more for this recipe.

1 Toss shrimp, 1 tablespoon oil, ½ teaspoon Cajun rub, lemon zest, and garlic in bowl. Cover and refrigerate for at least 30 minutes or up to 1 hour.

2 Adjust oven rack to middle position and heat oven to 200 degrees. Set wire rack in rimmed baking sheet and line plate with triple layer of paper towels. Add oil to large Dutch oven until it measures about 2 inches deep and heat over medium-high heat to 375 degrees. Whisk flour, cornstarch, pepper, baking powder, and remaining Cajun rub together in large bowl. Whisk in clam juice until smooth. Fold marinated shrimp into batter until evenly coated.

3 Add one-quarter of shrimp, one at a time, to hot oil. Fry, stirring gently to prevent pieces from sticking together, until shrimp are golden brown, about 2 minutes. Adjust burner, if necessary, to maintain oil temperature between 350 and 375 degrees.

4 Using wire skimmer or slotted spoon, transfer shrimp to prepared plate to drain briefly, then transfer shrimp to prepared wire rack and place in oven to keep warm. Return oil to 375 degrees and repeat with remaining shrimp in 3 batches. Serve with lemon wedges.

thick-cut steakhouse oven fries

serves 4

3 tablespoons vegetable oil

2 pounds Yukon Gold potatoes, unpeeled

3 tablespoons cornstarch

1 teaspoon Classic Steak Rub (page 73)

½ teaspoon coarse finishing salt

why this recipe works Crunchy potato wedges with fluffy-creamy interiors and a crisp shell are a treat, but they're even more fun to eat when they have a zesty spiced coating. Tossing the fries with a steak rub while they were piping hot woke up the spices, producing satisfyingly seasoned potatoes. We coated the fries in a cornstarch slurry that crisped up when baked—just like deep-fried fries. We coated the baking sheet with both vegetable oil spray and vegetable oil; the former contains lecithin, which prevents the oil from pooling and, in turn, prevents the potatoes from sticking. Choose potatoes that are 4 to 6 inches in length. This recipe's success is dependent on a heavy-duty rimmed baking sheet. The rate at which the potatoes brown is dependent on your baking sheet and oven. After removing the foil in step 4, monitor the color of the potatoes carefully to prevent scorching. You can substitute any of the spice rubs on pages 73–75 for the Classic Steak Rub. You can use your preferred coarse finishing salt in this recipe; for information on finishing salts, see pages 22–23.

1 Adjust oven rack to lowest position and heat oven to 425 degrees. Generously spray rimmed baking sheet with vegetable oil spray. Pour oil into prepared sheet and tilt sheet until surface is evenly coated with oil.

2 Halve potatoes lengthwise and turn halves cut sides down on cutting board. Trim thin slice from both long sides of each potato half; discard trimmings. Slice potatoes lengthwise into ⅓- to ½-inch-thick planks.

3 Combine ¾ cup water and cornstarch in large bowl, making sure no lumps of cornstarch remain on bottom of bowl. Microwave, stirring every 20 seconds, until mixture begins to thicken, 1 to 3 minutes. Remove from microwave and continue to stir until mixture thickens to pudding-like consistency. (If necessary, add up to 2 tablespoons water to achieve correct consistency.)

4 Transfer potatoes to bowl with cornstarch mixture and toss until each plank is evenly coated. Arrange planks on prepared sheet, leaving small gaps between planks. (Some cornstarch mixture will remain in bowl.) Cover sheet tightly with lightly greased aluminum foil and bake for 12 minutes. Remove foil from sheet and bake until bottom of each fry is golden brown, 10 to 18 minutes. Remove sheet from oven and, using thin metal spatula, carefully flip each fry. Return sheet to oven and continue to bake until second sides are golden brown, 10 to 18 minutes longer. Transfer fries to bowl and toss with steak rub and salt. Serve.

spice-roasted butternut squash with honey-lemon butter

serves 4

3 tablespoons extra-virgin olive oil

Salt and pepper

1 teaspoon ground cumin

1 teaspoon ground cinnamon

Pinch cayenne pepper

3 pounds butternut squash, peeled, seeded, and cut into 1-inch pieces

2 tablespoons unsalted butter

1 tablespoon honey

1 teaspoon chopped fresh thyme or ¼ teaspoon dried

1 teaspoon lemon juice

why this recipe works Butternut squash is great when cut into cubes and roasted on its own—until you taste it spiced up. We turned to the spice cabinet to accent squash's earthy, sweet flavor in a new way. We found that warm spices, such as cinnamon and cumin, have a delicate sweetness of their own, which complemented that quality in the squash. For a tender texture and nice browning, we cut the squash into 1-inch pieces and roasted it in a 425-degree oven after tossing the pieces with the mix of spices. We made this spiced squash a super-special side by drizzling it with an easy butter sauce, flavored with honey, lemon, and thyme. It was a rich and sweet but also a bright counterpoint to the spices. You'll never eat plain squash again. When peeling the squash, be sure to also remove the fibrous yellow flesh just beneath the skin.

1   Adjust oven rack to middle position and heat oven to 425 degrees. Line rimmed baking sheet with parchment paper. Whisk oil, 1 teaspoon salt, 1 teaspoon pepper, cumin, cinnamon, and cayenne together in large bowl. Add squash and toss until evenly coated. Arrange squash in even layer on prepared sheet and roast until tender and browned on bottom, 30 to 35 minutes.

2   Meanwhile, microwave butter, honey, and ¼ teaspoon salt in small bowl until butter is melted, about 30 seconds. Stir in thyme and lemon juice. Using spatula, transfer squash to serving platter. Drizzle with butter mixture and serve.

spice-roasted butternut squash with honey-lime butter

Substitute ground allspice for cinnamon, 1 tablespoon minced fresh chives for thyme, and lime juice for lemon juice.

spice-roasted butternut squash with honey-orange butter

Substitute ground coriander for cinnamon, oregano for thyme, and orange juice for lemon juice.

black pepper candied bacon

serves 4 to 6

¼ cup packed light brown sugar

1 teaspoon pepper

12 ounces center-cut bacon, halved crosswise

why this recipe works It might seem hard to imagine improving on bacon, but crispy bacon can become a cocktail party treat when layered with surprising sweet-savory flavor. For our sugar-and-spiced bacon, we sprinkled strips with brown sugar and black pepper. The sugar contributed a lovely caramel-toffee background flavor along with its sweetness, and a bit of black pepper provided the spice punch. Baking the seasoned strips ensured even cooking and prevented the coating from burning. Emboldened, we created two variations, each which delivered the same crunch but with even further dimension—one with the warmth of five-spice powder and the nuttiness of sesame seeds, and another with the smokiness of chipotle chile and the savoriness of cumin and garlic powder. We prefer center-cut bacon for this recipe, which is more uniform in thickness than traditional bacon. If your bacon has a range of thicknesses, place thinner slices on one tray and thicker pieces on the other for more even cooking. Do not substitute dark brown sugar here.

1 Adjust oven racks to upper-middle and lower-middle positions and heat oven to 350 degrees. Combine sugar and pepper in bowl. Arrange bacon on 2 aluminum foil–lined rimmed baking sheets and sprinkle with sugar mixture. Using fingers, spread sugar mixture evenly over one side of slices so that they are completely covered.

2 Bake bacon until dark brown and sugar is bubbling, 20 to 25 minutes, switching and rotating sheets halfway through baking. Set wire rack over triple-layer of paper towels. Remove sheets from oven as bacon finishes cooking and transfer bacon to prepared rack. Let cool for 5 minutes before serving.

five-spice and sesame candied bacon

We prefer to use our homemade Five-Spice Powder (page 74), but you can substitute store-bought five-spice powder.

Add 1 teaspoon five-spice powder to sugar mixture. After spreading sugar over bacon, sprinkle slices with 1 tablespoon sesame seeds.

chipotle candied bacon

Add ½ teaspoon chipotle chile powder, ½ teaspoon ground cumin, and ¼ teaspoon garlic powder to sugar mixture.

cinnamon-ginger spiced nuts

serves 8 to 10

⅔ cup superfine sugar

2 teaspoons ground cinnamon

1 teaspoon ground ginger

1 teaspoon ground coriander

1 large egg white

1 tablespoon water

1 teaspoon salt

1 pound raw whole almonds, cashews, walnuts, or shelled pistachios

why this recipe works Salty spiced nuts are deceptively easy, and they pack a triple-punch of flavor (salt, sugar, spice) that makes them a perfect snack to get a party started. Most recipes are made with a heavily sweetened syrup that causes the nuts to clump awkwardly and leaves your hands a sticky mess. We wanted to develop a recipe that was neat to eat. Tossing the nuts in a mixture of egg white, water, and salt gave them a nice crunchy (and dry) coating when baked and helped the spices adhere. The warmth of cinnamon and ginger, with some earthy notes of coriander, paired perfectly with the nuts' richness. Using this basic technique, we created a pair of variations so you can make a mix that fits your menu. If you can't find superfine sugar, process granulated sugar in a food processor for 1 minute. You can use a mixture of nuts instead of a single type.

1 Adjust oven racks to upper-middle and lower-middle positions and heat oven to 275 degrees. Line 2 rimmed baking sheets with parchment paper. Mix sugar, cinnamon, ginger, and coriander in bowl.

2 Whisk egg white, water, and salt together in bowl. Add nuts and toss to coat. Sprinkle spices over nuts, toss to coat, then spread evenly over prepared sheets. Bake until nuts are dry and crisp, about 50 minutes, stirring occasionally. Let nuts cool completely on sheets, about 30 minutes. Break nuts apart and serve.

chili-lime spiced nuts

We enjoy a combination of cashews and peanuts here.

Substitute 2½ teaspoons chili powder, 1 teaspoon ground cumin, and ½ teaspoon cayenne pepper for cinnamon, ginger, and coriander. Substitute 1 tablespoon lime juice for water and add 1 tablespoon grated lime zest to egg white mixture. (Nuts can be stored in airtight container for up to 3 weeks.)

orange-cardamom spiced nuts

We enjoy a combination of almonds and pistachios here.

Substitute 1 teaspoon ground cardamom and ½ teaspoon pepper for cinnamon, ginger, and coriander. Substitute 1 tablespoon orange juice for water and add 1 tablespoon grated orange zest and ¼ teaspoon vanilla extract to egg white mixture.

toast and bloom

maximizing flavor in braises, curries, chilis, and more

If you cook a lot, toasting and blooming may seem like routine actions, and they're often the first step to incorporating dried chiles into the chili pot or building a curry from complex curry powders. But do you know *why* so many recipes call for toasting or blooming spices? Spices contain a host of flavor compounds that give them character and complexity. But without the initial cooking, these compounds can remain largely dormant so that the dish tastes bland and dusty. Learn how toasting and blooming use heat differently to awaken spices' flavor.

BLOOMING SPICE BLENDS

TOAST IT

Toasting applies dry heat directly to spices. Just as with rich toasted nuts, toasting dried chiles and whole spices before stirring them into a dish brings their oils to the surface, resulting in a bolder aroma. Plus, it triggers flavorful browning and caramelization (like with toasted marshmallows) of the spices' proteins and sugars. (Yes, there are proteins and sugars in spices!) These flavors make the chilis of the Southwest complex and interesting rather than just hot, and allow the coating of leg of lamb to stand up to the robustly flavored meat. Note that we don't typically toast *ground* spices in the test kitchen; they develop a rounder flavor through blooming.

how to toast

Toasting spices and chiles is easy to do, but they can easily scorch. Be sure to keep an eye on the pan and use moderate heat.

whole spices and seeds

Whole spices need only be toasted until they become fragrant. If toasting spices alone, place them in a 10-inch skillet and cook over medium heat, stirring the spices constantly to prevent scorching, until you can smell the spice, 1 to 3 minutes. Immediately remove them from the skillet to stop the toasting. However, since toasting whole spices is sometimes the first step in a recipe, you can also toast in the same fashion in any pot or pan that the rest of your stovetop dish will cook in, such as the Dutch oven for our Black Bean Chili (page 121).

dried chiles

We also toast whole dried chiles right in the pot or pan we'll continue to cook in: Simply heat the chiles in the pan over medium heat, stirring frequently, until they're fragrant, 2 to 6 minutes, reducing the heat if the chiles begin to smoke. If a recipe calls for the chiles to be ripped into pieces and toasted with spices, they'll follow the shorter 1- to 3-minute cooking time of the spices. If you already have the oven on, you can use it as well: Arrange your chiles on a baking sheet and toast in a 350-degree oven just until fragrant and puffed, about 6 minutes.

working with dried chiles
You want to cook with dried, but not lifeless, chiles. Look for chiles that are pliable and smell slightly fruity. Avoid those that feel hard or crack when you bend them. Wipe the chiles with a damp cloth or paper towel to remove dust or dirt before using them. If not using straightaway, preserve the chiles' flavor and texture by sealing them in an airtight container or zipper-lock bag and store in a cool, dry place.

› common dried chiles

Chiles have a more intense character when dried, but that's about more than just incendiary heat. Because chiles for drying are allowed to ripen on the plant, many dried chiles often taste sweeter than fresh. Varieties range from earthy and fruit-sweet to bright and acidic. Chiles get their heat from a group of chemical compounds called capsaicinoids, the best known being capsaicin. Below we give a description of dried chiles we use in our recipes, rank their heat level on a scale of one to four, and offer substitutions to try.

ancho (dried poblano)
appearance Wrinkly, dark red.
flavor Rich, raisiny sweetness.
heat 1
substitutions Pasilla, mulato

chipotle (dried smoked jalapeño)
appearance Wrinkly, brownish red.
flavor Smoky, chocolaty, tobacco-like sweetness.
heat 2
substitution None

new mexican
appearance Smooth, brick red.
flavor Slightly acidic, earthy.
heat 2
substitution Cascabel

arbol
appearance Smooth, bright red.
flavor Bright, with smoky undertones.
heat 3
substitution Pequin

bird
appearance Narrow and petite, bright red.
flavor Rich, fruity.
heat 3½
substitution Arbol, pequin

BLOOM IT

Cooking ground spices in fat is another way to intensify flavor. Blooming changes fat-soluble flavor molecules from a solid state to liquid, where they mix and interact, thereby producing more complexity. But while heat unlocks the door, it's important to make sure the fat isn't too hot as it can scorch the spices. Blooming draws out maximum spice flavor without really adding an extra step—you'd need to add the spices to the dish at some point anyway!

› blooming spice blends

We often associate high levels of warm spice fragrance with the cuisines of Mexico, the Middle East and North Africa, and India. It comes as no surprise, then, that the spice blends we've created to bloom at the start of recipes largely come from those regions. By taking this step to develop flavor, we're able to closely recreate the tastes of these global dishes, even with a more limited pantry. As with our rub recipes (see pages 73–75), we do not toast the whole spices before creating these blends. We like the clean flavor of untoasted blends, and they lend themselves to many versatile applications. All of these blends make about ½ cup. They can be stored in an airtight container for up to 1 month, except for Thai Panang Curry Paste.

everyday chili powder
This balanced all-purpose powder is mild but has perceptible smoke and heat. We prefer the robust flavor of Mexican oregano, but you can substitute any dried oregano.

- 2 **ounces (7 to 8) dried New Mexican chiles, stemmed, seeded, and torn into ½-inch pieces (1½ cups)**
- 1 **teaspoon cumin seeds**
- ½ **teaspoon dried Mexican oregano**
- 1 **tablespoon paprika**
- ½ **teaspoon garlic powder**
- ¼ **teaspoon cayenne pepper**

Working in batches, process New Mexican chiles, cumin seeds, and oregano in spice grinder until finely ground, about 30 seconds. Stir in paprika, garlic powder, and cayenne.

grinding dried chiles for blends

While we want to cook with the freshest dried chiles (see pages 114–115), the pliable chiles we like are too sticky to grind for our blends. We don't like to toast chiles before grinding so they can be used in a variety of applications. To take away some tackiness—without toasting the chiles—before grinding, we dehydrate them: Adjust an oven rack to the middle position and heat the oven to 225 degrees. Place the chiles on a wire rack set in a rimmed baking sheet and dry until no longer tacky or leathery, about 2 hours. Let the chiles cool completely before grinding.

smoky cocoa chili powder

This powder is spicy and warm. We prefer Mexican oregano, but you can substitute any dried oregano.

1½ ounces (about 6) dried chipotle chiles, stemmed, seeded, and torn into ½-inch pieces (1 cup)
½ ounce (about 2) dried New Mexican chiles, stemmed, seeded, and torn into ½-inch pieces (⅓ cup)
1 teaspoon cumin seeds
½ teaspoon dried Mexican oregano
1 tablespoon cocoa powder
1 tablespoon paprika
½ teaspoon garlic powder
¼ teaspoon cayenne pepper

Working in batches, process chipotles, New Mexican chiles, cumin seeds, and oregano in spice grinder until finely ground, about 30 seconds. Stir in cocoa, paprika, garlic powder, and cayenne.

ras el hanout

This North African blend delivers complex flavor from a mix of warm spices. If you can't find Aleppo pepper, you can substitute ½ tea-spoon paprika plus ½ teaspoon red pepper flakes.

16 cardamom pods
4 teaspoons coriander seeds
4 teaspoons cumin seeds
2 teaspoons anise seeds
2 teaspoons ground dried Aleppo pepper
½ teaspoon allspice berries
¼ teaspoon black peppercorns
4 teaspoons ground ginger
2 teaspoons ground nutmeg
2 teaspoons ground cinnamon

Process cardamom pods, coriander seeds, cumin seeds, anise seeds, Aleppo, allspice, and peppercorns in spice grinder until finely ground, about 30 seconds. Stir in ginger, nutmeg, and cinnamon.

garam masala

The warm, floral, and earthy flavor profile of garam masala ("warm spice blend") makes it a welcome addition to most curries or a great seasoning for meat.

3 tablespoons black peppercorns
8 teaspoons coriander seeds
4 teaspoons cardamom pods
2½ teaspoons cumin seeds
1½ (3-inch) cinnamon sticks

Process all ingredients in spice grinder until finely ground, about 30 seconds.

› blooming spice blends

mild curry powder
Mild, vegetal, and sweet, this curry powder has a unique flavor due to the combination of savory and sweet spices.

2 tablespoons coriander seeds
1½ tablespoons cumin seeds
1 tablespoon yellow mustard seeds
1½ teaspoons black peppercorns
1½ tablespoons ground turmeric
1 teaspoon ground ginger
¼ teaspoon ground cinnamon

Process coriander seeds, cumin seeds, mustard seeds, and peppercorns in spice grinder until finely ground, about 30 seconds. Stir in turmeric, ginger, and cinnamon.

vindaloo curry powder
A healthy dose of arbol chiles, cayenne, and paprika creates fiery complex heat in this blend. For a spicier curry powder, use the larger amount of chiles.

6–8 dried arbol chiles, stemmed
1½ tablespoons coriander seeds
1½ tablespoons cumin seeds
1 tablespoon fenugreek seeds
1½ teaspoons black peppercorns
1 whole clove
1 teaspoon cayenne pepper
1 teaspoon paprika
½ teaspoon ground cinnamon

Process arbols, coriander seeds, cumin seeds, fenugreek seeds, peppercorns, and clove in spice grinder until finely ground, about 30 seconds. Stir in cayenne, paprika, and cinnamon.

vadouvan curry powder
Vadouvan is a French-influenced curry powder, with dried onion adding sweet allium flavor to the Indian profile.

4 teaspoons cumin seeds
1 tablespoon yellow mustard seeds
1 cardamom pod
5 teaspoons dried minced onion
4 teaspoons ground turmeric
1½ teaspoons fennel seeds, cracked
¼ teaspoon ground cinnamon

Process cumin seeds, mustard seeds, and cardamom pod in spice grinder until finely ground, about 30 seconds. Stir in dried onion, turmeric, fennel seeds, and cinnamon.

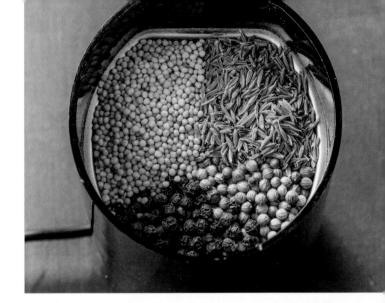

thai panang curry paste

This red paste balances sweet and spicy aromatic flavors. The makrut lime leaves are worth seeking out, but you can substitute 1 (3-inch) strip each of lemon and lime zest.

½ ounce (about 20) bird chiles, stemmed
1 teaspoon coriander seeds
½ teaspoon cumin seeds
2 lemon grass stalks, trimmed to bottom 6 inches and sliced thin
6 tablespoons water
8 garlic cloves, peeled and smashed
2 tablespoons packed dark brown sugar
2 makrut lime leaves
1 tablespoon tomato paste
1 teaspoon grated fresh ginger

1 Process bird chiles, coriander seeds, and cumin seeds in spice grinder until finely ground, about 30 seconds; transfer to blender.

2 Microwave lemon grass and water in covered bowl until steaming, about 2 minutes; transfer to blender with spices. Add garlic, sugar, lime leaves, tomato paste, and ginger and process until smooth paste forms, about 4 minutes, scraping down sides of blender jar as needed. (Paste can be refrigerated for up to 1 week.)

black bean chili

serves 6 to 8

- 1 pound white mushrooms, trimmed and chopped coarse
- 1 tablespoon mustard seeds
- 2 teaspoons cumin seeds
- 3 tablespoons vegetable oil
- 1 onion, chopped fine
- 9 garlic cloves, minced
- 3 tablespoons Everyday Chili Powder (page 116)
- 1 tablespoon minced canned chipotle chile in adobo sauce
- 2½ cups vegetable broth
- 2½ cups water, plus extra as needed
- 1 pound (2½ cups) dried black beans, picked over and rinsed
- 1 tablespoon packed light brown sugar
- ⅛ teaspoon baking soda
- 2 bay leaves
- 1 (28-ounce) can crushed tomatoes
- 2 red bell peppers, stemmed, seeded, and cut into ½-inch pieces
- ½ cup minced fresh cilantro
- Salt
- Lime wedges

why this recipe works Unsurprisingly, chili is often a lot about chili powder and, true to form, our black bean chili is a platform for our homemade chili powder to shine. We found that a generous 3 tablespoons infused our chili with round, earthy flavor from the New Mexican chiles we grind for the blend along with a bit of heat from cayenne. To provide depth and smokiness to back up the chili powder, we added toasted whole cumin seeds and minced chipotle in adobo. A surprise addition, toasted mustard seeds, provided more complexity and bite. After getting the spices right, we turned to the beans, which we wanted to be creamy and tender. Knowing that dried beans supply that superior texture, we looked for ways to boost the meaty flavor of the chili. The answer was glutamate-rich white mushrooms, which also added body to the chili. This rich, hearty chili was so satisfying that no one missed the meat. We prefer to use our homemade Everyday Chili Powder (page 116), but you can substitute store-bought chili powder. Serve with your favorite toppings.

1 Adjust oven rack to lower-middle position and heat oven to 325 degrees. Pulse mushrooms in food processor until chopped, about 10 pulses.

2 Toast mustard seeds and cumin seeds in Dutch oven over medium heat, stirring constantly, until fragrant, about 1 minute. Stir in oil, onion, and mushrooms, cover, and cook until vegetables have released their liquid, about 5 minutes. Uncover and continue to cook until vegetables are browned, 5 to 10 minutes.

3 Add garlic, chili powder, and chipotle and cook, stirring constantly, until fragrant, about 1 minute. Stir in broth, water, beans, sugar, baking soda, and bay leaves and bring to simmer. Using wide, shallow spoon, skim any foam from surface of liquid. Cover, transfer pot to oven, and cook for 1 hour.

4 Stir in tomatoes and bell peppers and cook, covered, until beans are fully tender, about 1 hour, stirring occasionally. (If chili begins to stick to bottom of pot or is too thick, add extra water as needed.)

5 Remove pot from oven and discard bay leaves. Stir in cilantro and season with salt to taste. Serve with lime wedges.

best ground beef chili

serves 8 to 10

- 2 pounds 85 percent lean ground beef
- 2 tablespoons plus 2 cups water
- Salt
- ¾ teaspoon baking soda
- 3 ounces (6 to 8) dried ancho chiles, stemmed, seeded, and torn into ½-inch pieces (1½ cups)
- 1 ounce tortilla chips, crushed (¼ cup)
- 2 tablespoons cumin seeds
- 4 teaspoons coriander seeds
- 1 tablespoon paprika
- 1 tablespoon garlic powder
- 2 teaspoons dried Mexican oregano
- 1½ teaspoons black peppercorns
- ½ teaspoon dried thyme
- 1 (14.5-ounce) can whole peeled tomatoes
- 1 tablespoon vegetable oil
- 1 onion, chopped fine
- 3 garlic cloves, minced
- 1–2 teaspoons minced canned chipotle chile in adobo sauce
- 1 (15-ounce) can pinto beans
- 2 teaspoons sugar
- 2 tablespoons cider vinegar
- Lime wedges
- Coarsely chopped fresh cilantro
- Chopped red onion

why this recipe works Perfectly tender—not pebbly—ground beef, a judicious amount of beans, and a stew with nice body are requisites for a chili with the title "Best." But it's the chiles that give this chili its blue-ribbon flavor: A generous amount of toasted dried anchos provided deep, fruity flavor, while smoky chipotle in adobo heated things up. The result is a chili with a whole lot of dimension. To keep the meat tender and help it hold onto moisture, we first treated it with salt and baking soda. Cornmeal was perfect for thickening and adding a subtle corn flavor, but we simply used ground tortilla chips since we like serving the chili with them anyway. Before serving, we made sure to stir in the fat that collected on the top (don't skim it!), since it contains much of the bloomed flavor from the fat-soluble spices. We prefer the robust flavor of Mexican oregano, but you can substitute any dried oregano. For a spicier chili, use the larger amount of chipotle. You can serve the chili with any additional favorite toppings and tortilla chips.

1   Adjust oven rack to lower-middle position and heat oven to 275 degrees. Toss beef with 2 tablespoons water, 1 teaspoon salt, and baking soda in bowl until thoroughly combined. Set aside for 20 minutes.

2   Meanwhile, toast anchos in Dutch oven over medium-high heat, stirring frequently, until fragrant, 2 to 6 minutes; reduce heat if they begin to smoke. Transfer to food processor and let cool for 5 minutes. Add tortilla chips, cumin seeds, coriander seeds, paprika, garlic powder, oregano, peppercorns, and thyme to food processor with anchos and process until finely ground, about 3 minutes; transfer to bowl. Process tomatoes and their juice in now-empty processor until smooth, about 30 seconds.

3   Heat oil in now-empty pot over medium-high heat until shimmering. Add onion and cook until softened, about 5 minutes. Stir in garlic and cook until fragrant, about 30 seconds. Add beef and cook, breaking up meat into ¼-inch pieces with wooden spoon, until browned and fond begins to form on pot bottom, 12 to 14 minutes. Add ancho mixture and chipotle and cook, stirring frequently, until fragrant, 1 to 2 minutes. Stir in beans and their liquid, sugar, processed tomatoes, and remaining 2 cups water, scraping up any browned bits, and bring to simmer. Cover, transfer pot to oven, and cook, stirring occasionally, until beef is tender and chili is slightly thickened, 1½ to 2 hours. Remove pot from oven and let sit, uncovered, for 10 minutes. Add vinegar and stir chili well to recombine. Season with salt to taste. Serve, passing lime wedges, cilantro, and onion separately.

tex-mex cheese enchiladas

serves 4 to 6

- 1 ounce (about 2) dried ancho chiles, stemmed, seeded, and torn into ½-inch pieces (½ cup)
- 1 tablespoon cumin seeds
- ½ teaspoon black peppercorns
- 2 teaspoons dried Mexican oregano
- 5 tablespoons vegetable oil
- 1 tablespoon garlic powder
- 3 tablespoons all-purpose flour
- Salt and pepper
- 2 cups chicken or vegetable broth
- 2 teaspoons distilled white vinegar
- 8 ounces Monterey Jack cheese, shredded (2 cups)
- 6 ounces sharp cheddar cheese, shredded (1½ cups)
- 12 (6-inch) corn tortillas
- 1 cup finely chopped onion

why this recipe works Unlike their Mexican kin, Tex-Mex enchiladas have no meat or tomatoey sauce; instead, a smoky chile gravy provides most of the flavor. Dried ancho chiles, toasted and ground, along with cumin, garlic powder, and oregano, were the perfect backbone for our roux-based sauce, giving it smoky, slightly fruity flavor with a touch of bitterness. A splash of vinegar brightened it up. Instead of using the processed cheese typical of the dish, we opted for a mixture of cheddar for sharp, distinctly "cheesy" flavor and Monterey Jack for smooth meltability. Finally, while traditional recipes call for frying the corn tortillas one at a time, we found a shortcut that reduced the time (and excess grease): We brushed the tortillas with oil and microwaved them for a minute before wrapping them around our cheesy filling. We prefer the robust flavor of Mexican oregano, but you can substitute any dried oregano.

1 Toast anchos and cumin seeds in 12-inch skillet over medium heat, stirring constantly, until fragrant, about 1 minute. Transfer to spice grinder and let cool for 5 minutes. Add peppercorns and oregano and process until finely ground, about 30 seconds.

2 Heat 3 tablespoons oil in now-empty skillet over medium-high heat until shimmering. Add chile mixture, garlic powder, flour, and ½ teaspoon salt and cook, stirring constantly, until fragrant and slightly deepened in color, about 1 minute. Slowly whisk in broth, scraping up any browned bits and smoothing out any lumps. Bring to simmer and cook, whisking often, until sauce has thickened and measures 1½ cups, about 5 minutes. Whisk in vinegar and season with salt and pepper to taste. Remove from heat and cover to keep warm.

3 Adjust oven rack to middle position and heat oven to 450 degrees. Spread ½ cup sauce over bottom of 13 by 9-inch baking dish. Combine Monterey Jack and cheddar in bowl; set ½ cup aside for topping. Brush both sides of tortillas with remaining 2 tablespoons oil. Stack tortillas, wrap in damp dish towel, place on plate, and microwave until warm and pliable, about 1 minute.

4 Working with 1 warm tortilla at a time, spread ¼ cup cheese mixture across center of each tortilla and sprinkle with 1 tablespoon onion. Roll tortilla tightly around filling and place, seam side down, in baking dish, arranging enchiladas in 2 columns across width of dish.

5 Pour remaining sauce over top to cover completely and sprinkle with reserved cheese. Cover dish tightly with greased aluminum foil. Bake until sauce is bubbling and cheese is melted, about 15 minutes. Sprinkle with remaining ¼ cup onion and serve.

crispy spiced ground beef tacos

serves 4

1 tablespoon water

¼ teaspoon baking soda

12 ounces 90 percent lean ground beef

7 tablespoons vegetable oil

1 onion, chopped fine

¼ cup Smoky Cocoa Chili Powder (page 117)

Salt

2 tablespoons tomato paste

2 ounces cheddar cheese, shredded (½ cup), plus extra for serving

12 (6-inch) corn tortillas

Shredded iceberg lettuce

Chopped tomato

Sour cream

Pickled jalapeño slices

Hot sauce

why this recipe works The combination of meat, creamy cheese, and cool, crisp lettuce has made the hard-shell taco an American staple. But the seasonings in commercial taco kits are dusty and one-note, and the corn shells brittle and stale-tasting. We wanted to fix up and spice up the taco Tuesday standard, and we got inspiration from *tacos dorados*, a Mexican preparation in which corn tortillas are stuffed with a beef filling before being folded in half and fried. The tacos are then opened and loaded with garnishes. We thought this was a great place to employ some depth with heat so we used our Smoky Cocoa Chili Powder (page 117). We tossed ground beef with a bit of baking soda to help it stay juicy before adding it to a savory base of sautéed onion, the spice blend, and tomato paste. Next, we stirred in cheese to make the filling more cohesive and to add richness to temper the savory heat. To build the tacos, we brushed corn tortillas with oil, warmed them in the oven to make them pliable, and stuffed them with filling. Finally, we pan-fried the tacos until they were supercrispy and golden. These were one part nostalgic, one part sophisticated, and all parts delicious. Arrange the tacos so they face the same direction in the skillet. To ensure crispy tacos, cook the tortillas until they are deeply browned. Open each taco like a book and load it with your preferred toppings; close it to eat.

1 Adjust oven rack to middle position and heat oven to 400 degrees. Combine water and baking soda in large bowl. Add beef and mix until thoroughly combined. Set aside.

2 Heat 1 tablespoon oil in 12-inch nonstick skillet over medium heat until shimmering. Add onion and cook, stirring occasionally, until softened, 4 to 6 minutes. Add chili powder and 1 teaspoon salt and cook, stirring frequently, until fragrant, about 1 minute. Stir in tomato paste and cook until paste is rust-colored, 1 to 2 minutes. Add beef mixture and cook, using wooden spoon to break meat into pieces no larger than ¼ inch, until beef is no longer pink, 5 to 7 minutes. Transfer beef mixture to bowl; stir in cheddar until cheese has melted and mixture is homogeneous. Wipe skillet clean with paper towels.

3 Thoroughly brush both sides of tortillas with 2 tablespoons oil. Arrange tortillas, overlapping, on rimmed baking sheet in 2 rows (6 tortillas each). Bake until tortillas are warm and pliable, about 5 minutes. Remove tortillas from oven and reduce oven temperature to 200 degrees.

4 Place 2 tablespoons filling on 1 side of 1 tortilla. Fold and press to close tortilla (edges will be open, but tortilla will remain folded). Repeat with remaining tortillas and remaining filling. (At this point, filled tortillas can be covered and refrigerated for up to 12 hours.)

5   Set wire rack in second rimmed baking sheet and line rack with double layer of paper towels. Heat remaining ¼ cup oil in now-empty skillet over medium-high heat until shimmering. Arrange 6 tacos in skillet with open sides facing away from you. Cook, adjusting heat so oil actively sizzles and bubbles appear around edges of tacos, until tacos are crispy and deeply browned on 1 side, 2 to 3 minutes. Using tongs and thin spatula, carefully flip tacos. Cook until deeply browned on second side, 2 to 3 minutes, adjusting heat as necessary.

6   Remove skillet from heat and transfer tacos to prepared wire rack. Blot tops of tacos with double layer of paper towels. Place sheet with fried tacos in oven to keep warm. Return skillet to medium-high heat and cook remaining tacos. Serve tacos immediately, passing extra cheddar, lettuce, tomato, sour cream, jalapeños, and hot sauce separately.

roast butterflied leg of lamb with coriander, fennel, and black pepper

serves 10 to 12

lamb

- 1 (6- to 8-pound) butterflied leg of lamb

  Kosher salt

- ⅓ cup vegetable oil
- 3 shallots, sliced thin
- 4 garlic cloves, peeled and smashed
- 1 (1-inch) piece ginger, sliced into ½-inch-thick rounds and smashed
- 1 tablespoon coriander seeds
- 1 tablespoon fennel seeds
- 1 tablespoon black peppercorns
- 3 bay leaves
- 2 (2-inch) strips lemon zest

sauce

- ⅓ cup chopped fresh parsley
- ⅓ cup chopped fresh cilantro
- 1 shallot, minced
- 2 tablespoons lemon juice

  Salt and pepper

why this recipe works Leg of lamb has a richness of flavor unmatched by beef or pork, so it pairs well with a wide range of robust spices. A rub is common, but we found a way to infuse our butterflied and pounded lamb with spice in a unique way: by roasting it right on top of a bed of whole spices. Why? Our standard method for cooking this cut is to start it in a very low oven (just 250 degrees) and then finish with a blast under the broiler for juicy, tender lamb with a burnished, crisp crust. But the broiler scorched any superficial application of spice, so we had to find a hiding place for flavor. We placed whole coriander and fennel seeds, as well as peppercorns, bay leaves, smashed garlic, sliced ginger, and lemon zest, on a baking sheet along with a glug of oil and popped it in the oven to first toast and bloom the spices. Then we placed the lamb on top of the complexly flavored spices and returned the pan to the oven. The aromatics and spice-infused oil clung to the bottom and provided rich flavor, and then became the base for a quick sauce to serve alongside the juicy, boldly spiced lamb. We prefer the milder taste and bigger size of domestic lamb, but you may substitute imported lamb from New Zealand and Australia. The 2 tablespoons of kosher salt in step 1 is for a 6-pound leg. If using a larger leg (7 to 8 pounds), add an additional teaspoon of salt for every pound. We prefer this lamb cooked to medium-rare, but if you prefer it more or less done, see our guidelines on page 280.

---

1 **for the lamb** Place roast on cutting board with fat cap facing down. Using sharp knife, trim any pockets of fat and connective tissue from underside of roast. Flip roast over, trim fat cap to between ⅛ and ¼ inch thick, and pound lamb to even 1-inch thickness. Using sharp knife, cut slits ½ inch apart in crosshatch pattern in fat cap of roast, being careful not to cut into meat. Rub 2 tablespoons salt over entire roast and into slits. Let sit, uncovered at room temperature, for 1 hour.

2 Meanwhile, adjust oven racks to upper-middle and lower-middle positions and heat oven to 250 degrees. Stir oil, shallots, garlic, ginger, coriander seeds, fennel seeds, peppercorns, bay leaves, and lemon zest together in rimmed baking sheet and bake on lower rack until spices are softened and fragrant and shallots and garlic turn golden, about 1 hour. Remove sheet from oven and discard bay leaves.

3   Thoroughly pat roast dry with paper towels and transfer, fat side up, to sheet (directly on top of spices). Roast on lower rack until lamb registers 120 degrees, 30 to 40 minutes. Remove sheet from oven and heat broiler. Broil roast on upper rack until surface is well browned and charred in spots and lamb registers 125 degrees (for medium-rare), 3 to 8 minutes.

4   Remove sheet from oven, transfer roast to carving board (some spices will cling to roast), and let rest for 20 minutes.

5   **for the sauce** Meanwhile, carefully pour pan juices through fine-mesh strainer into medium bowl, pressing on solids to extract as much liquid as possible; discard solids. Stir in parsley, cilantro, minced shallot, and lemon juice. Add any accumulated lamb juices to sauce and season with salt and pepper to taste.

6   With long side facing you, slice roast with grain into 3 equal pieces. Turn each piece and slice against grain into ¼-inch-thick slices. Serve with sauce. (Briefly warm sauce in microwave if it has cooled and thickened.)

lamb vindaloo

serves 6 to 8

- 4 pounds boneless lamb shoulder roast, trimmed and cut into 1½-inch pieces

  Salt and pepper

- 2 tablespoons vegetable oil

- 3 onions, chopped

- ¼ cup Vindaloo Curry Powder (page 118)

- 8 garlic cloves, minced

- 2 tablespoons all-purpose flour

- 3 cups chicken broth, plus extra as needed

- 2 teaspoons sugar

- 1 (14.5-ounce) can diced tomatoes

- ¼ cup minced fresh cilantro

- 2 tablespoons red wine vinegar

why this recipe works If you're familiar only with mild Indian curry powder and yellow-tinted stews made with it, let us introduce you to something a bit more spicy: vindaloo. Vindaloo curry is a complex dish that has both Indian and Portuguese influences. The hallmark of vindaloo is its interplay of sweet and sour flavors in a thick reddish-orange sauce. The heat of the spices in our vindaloo curry powder, including ground dried arbol chiles and cayenne pepper, is tamed by the sweetness of the sugar and the acidity of the tomatoes and vinegar in the dish. Traditional vindaloos are made with pork, but as vindaloo curries became popular all over, lamb, chicken, and sometimes even chunks of potatoes found their way into this dynamic stew. We decided to use a hearty boneless lamb shoulder roast, as the lengthy cooking time helped to concentrate and further bloom the spice blend in the sauce. You can substitute an equal amount of boneless leg of lamb for the lamb shoulder, if desired. We prefer to use our homemade Vindaloo Curry Powder (page 118), but you can substitute store-bought vindaloo curry powder. Serve with basmati rice.

1   Adjust oven rack to lower-middle position and heat oven to 325 degrees. Pat lamb dry with paper towels and season with salt and pepper. Heat 1 tablespoon oil in Dutch oven over medium-high heat until just smoking. Brown half of lamb on all sides, 7 to 10 minutes; transfer to bowl. Repeat with remaining 1 tablespoon oil and remaining lamb; transfer to bowl.

2   Add onions to fat left in pot and cook over medium heat, stirring often, until softened and lightly browned, 6 to 8 minutes. Stir in curry powder, garlic, and ¼ teaspoon salt and cook until fragrant, about 1 minute. Add flour and cook, stirring constantly, for 1 minute. Slowly stir in broth and sugar, scraping up any browned bits and smoothing out any lumps. Stir in tomatoes and their juice and lamb with any accumulated juices and bring to simmer. Cover, transfer pot to oven, and cook until lamb is tender, about 2 hours.

3   Remove pot from oven. Using wide, shallow spoon, skim excess fat from surface of stew. Adjust consistency with extra hot broth as needed. Stir in cilantro and vinegar and season with salt and pepper to taste. Serve.

thai panang curry with shrimp

serves 4

 2 tablespoons vegetable oil

2–4 tablespoons Thai Panang Curry Paste (page 119)

 1 (14-ounce) can coconut milk

 2 tablespoons fish sauce

 6 ounces sugar snap peas, strings removed

 1 red bell pepper, stemmed, seeded, and cut into ¼-inch-wide strips

1½ pounds large shrimp (26 to 30 per pound), peeled, deveined, and tails removed

 ¼ cup chopped fresh mint

 ¼ cup chopped fresh basil

 ⅓ cup dry-roasted peanuts, chopped

why this recipe works Panang curry is a sweeter, more full-bodied version of Thai red curry that's often enriched with ground peanuts and seasoned with sugar, fish sauce, deeply fragrant makrut lime leaves, and a touch of fiery chile. And unlike more familiar curries, which are typically brothy, panang curry has a thick, velvety consistency (from a judicious amount of coconut milk) that steadfastly clings to the shrimp. To start, we sizzled a few tablespoons of homemade curry paste in vegetable oil; blooming the paste ensured that the fresh aromatics and spices reached their full flavor potential despite the dish's short cooking time. This is a departure from traditional recipes that call for frying the paste in coconut cream that has been "cracked"—that is, simmered until its oil separates out. We've found that coconut milks from different brands yield varying amounts of cream, so the vegetable oil method was more foolproof. Peanut is a final key flavor component; a scattering of finely chopped roasted peanuts over the top before serving lent the dish subtle nuttiness as well as a nice crunch. We prefer to use our homemade Thai Panang Curry Paste (page 119), but you can substitute store-bought Thai red curry paste if you wish. For a spicier curry, use the larger amount of curry paste.

---

1 Heat oil in 12-inch nonstick skillet over medium heat until shimmering. Add curry paste and cook, stirring frequently, until paste is fragrant and darkens in color to brick red, 5 to 8 minutes. Whisk in coconut milk and fish sauce, bring to simmer, and cook until sauce is slightly thickened, 10 to 12 minutes.

2 Add snap peas and bell pepper and simmer for 3 minutes. Add shrimp, cover, and cook, stirring occasionally, until shrimp are opaque throughout and vegetables are crisp-tender, about 4 minutes. Off heat, stir in mint and basil. Sprinkle with peanuts and serve.

classic vegetable curry with potatoes and cauliflower

serves 4 to 6

- 3 tablespoons vegetable oil
- 2 onions, chopped fine
- 12 ounces red potatoes, unpeeled, cut into ½-inch pieces
- 3 tablespoons Mild Curry Powder (page 118)

  Salt and pepper
- 3 garlic cloves, minced
- 1 tablespoon grated fresh ginger
- 1 tablespoon tomato paste
- 1½ cups vegetable broth, plus extra as needed
- ½ head cauliflower (1 pound), cored and cut into 1-inch florets
- 1 (15-ounce) can chickpeas, rinsed
- 1 (14.5-ounce) can diced tomatoes
- 1½ cups frozen peas, thawed
- ½ cup canned coconut milk
- ¼ cup chopped fresh cilantro

Vary your curry powder or paste and you'll find that it takes better to different ingredients—and gives you a whole new dish. After all, robust spices stand up to robust ingredients and vice versa. These are some interesting curries using our different powders. We prefer to use our home-made curry powders and paste, but you can substitute store-bought. Mild curry powder is also known as "sweet" curry powder in the grocery store.

1   Heat oil in Dutch oven over medium-high heat until shimmering. Add onions, potatoes, curry powder, and ¾ teaspoon salt and cook, stirring occasionally, until onions are browned and potatoes are golden brown at edges, 8 to 10 minutes. Stir in garlic, ginger, and tomato paste and cook until fragrant, about 1 minute.

2   Slowly stir in broth, scraping up any browned bits. Stir in cauliflower, chickpeas, and tomatoes and their juice and bring to simmer. Reduce heat to low, cover, and simmer gently until vegetables are tender, 20 to 25 minutes, stirring occasionally.

3   Stir in peas and coconut milk and cook, uncovered, until heated through, about 2 minutes. Adjust consistency with extra hot broth as needed. Off heat, stir in cilantro and season with salt and pepper to taste. Serve.

vindaloo vegetable curry with okra and tomatoes

Omit potatoes, broth, and coconut milk. Substitute Vindaloo Curry Powder (page 118) for Mild Curry Powder, 1 pound frozen okra for cauliflower, and parsley for cilantro. Increase chickpeas to 2 (15-ounce) cans and tomatoes to 3 (14.5-ounce) cans. Stir 2 tablespoons red wine vinegar into curry before serving.

vadouvan vegetable curry with sweet potatoes and green beans

Omit peas and coconut milk. Substitute Vadouvan Curry Powder (page 118) for Mild Curry Powder; sweet potatoes for red potatoes; 12 ounces green beans, trimmed and cut into 2-inch pieces, for cauliflower; and minced fresh chives for cilantro. Reduce simmering time to 10 to 15 minutes.

panang vegetable curry with eggplant and red bell peppers

Omit peas. Substitute 5 tablespoons Thai Panang Curry Paste (page 119) for Mild Curry Powder; 1½ pounds eggplant, cut into 1-inch pieces, for potatoes; 2 red bell peppers, cut into 1-inch pieces, for cauliflower; and fresh basil for cilantro. Reduce simmering time to about 10 minutes.

hungarian beef stew

serves 6 to 8

- 4 pounds boneless beef chuck-eye roast, pulled apart at seams, trimmed, and cut into 1½-inch pieces

  Kosher salt and pepper

- 1 (12-ounce) jar roasted red peppers, rinsed

- ⅓ cup paprika

- 2 tablespoons tomato paste

- 1 tablespoon distilled white vinegar

- 3 pounds onions, chopped fine

- 2 tablespoons vegetable oil

- 4 carrots, peeled and sliced 1 inch thick

- 1 bay leaf

- 1 cup beef broth, plus extra as needed

why this recipe works Though you'd never guess it from the Americanized versions with ultralong ingredient lists, traditional Hungarian goulash is the simplest of stews, calling for little more than beef and onions. Oh, and a whole lot of paprika. Tasters preferred traditional sweet paprika to hot or smoked because of its floral, fruity qualities, but when we used enough to pack the flavor punch we wanted, the spice contributed a gritty, dusty texture. Consulting a few Hungarian restaurants, we discovered they used "paprika cream," a hard-to-find smooth product made from a blend of paprika and red bell peppers. So we created our own by pureeing a drained jar of roasted red peppers with a little tomato paste, vinegar, and the paprika; this gave the stew the bold flavor and smooth texture we were after. Searing the meat competed with the paprika's flavor, so we simply softened the onions first and then stirred in the paprika mixture and the meat and left everything to cook. Paprika is vital to this recipe, so it's best to use a fresh container. Don't substitute hot or smoked paprika for the sweet paprika. Serve with sour cream and buttered egg noodles.

1 Adjust oven rack to lower-middle position and heat oven to 325 degrees. Season beef with 2 teaspoons salt. Process red peppers, paprika, tomato paste, and 2 teaspoons vinegar in food processor until smooth, 1 to 2 minutes, scraping down sides of bowl as needed.

2 Combine onions, oil, and 2 teaspoons salt in Dutch oven, cover, and cook over medium heat, stirring occasionally, until onions soften but have not yet begun to brown, 8 to 10 minutes. (If onions begin to brown, reduce heat to medium-low and stir in 1 tablespoon water.)

3 Stir in pepper mixture and cook, uncovered, until onions begin to stick to bottom of pot, about 2 minutes. Stir in beef, carrots, and bay leaf and use rubber spatula to scrape down sides of pot. Cover, transfer pot to oven, and cook until beef is almost tender and surface of liquid is ½ inch below top of meat, 2 to 2½ hours, stirring every 30 minutes.

4 Stir in broth until surface of liquid measures ¼ inch from top of meat (beef should not be fully submerged). Cover and continue to cook until beef is tender, about 30 minutes.

5 Remove pot from oven and discard bay leaf. Using wide, shallow spoon, skim excess fat from surface of stew. Adjust consistency with extra hot broth as needed. Stir in remaining 1 teaspoon vinegar and season with salt and pepper to taste. Serve.

spanish shellfish stew

serves 4 to 6

picada

¼ cup slivered almonds

2 slices hearty white sandwich bread, torn into quarters

2 tablespoons extra-virgin olive oil

⅛ teaspoon salt

Pinch pepper

stew

¼ cup extra-virgin olive oil

8 ounces medium-large shrimp (31 to 40 per pound), peeled and deveined, shells reserved

1½ cups dry white wine or dry vermouth

1 onion, chopped fine

1 red bell pepper, stemmed, seeded, and chopped fine

3 garlic cloves, minced

1 teaspoon paprika

¼ teaspoon saffron threads, crumbled

⅛ teaspoon red pepper flakes

2 tablespoons brandy

1 (28-ounce) can whole peeled tomatoes, drained with juice reserved, chopped

2 bay leaves

1½ pounds littleneck clams, scrubbed

8 ounces mussels, scrubbed and debearded

12 ounces large sea scallops, tendons removed

1 tablespoon minced fresh parsley

Salt and pepper

why this recipe works One of the most recognizable dishes from Spanish cuisine, paella, teaches that floral saffron is a fitting pairing for delicate seafood, adding beautiful color and a flavor that perfumes without overwhelming. Another favorite Spanish dish that pairs the two is *zarzuela*, a shellfish stew you can think of as Spain's version of France's bouillabaisse. Chock-full of shellfish, this full-flavored tomato-based stew is seasoned (and colored) with not just saffron but also sweet, peppery paprika, and thickened with a *picada*, a mixture of ground almonds, bread crumbs, and olive oil. To create our version, we followed Spanish tradition and began with a *sofrito* of onion, red bell pepper, and garlic and next added our spices so they could bloom and create a rich foundation of flavor. For the liquid we used canned tomatoes and dry white wine, plus a little brandy for depth. Knowing that seafood shells contribute significant flavor to dishes, we enriched the broth by steeping the shrimp shells in the wine while we prepared the other ingredients. Be sure to buy shrimp with their shells on and reserve the shells when cleaning the shrimp. We like to serve the stew with lemon wedges.

---

1 **for the picada** Adjust oven rack to middle position and heat oven to 375 degrees. Pulse almonds in food processor to fine meal, about 20 pulses. Add bread, oil, salt, and pepper and pulse to coarse crumbs, about 10 pulses. Spread mixture evenly in rimmed baking sheet and bake, stirring often, until golden brown, about 10 minutes. Set aside and let cool.

2 **for the stew** Heat 1 tablespoon oil in medium saucepan over medium heat until shimmering. Add shrimp shells and cook, stirring frequently, until shells begin to turn spotty brown and pot starts to brown, 2 to 4 minutes. Off heat, stir in wine, cover, and let steep until ready to use.

3 Heat remaining 3 tablespoons oil in Dutch oven over medium-high heat until shimmering. Add onion and bell pepper and cook until softened and lightly browned, 5 to 7 minutes. Stir in garlic, paprika, saffron, and pepper flakes and cook until fragrant, about 30 seconds. Stir in brandy, scraping up any browned bits. Stir in tomatoes and their juice and bay leaves and cook until slightly thickened, 5 to 7 minutes.

4 Strain wine mixture into Dutch oven, pressing on shells to extract as much liquid as possible; discard shells. Bring to simmer and cook until flavors meld, 3 to 5 minutes.

5   Nestle clams into pot, cover, and cook for 4 minutes. Nestle mussels and scallops into pot, cover, and continue to cook until most clams have opened, about 3 minutes. Arrange shrimp evenly over stew, cover, and continue to cook until shrimp are opaque throughout, scallops are firm and opaque in center, and clams and mussels have opened, 1 to 2 minutes.

6   Off heat, discard bay leaves and any clams and mussels that refuse to open. Stir in picada and parsley and season with salt and pepper to taste. Serve in wide, shallow bowls.

chicken tagine with fennel, chickpeas, and apricots

serves 4 to 6

- 2 tablespoons extra-virgin olive oil, plus extra as needed
- 5 garlic cloves, minced
- 1½ teaspoons paprika
- ½ teaspoon ground turmeric
- ½ teaspoon ground cumin
- ¼ teaspoon ground ginger
- ¼ teaspoon cayenne pepper
- 2 (15-ounce) cans chickpeas, rinsed
- 8 (5- to 7-ounce) bone-in chicken thighs, trimmed
  Salt and pepper
- 1 large fennel bulb, stalks discarded, bulb halved and cut into ½-inch-thick wedges through core
- 3 (2-inch) strips lemon zest, plus lemon wedges for serving
- 1 cinnamon stick
- ½ cup dry white wine
- 1 cup chicken broth
- 1 cup pitted large brine-cured green or black olives, halved
- ½ cup dried apricots, halved
- 2 tablespoons chopped fresh parsley

why this recipe works While traditional spice blends for Moroccan tagines can contain upwards of 30 spices, we found just a few everyday spices were necessary to re-create the authentic notes of Moroccan chicken tagine in a simple skillet supper. We used skin-on chicken thighs and browned the meat; then we browned fennel in the rendered fat and bloomed a blend of spicy, earthy, and warm ground spices and a whole cinnamon stick, which cooked with the dish and infused the whole thing with flavor. We added a few broad ribbons of lemon zest as well to give the tagine a rich citrus back note. Brine-cured olives provided the meatiness and piquant flavor of hard-to-find Moroccan ones, and some dried apricots, which plumped among the chickpeas and broth, created well rounded sweetness for this well-spiced dish. Chopped parsley, stirred in right before serving, was the perfect finishing touch to freshen the flavors.

1   Adjust oven rack to upper-middle position and heat oven to 350 degrees. Combine 1 tablespoon oil, garlic, paprika, turmeric, cumin, ginger, and cayenne in bowl; set aside. Place ½ cup chickpeas in second bowl and mash to coarse paste with potato masher.

2   Pat chicken dry with paper towels and season with salt and pepper. Heat remaining 1 tablespoon oil in 12-inch ovensafe skillet over medium-high heat until just smoking. Cook chicken skin side down until skin is crisped and well browned, 8 to 10 minutes; transfer chicken skin side up to plate.

3   Pour off all but 2 tablespoons fat from skillet (or, if necessary, add extra oil to equal 2 tablespoons). Heat fat left in skillet over medium heat until shimmering. Arrange fennel cut side down in skillet and sprinkle with ¼ teaspoon salt. Cover and cook until lightly browned, 3 to 5 minutes per side. Push fennel to sides of skillet. Add spice mixture, lemon zest, and cinnamon stick to center and cook, mashing spice mixture into skillet, until fragrant, about 30 seconds. Stir spice mixture into fennel. Stir in wine, scraping up any browned bits, and cook until almost evaporated, about 2 minutes.

4   Stir in broth, olives, apricots, mashed chickpeas, and whole chickpeas and bring to simmer. Nestle chicken skin side up into skillet, keeping skin above liquid. Roast until fennel is tender and chicken registers 185 degrees, 35 to 40 minutes. Using pot holders, carefully remove skillet from oven. Discard lemon zest and cinnamon stick. Season with salt and pepper to taste. Sprinkle with parsley and serve with lemon wedges.

tandoori chicken with raita

serves 4

raita

- 1 cup plain whole-milk yogurt
- 2 tablespoons minced fresh cilantro
- 1 garlic clove, minced
- Salt
- Cayenne pepper

chicken

- 2 tablespoons vegetable oil
- 6 garlic cloves, minced
- 2 tablespoons grated fresh ginger
- 1 tablespoon Garam Masala (page 117)
- 2 teaspoons ground cumin
- 2 teaspoons Everyday Chili Powder (page 116)
- 1 cup plain whole-milk yogurt
- ¼ cup lime juice (2 limes), plus lime wedges for serving
- 2 teaspoons salt
- 3 pounds bone-in chicken pieces (split breasts cut in half, drumsticks, and/or thighs), skin removed, trimmed

why this recipe works Traditional tandoori chicken is marinated in yogurt and spices and roasted in a superhot tandoor oven to produce tender, flavorful meat and a beautiful char. To make it at home, we built a fragrant paste, blooming ginger and garlic in oil before adding garam masala, cumin, and chili powder. We used this paste twice, applying some directly to the meat, which we slashed so the flavors penetrated, and stirring the rest into yogurt for our marinade. Arranged on a wire rack set in a baking sheet, our chicken roasted gently and evenly in a moderate oven; a few minutes under the broiler delivered char. A quick raita cooled things down. If you are using large chicken breasts (about 1 pound each), cut each breast into three pieces. We prefer to use our homemade Garam Masala (page 117) and Everyday Chili Powder (page 116), but you can substitute store-bought spices. Serve with rice.

---

1 for the raita Combine yogurt, cilantro, and garlic in bowl and season with salt and cayenne to taste. Refrigerate until ready to serve. (Raita can be refrigerated for up to 24 hours).

2 for the chicken Heat oil in 10-inch skillet over medium heat until shimmering. Add garlic and ginger and cook until fragrant, about 30 seconds. Stir in garam masala, cumin, and chili powder and cook until fragrant, about 30 seconds. Transfer half of garlic mixture to bowl and stir in yogurt and 2 tablespoons lime juice; set marinade aside. Combine remaining garlic mixture, remaining 2 tablespoons lime juice, and salt in large bowl. Using sharp knife, make 2 or 3 short slashes in each piece of chicken. Transfer chicken to large bowl and gently rub with garlic–lime juice mixture until all pieces are evenly coated. Let sit at room temperature for 30 minutes.

3 Adjust oven rack to upper-middle position and heat oven to 325 degrees. Set wire rack in aluminum foil–lined rimmed baking sheet. Pour yogurt marinade over chicken and toss until chicken is evenly and thickly coated. Arrange chicken pieces, scored sides down, on prepared rack; discard excess marinade. Roast chicken until breasts register 125 degrees and drumsticks/thighs register 130 degrees, 15 to 25 minutes. (Smaller pieces may cook faster than larger pieces. Remove pieces from oven as they reach correct temperature.)

4 Adjust oven rack 6 inches from broiler element and heat broiler. Return chicken to wire rack in pan, scored sides up, and broil until chicken is lightly charred in spots and breasts register 160 degrees and drumsticks/thighs register 175 degrees, 8 to 15 minutes. Transfer chicken to serving platter, tent with foil, and let rest for 5 minutes. Serve with raita and lime wedges.

pomegranate-braised beef short ribs with prunes and sesame

serves 6 to 8

4 pounds bone-in English-style short ribs, trimmed

Salt and pepper

4 cups unsweetened pomegranate juice

1 cup water

2 tablespoons extra-virgin olive oil

1 onion, chopped fine

1 carrot, peeled and chopped fine

2 tablespoons Ras el Hanout (page 117)

4 garlic cloves, minced

¾ cup prunes, halved

1 tablespoon red wine vinegar

2 tablespoons toasted sesame seeds

2 tablespoons chopped fresh cilantro

why this recipe works Meltingly tender classic braised short ribs take a trip to the Mediterranean with this spin that features a warm-spiced sweet-but-tart sauce made with pomegranate juice and prunes. A good dose—2 tablespoons—of *ras el hanout* added a pleasing, piquant aroma; we bloomed it by sautéing it with our onions and carrots to bring out its warmth from the start. Rather than simply brown the ribs, we started by roasting them in the oven; this rendered a significant amount of fat that we could discard. After braising, we defatted the cooking liquid, then blended it with the vegetables and some of the prunes to create a velvety sauce. We added the remaining prunes to the sauce and garnished the dish with toasted sesame seeds and cilantro. We prefer the less expensive and more readily available English-style ribs here. If using flanken-style ribs, flip the ribs halfway through roasting in step 1. We prefer to use our homemade Ras el Hanout (page 117), but you can use store-bought ras el hanout.

1 Adjust oven rack to lower-middle position and heat oven to 450 degrees. Pat ribs dry with paper towels and season with salt and pepper. Arrange ribs, bone side down, in single layer in large roasting pan and roast until meat begins to brown, about 45 minutes.

2 Discard any accumulated fat and juices in pan and continue to roast until meat is well browned, 15 to 20 minutes. Transfer ribs to bowl and tent with aluminum foil; set aside. Stir pomegranate juice and water into now-empty pan, scraping up any browned bits; set aside.

3 Reduce oven temperature to 300 degrees. Heat oil in Dutch oven over medium heat until shimmering. Add onion, carrot, and ¼ teaspoon salt and cook until softened, about 5 minutes. Stir in ras el hanout and garlic and cook until fragrant, about 30 seconds.

4 Stir in pomegranate mixture from roasting pan and half of prunes and bring to simmer. Nestle ribs, bone side up, into pot and return to simmer. Cover, transfer pot to oven, and cook until ribs are tender, about 2½ hours.

5 Using pot holders, remove pot from oven. Being careful of hot pot handles, transfer ribs to bowl; discard any loose bones and tent with aluminum foil. Strain braising liquid through fine-mesh strainer into fat separator; transfer solids to blender. Let braising liquid settle for 5 minutes, then pour defatted liquid into blender with solids and process until smooth, about 1 minute.

6 Transfer sauce to now-empty pot and stir in vinegar and remaining prunes. Return ribs and any accumulated juices to pot, bring to gentle simmer over medium heat, and cook, spooning sauce over ribs occasionally, until heated through, about 5 minutes. Season with salt and pepper to taste. Transfer ribs to serving platter, spoon 1 cup sauce over top, and sprinkle with sesame seeds and cilantro. Serve, passing remaining sauce separately.

rigatoni with spiced beef ragu

serves 4 to 6

1½ cups beef broth

½ ounce dried porcini mushrooms, rinsed

1 tablespoon extra-virgin olive oil

1 onion, chopped fine

2 garlic cloves, minced

1 tablespoon tomato paste

3 anchovy fillets, rinsed, patted dry, and minced

½ teaspoon Five-Spice Powder (page 74)

½ cup dry red wine

1 (14.5-ounce) can whole peeled tomatoes, drained with juice reserved, chopped fine

2 pounds boneless beef short ribs, trimmed

Salt and pepper

1 pound rigatoni

why this recipe works Sometimes Italian beef ragu recipes call for a touch of warm spice, a nod to the importance of the spice route that passed through Italy from the 15th to the 17th century. And while this ragu is definitely Italian, you'll find a distinctly Asian ingredient in the list: five-spice powder. We found that we could trade in separate spices for this single blend. Boneless beef short ribs contributed a velvety texture and robust flavor, while porcini mushrooms, tomato paste, and anchovies added savory notes to make this relatively quick sauce taste as though it had taken all day to make. If you can't find boneless short ribs, you can substitute 2½ pounds boneless chuck-eye roast, trimmed and cut into 1-inch pieces. We prefer to use our home-made Five-Spice Powder (page 74), but you can substitute store-bought five-spice powder. Serve with grated Parmesan if desired. The sauce is great served over polenta as well.

1 Adjust oven rack to lower-middle position and heat oven to 325 degrees. Microwave ½ cup broth and mushrooms in covered bowl until steaming, about 1 minute. Let sit until softened, about 5 minutes. Drain mushrooms in fine-mesh strainer lined with coffee filter, pressing to extract all liquid. Reserve liquid and chop mushrooms fine.

2 Heat oil in Dutch oven over medium heat until shimmering. Add onion and cook until softened, about 5 minutes. Stir in garlic and cook until fragrant, about 1 minute. Add tomato paste, anchovies, and five-spice powder and cook, stirring frequently, until mixture has darkened and fond forms on pot bottom, about 4 minutes. Stir in wine, scraping up any browned bits. Bring to simmer and cook, stirring occasionally, until wine is almost completely evaporated, 2 to 4 minutes. Stir in tomatoes and reserved juice, remaining 1 cup broth, reserved mush-room soaking liquid, and mushrooms and bring to simmer.

3 Season beef with salt and pepper and nestle into pot. Cover, transfer pot to oven and cook for 1 hour. Uncover and continue to cook until beef is tender, 1 to 1¼ hours. Using pot holders, remove pot from oven. Being careful of hot pot handles, use slotted spoon to transfer beef to cutting board. Let beef cool slightly, then shred into bite-size pieces using 2 forks; discard excess fat. Using wide, shallow spoon, skim excess fat from surface of sauce. Return beef to sauce and season with salt and pepper to taste.

4 Meanwhile, bring 4 quarts water to boil in large pot. Add pasta and 1 tablespoon salt and cook, stirring often, until al dente. Reserve ½ cup cooking water, then drain pasta and return it to pot. Add sauce and toss to combine. Before serving, adjust consistency with reserved cooking water as needed.

sichuan braised tofu with beef

serves 4 to 6

- 1 tablespoon Sichuan peppercorns, toasted
- 28 ounces soft tofu, cut into ½-inch cubes
- 2 cups chicken broth
- 12 scallions, cut into 1-inch pieces, white parts lightly crushed
- 9 garlic cloves, peeled
- 1 (3-inch) piece ginger, peeled and sliced into ¼-inch-thick rounds
- ⅓ cup Asian broad bean chili paste
- 1 tablespoon fermented black beans
- 6 tablespoons vegetable oil
- 1 tablespoon Sichuan chili powder
- 8 ounces 85 percent lean ground beef
- 2 tablespoons hoisin sauce
- 2 teaspoons toasted sesame oil
- 2 tablespoons water
- 1 tablespoon cornstarch

why this recipe works *Mapo* tofu is bold in flavor, balanced in tingly spiciness, and downright interesting. This comes from the sauce base that features plenty of ginger and garlic along with four Sichuan pantry powerhouses: Asian broad bean chili paste, fermented black beans, Sichuan chili powder, and Sichuan peppercorns. The resulting paste is cooked for a few minutes until the magic happens: The paste darkens and the oil begins to separate from the paste. What does this mean? It's at this point that you know all the ingredients have bloomed to their full potential. Before adding the soft tofu to the sauce, we gently poached it in broth to keep the cubes intact. A small amount of ground beef acted as a seasoning, not as a primary component. Asian broad bean chili paste (or sauce) is also known as *doubanjiang* or *toban djan;* our favorite, Pixian, is available online. Lee Kum Kee Chili Bean Sauce is a good supermarket option. If you can't find Sichuan chili powder, an equal amount of Korean red pepper flakes (*gochugaru*) is a good substitute. In a pinch, use 2½ teaspoons of ancho chile powder and ½ teaspoon of cayenne pepper. If you can't find fermented black beans, you can use an equal amount of fermented black bean paste or sauce, or 2 additional teaspoons of Asian broad bean chili paste. Serve with steamed white rice.

1 Process peppercorns in spice grinder until coarsely ground, about 20 seconds (you should have 1½ teaspoons). Place tofu, broth, and scallions in large bowl and microwave, covered, until steaming, 5 to 7 minutes. Let sit while preparing remaining ingredients.

2 Process garlic, ginger, chili paste, and black beans in food processor until coarse paste forms, 1 to 2 minutes, scraping down sides of bowl as needed. Add ¼ cup vegetable oil, chili powder, and 1 teaspoon ground peppercorns and process until smooth paste forms, 1 to 2 minutes; transfer to small bowl.

3 Heat 1 tablespoon vegetable oil and beef in large saucepan over medium heat. Cook, breaking up meat with wooden spoon, until meat just begins to brown, 5 to 7 minutes; transfer to separate bowl. Add remaining 1 tablespoon vegetable oil and spice paste to now-empty saucepan and cook, stirring frequently, until paste darkens and oil begins to separate from paste, 2 to 3 minutes. Gently pour tofu, scallions, and broth into saucepan, followed by hoisin, sesame oil, and beef with any accumulated juices. Cook, stirring gently and frequently, until dish comes to simmer, 2 to 3 minutes. Whisk water and cornstarch together in small bowl. Add cornstarch mixture to saucepan and continue to cook, stirring frequently, until thickened, 2 to 3 minutes. Transfer to serving platter and sprinkle with remaining ground peppercorns. Serve.

sautéed radishes with vadouvan curry and almonds

serves 4 to 6

3 tablespoons unsalted butter, cut into 3 pieces

1½ pounds radishes with their greens, radishes trimmed and quartered, 8 cups greens reserved

Salt

1½ teaspoons Vadouvan Curry Powder (page 118)

2 tablespoons whole almonds, toasted and coarsely chopped

why this recipe works Blooming doesn't have to be a long process; in fact, ground spices really take just a 30-second sauté to come alive. Here we use a commonly bloomed soup, stew, and braise spice, curry powder, to coat something different—a vegetable side— with flavor. Earthy-sweet Vadouvan curry powder pairs nicely, with the spicy radishes, which themselves sweeten when cooked. (Heat degrades many of the compounds responsible for a radish's pungent, peppery flavor and concentrates its natural sugars.) We started by cooking quartered radishes in butter over moderate heat until they were browned and nutty, and then we stirred in the curry powder to release its flavor in the heat and thoroughly coat the radishes. To provide some textural variety and color, we cooked the radish greens at the end in plenty of garlic. The greens retained a slight crispness that complements the heartier radish pieces. If you can't find radishes with their greens, skip step 2. We prefer to use our homemade Vadouvan Curry Powder (page 118), but you can substitute any store-bought curry powder.

1 Melt 2 tablespoons butter in 12-inch skillet over medium-high heat. Add radishes and ¼ teaspoon salt and cook, stirring occasionally, until radishes are lightly browned and crisp-tender, 10 to 12 minutes. Stir in curry powder and cook until fragrant, about 30 seconds; transfer to bowl.

2 Melt remaining 1 tablespoon butter in now-empty skillet over medium heat. Add radish greens and ⅛ teaspoon salt and cook, stirring frequently, until wilted, about 1 minute. Off heat, stir in radishes and season with salt to taste. Sprinkle with almonds and serve.

shakshuka

serves 4

- 3 tablespoons vegetable oil
- 2 onions, chopped fine
- 2 yellow bell peppers, stemmed, seeded, and cut into ¼-inch pieces
- 4 garlic cloves, minced
- 2 teaspoons tomato paste
- 1 teaspoon ground cumin
- 1 teaspoon ground turmeric
- Salt and pepper
- ⅛ teaspoon cayenne pepper
- 1½ cups jarred piquillo peppers, chopped coarse
- 1 (14.5-ounce) can diced tomatoes
- ¼ cup water
- 2 bay leaves
- ⅓ cup chopped fresh cilantro
- 8 large eggs
- 2 ounces feta cheese, crumbled (½ cup)

why this recipe works *Shakshuka,* a dish that originated in Tunisia but has long been made in various regions of the Mediterranean and Middle East, features eggs poached in a spiced tomato, onion, and pepper sauce. The name is derived from a term meaning "all mixed up," and the key to a great one is balancing the piquancy, acidity, richness, and sweetness of its ingredients. Spices can vary from region to region; we liked the warmth of cumin, turmeric, and some cayenne: Bloomed at the start, their warmth and earthiness were the right foil for the sweet peppers. Piquillo peppers were the favorite we tried in the dish, boasting spicy-sweet and vibrant flavors. These small red peppers from Spain, sold in jars or cans, have a subtle hint of smokiness from being roasted over a wood fire. We added yellow bell peppers to the mix for a clean, fresh flavor and a bright contrast to the deep red sauce. After poaching the eggs in the spiced sauce, we finished our shakshuka with a sprinkling of bright cilantro and salty, creamy feta cheese. Jarred roasted red peppers can be substituted for the piquillo peppers. You will need a 12-inch skillet with a tight-fitting lid for this recipe. Serve with pita or crusty bread to mop up the sauce.

---

1 Heat oil in 12-inch skillet over medium-high heat until shimmering. Add onions and bell peppers and cook until softened and beginning to brown, 8 to 10 minutes. Add garlic, tomato paste, cumin, turmeric, 1½ teaspoons salt, ¼ teaspoon pepper, and cayenne and cook, stirring frequently, until tomato paste begins to darken, about 3 minutes.

2 Stir in piquillo peppers, tomatoes and their juice, water, and bay leaves and bring to simmer. Reduce heat to medium-low and cook, stirring occasionally, until sauce is slightly thickened, 10 to 15 minutes.

3 Off heat, discard bay leaves and stir in ¼ cup cilantro. Transfer 2 cups sauce to blender and process until smooth, about 60 seconds. Return puree to skillet and bring sauce to simmer over medium-low heat.

4 Off heat, make 4 shallow indentations (about 2 inches wide) in surface of sauce using back of spoon. Crack 2 eggs into each indentation and season eggs with salt and pepper. Cover and cook over medium-low heat until egg whites are just set and yolks are still runny, 5 to 10 minutes. Sprinkle with feta and remaining cilantro and serve.

finish with flair

making food livelier with just a sprinkle or drizzle

There are many ways to flavor foods with spice and they don't always happen during cooking: Sprinkling a spice, herb, and seed blend—like the punchy, lemony, rich Middle Eastern seasoning blend za'atar— on a dish at the last moment adds bright, herbal flavor and appealing crunch. Spicing up sauces lets you dollop and drizzle flavor onto food; with spices in the mix, sauces aren't just rich or acidic but also complex. A splash of spice-enhanced cider dressing perks up vegetables and proteins with the brightness of vinaigrette and the complementary aroma of caraway seed; a spread of wasabi mayonnaise turns up the heat on sandwiches.

SPRINKLE IT

We love to make and have on hand the following spice blends to quickly and easily dress up finished dishes. With just a sprinkle, these combinations add texture and dimension in addition to flavor. And they nicely display the concept of seeds as spices: The sesame seeds in za'atar or the nigella seeds in hazelnut dukkah offset dishes with their depth, richness, and appealing crunch. None of these need to be cooked with the food—just dash and go. All of these blends make about ½ cup.

› finishing spice blends

za'atar

Za'atar is an aromatic eastern Mediterranean spice blend that is used as both a seasoning and a condiment. The thyme gives it a round herbal flavor, the sumac lemony tartness, and the sesame seeds richness and subtle crunch.

- ½ cup dried thyme
- 2 tablespoons sesame seeds, toasted
- 1½ tablespoons ground sumac

Working in batches, process thyme in spice grinder until finely ground, about 30 seconds; transfer to small bowl. Stir in sesame seeds and sumac. (Za'atar can be stored in airtight container for up to 3 months.)

› how to use Add to olive oil and use as a dip for bread, sprinkle over roasted vegetables, top hummus and yogurt dips, dust over just-cooked rich meats, stir into lemony vinaigrette or tahini sauce, rub on whole chicken before cooking, dust over hard-boiled eggs.

advieh

Advieh means "spice" in Farsi, and the blend is fundamental to Persian cooking. Complexly flavored, deeply warm, and floral, it's traditionally used to flavor all manner of rice dishes and stews (khoresh). Be sure to use food-grade dried rose buds, which you can find at spice shops and specialty markets.

- 1 (3-inch) cinnamon stick, broken into pieces
- 1 tablespoon cumin seeds, toasted
- 1 teaspoon cardamom pods
- ½ teaspoon black peppercorns
- ¼ ounce (½ cup) dried rose buds, stems removed
- ½ teaspoon flake sea salt, such as Maldon (see page 22)

Process cinnamon stick in spice grinder until finely ground, about 30 seconds. Add cumin seeds, cardamom pods, and peppercorns and process until coarsely ground, about 15 seconds. Add rose buds and pulse until coarsely ground and pieces of petal are no larger than ⅛ inch, about 5 pulses. Transfer to small bowl and stir in salt. (*Advieh* can be stored in airtight container for up to 1 year.)

› how to use Sprinkle over rice or roasted vegetables; stir into stews or braised dishes; rub on whole chicken before roasting; add to ground meat for *kofte*; season chicken, lamb, or beef kebabs before grilling; use as a seasoning for brining pickles; toss with pistachios before oven-toasting; substitute for cinnamon or cardamom in baked goods.

› finishing spice blends

pistachio dukkah

North African dukkah blends vary in ingredients and can provide different flavor profiles. This blend is warmly spiced and delightfully coarse and nutty from the finely chopped pistachios.

- 1½ teaspoons coriander seeds, toasted
- ¾ teaspoon cumin seeds, toasted
- ½ teaspoon fennel seeds, toasted
- 2 tablespoons sesame seeds, toasted
- 3 tablespoons shelled pistachios, toasted and chopped fine
- ½ teaspoon flake sea salt, such as Maldon (see page 22)
- ½ teaspoon pepper

Process coriander seeds, cumin seeds, and fennel seeds in spice grinder until finely ground, about 30 seconds. Add sesame seeds and pulse until coarsely ground, about 4 pulses; transfer to small bowl. Stir in pistachios, salt, and pepper. (Dukkah can be refrigerated for up to 3 months.)

› **how to use** Sprinkle over cooked greens or other earthy vegetables such as green beans or mushrooms; finish pureed soups; serve with oil as a dip for bread; garnish salads or bean, rice, or grain dishes.

hazelnut-nigella dukkah

This dukkah is a bit warmer from the hazelnuts and more intense from the nigella seeds than the sweeter pistachio dukkah. Use it when you want more aggressive flavor. You can find nigella seeds at spice shops and specialty markets.

- 1 teaspoon fennel seeds, toasted
- 1 teaspoon coriander seeds, toasted
- 1½ tablespoons raw sunflower seeds, toasted
- 1 tablespoon sesame seeds, toasted
- 1½ teaspoons nigella seeds
- 3 tablespoons hazelnuts, toasted, skinned, and chopped fine
- 1½ teaspoons paprika
- ½ teaspoon flake sea salt, such as Maldon (see page 22)

Process fennel seeds and coriander seeds in spice grinder until finely ground, about 30 seconds. Add sunflower seeds, sesame seeds, and nigella seeds and pulse until coarsely ground, about 4 pulses; transfer to small bowl. Stir in hazelnuts, paprika, and salt. (Dukkah can be refrigerated for up to 3 months.)

› **how to use** Sprinkle over roasted cauliflower, top salads, serve with yogurt and pita, sprinkle on morning fried eggs, garnish marinated feta cheese, finish grain dishes.

shichimi togarashi

This Japanese seven-spice blend is pungent and spicy from chile heat, aromatic from additional spices, and fragrant from orange zest, which we microwave to dry. This complexity makes basic noodle dishes utterly intriguing and the spice really heats up a dish.

- 1½ teaspoons grated orange zest
- 4 teaspoons sesame seeds, toasted
- 1 tablespoon paprika
- 2 teaspoons pepper
- ½ teaspoon garlic powder
- ½ teaspoon ground ginger
- ¼ teaspoon cayenne pepper

Microwave orange zest in small bowl, stirring occasionally, until dry and no longer clumping together, about 2 minutes. Stir in sesame seeds, paprika, pepper, garlic powder, ginger, and cayenne. (Shichimi togarashi can be stored in airtight container for up to 1 week.)

› **how to use** Sprinkle over udon or soba noodles, rice, steamed vegetables, or French fries; stir into dressings and marinades; apply to grilled meats; toss with popcorn; season soft-boiled eggs; dress up tofu dishes.

furikake

Another Japanese condiment, this blend is a surprise to the taste buds no matter what it's dressing: It's at once briny, earthy, nutty, and sweet. You can find nori sheets and bonito flakes in most well-stocked supermarkets.

- **2 nori sheets, torn into 1-inch pieces**
- **3 tablespoons sesame seeds, toasted**
- **1½ tablespoons bonito flakes**
- **1½ teaspoons sugar**
- **1½ teaspoons flake sea salt, such as Maldon (see page 22)**

Process nori in spice grinder until coarsely ground and pieces are no larger than ½ inch, about 15 seconds. Add sesame seeds, bonito flakes, and sugar and pulse until coarsely ground and pieces of nori are no larger than ¼ inch, about 2 pulses. Transfer to small bowl and stir in salt. (Furikake can be stored in airtight container for up to 3 months.)

> **how to use** Sprinkle over rice, serve with fish, top avocado toast, toss with sautéed vegetables, sprinkle on cucumber spears, season snack mixes.

everything bagel blend

A trendy newcomer in non-bagel contexts, this blend gives everything you sprinkle it on the aroma of everyone's favorite bagel and appealing crunch.

- **2 tablespoons sesame seeds, toasted**
- **2 tablespoons poppy seeds**
- **1 tablespoon caraway seeds, toasted**
- **1 tablespoon kosher salt**
- **1 tablespoon dried minced onion**
- **1 tablespoon dried minced garlic**

Combine all ingredients in bowl. (Blend can be stored in airtight container for up to 3 months.)

> **how to use** Sprinkle on savory doughs before baking, season meat before roasting and grilling, dress up plain bagels by adding to the cream cheese, sprinkle over potato salad or deviled eggs, top vegetable dips.

single-spice sprinklers

In addition to the blends on these pages, there are also single spices that we like to sprinkle over finished dishes to add flavor.

aleppo pepper Try these fruity pepper flakes sprinkled on avocado toast, marinated feta, braised greens, or bean dips.

celery salt In addition to coating the rim of cocktail glasses, the mix adds vegetal flavor, minerality, and salinity to soft-boiled eggs or roasted potatoes.

cinnamon As is common, a shake is nice on your latte— or on your peanut butter toast, oatmeal, or ice cream.

dried mint This dried herb is important in Middle Eastern cooking. Dust over bright green or bean salads, rich stews, or yogurt dips. Crushing it between your fingers unlocks its flavor.

espelette pepper This French Basque country staple can add warm heat and paprika-like sweetness to pureed soups or mashed potatoes, vibrant shellfish stews, or braised beans.

fennel pollen From wild fennel, fennel pollen has a honey-like but savory flavor that enhances goat cheese or ricotta, lemony pasta, and roasted vegetables.

nigella, sesame, and poppy seeds These blend ingredients also provide richness, earthiness, and crunch when sprinkled on independently.

sumac A dusting of sumac hits Middle Eastern food with lemony bite. Sprinkle over salads, kebabs, rich meats, buttered rice, or roasted root vegetables.

homemade yogurt cheese with hazelnut-nigella dukkah

serves 6 to 8

2 cups plain yogurt

2 tablespoons Hazelnut-Nigella Dukkah (page 158)

Extra-virgin olive oil

why this recipe works Soft cheeses and dips are natural choices for a finishing spice blend—their creamy texture and rich profile benefit from a boost of contrasting flavor and texture. Yogurt cheese is a perfect example. Also called *labneh,* this Middle Eastern ingredient isn't really a cheese at all; rather, it's yogurt that's been strained to remove the whey, giving it a thick, lush consistency and a rich, tangy flavor. It makes a great fresh dip or spread for bread or vegetables— and is even more lively with a sprinkle of spice. We like to top it with another Middle Eastern ingredient, *dukkah*, as the thickened yogurt's tang is a nice foil to the blend's concentrated, toasty flavors. Yogurt cheese couldn't be easier to make at home, requiring only one ingredient and a couple hours of hands-off time. To end up with about 1 cup of yogurt cheese, we started with 2 cups of traditional yogurt. A strainer lined with a triple layer of cheesecloth was ideal for allowing the whey to drain off. After about 8 hours, a full cup of whey had drained off, leaving velvety strained yogurt. Both regular and low-fat yogurt will work well here; do not use nonfat yogurt. Avoid yogurts containing modified food starch, gelatin, or gums since they prevent the yogurt from draining. We particularly like our more strongly flavored Hazelnut-Nigella Dukkah with the labneh, but feel free to substitute any of the finishing spice blends on pages 156–159. Serve with warm pita, pita chips, or fresh crudités.

1   Line colander or fine-mesh strainer with triple layer of cheesecloth and place over large bowl or measuring cup. Place yogurt in colander, cover with plastic wrap (plastic should not touch yogurt), and refrigerate until 1 cup whey has drained from yogurt, at least 8 hours or up to 12 hours. (If more than 1 cup whey drains from yogurt, stir extra back into yogurt.)

2   Spread drained yogurt attractively over serving plate. Sprinkle with dukkah and drizzle with oil to taste. Serve.

parmesan–black pepper popcorn

makes 4 quarts; serves 6 to 8

3 tablespoons unsalted butter

Salt and pepper

2 tablespoons vegetable oil

½ cup popcorn kernels

1 ounce Parmesan cheese, grated (½ cup)

why this recipe works Most of us reach for those preseasoned, microwavable bags when we're in the mood for flavored popcorn, but between the artificial flavors and the high probability of burning, they usually disappoint. Nearly any finishing spice in this chapter would be great sprinkled on buttered popcorn as it's a blank-canvas snack. But we also wanted to nail down a couple of go-to recipes for dressed-up combos—as well as a cooking technique that would be easy enough to supplant the microwave. Before we spiced up the popcorn, we needed a foolproof way of popping it. A Dutch oven did the best job of heating the oil evenly, which ensured that the kernels heated and popped at the same rate, giving us few unpopped kernels and less risk of burning. For a more refined popcorn that made just as much sense served at the start of a dinner party as eaten out of the bowl during a movie, we seasoned the popcorn with salty, nutty Parmesan cheese and plenty of spicy black pepper to cut the richness. For something a bit more zesty, we went with a sweet-and-spicy profile: cinnamon and sugar and chili powder. Heating the spices with the butter as it melted allowed their flavors to bloom, and tossing the popcorn with spiced butter ensured the seasoning was evenly distributed. Be sure to shake the pot vigorously when cooking to prevent the popcorn from scorching.

Microwave butter and ½ teaspoon pepper in small bowl at 50 percent power until just melted, 1 to 3 minutes. Combine oil and popcorn in Dutch oven. Cover and place over medium-high heat, shaking occasionally, until first few kernels begin to pop. Continue to cook, shaking pot vigorously, until popping has mostly stopped. Transfer to large bowl, toss with melted butter and Parmesan, and season with salt to taste. Serve.

hot-and-sweet popcorn

Substitute 2 tablespoons sugar, 1 teaspoon ground cinnamon, and ½ teaspoon chili powder for pepper. Omit Parmesan.

spiced roasted chickpeas

serves 6

2 (15-ounce) cans chickpeas

3 tablespoons extra-virgin olive oil

2 teaspoons paprika

1 teaspoon ground coriander

½ teaspoon ground turmeric

½ teaspoon ground allspice

½ teaspoon ground cumin

½ teaspoon sugar

Salt

⅛ teaspoon cayenne pepper

why this recipe works Tossed with appealing spice, roasted chickpeas have a crisp, airy texture that make them a most poppable snack—or salad topper or roasted vegetable accompaniment or hummus garnish. Chickpeas are used throughout India, so a version with spices from the region—coriander, turmeric, allspice, and cumin—seemed appropriate. We achieved crispiness by first microwaving the chickpeas for about 10 minutes to burst them open at the seams so they released interior moisture. We then baked them in a 350-degree oven. To prevent burning, we crowded them toward the center of the pan near the end of roasting. We finished with a dusting of spices. You will need a 13 by 9-inch metal baking pan for this recipe; a glass or ceramic baking dish will result in uneven cooking.

1   Adjust oven rack to middle position and heat oven to 350 degrees. Place chickpeas in colander and drain for 10 minutes. Line large plate with double layer of paper towels. Spread chickpeas over plate in even layer. Microwave until exteriors of chickpeas are dry and many have ruptured, 8 to 12 minutes.

2   Transfer chickpeas to 13 by 9-inch metal baking pan. Add oil and stir until evenly coated. Using spatula, spread chickpeas into single layer. Transfer to oven and roast for 30 minutes. Stir chickpeas and crowd toward center of pan. Continue to roast until chickpeas appear dry, slightly shriveled, and deep golden brown, 20 to 40 minutes. (To test for doneness, remove a few paler chickpeas and let cool briefly before tasting; if interiors are soft, return to oven and test again in 5 minutes.)

3   Combine paprika, coriander, turmeric, allspice, cumin, sugar, ⅛ teaspoon salt, and cayenne in small bowl. Transfer chickpeas to large bowl and toss with spice mixture to coat. Season with salt to taste. Let cool fully before serving, about 30 minutes. (Chickpeas can stored in airtight container for up to 7 days.)

barbecue-spiced roasted chickpeas

Omit allspice and cumin. Increase sugar to 1½ teaspoons. Substitute 1 tablespoon smoked paprika for paprika, garlic powder for coriander, and onion powder for turmeric.

spanish-spiced roasted chickpeas

Omit turmeric, allspice, and sugar. Decrease coriander to ½ teaspoon and cumin to ¼ teaspoon. Substitute 1 tablespoon smoked paprika for paprika.

smoky shishito peppers with espelette and lime

serves 4

- 1 teaspoon ground dried Espelette pepper
- 1 teaspoon smoked paprika
- ½ teaspoon coarse finishing salt
- ¼ teaspoon grated lime zest, plus lime wedges for serving
- 2 tablespoons vegetable oil
- 8 ounces shishito peppers

why this recipe works Japanese shishito peppers—slender little peppers with thin skins, delicate flesh, and a fruity, grassy flavor that's neither sweet nor hot—are a popular bar snack when blistered. A sprinkle of coarse salt is a must, but these tame peppers are also the perfect base to showcase finishing spices, their dusting as special as the appetizer itself. We've provided combinations from the more basic—the always appetite-whetting combo of heat and acid with dried chile and lime—to the refined and aromatic such as fennel pollen, Aleppo pepper, and lemon. You can find shishito peppers at most well-stocked supermarkets or the farmers' market. If you can't find Basque Espelette chile powder, also referred to as *Piment d'Espelette,* you can substitute 1 teaspoon Aleppo pepper or ¼ teaspoon paprika plus ¼ teaspoon red pepper flakes. The skillet will look full. You can use your preferred coarse finishing salt in this recipe; for more information on finishing salts, see pages 22–23.

Combine Espelette pepper, paprika, salt, and lime zest in small bowl; set aside. Heat oil in 12-inch skillet over medium-high heat until just smoking. Add shishitos and cook, without moving, until skins are blistered, about 3 minutes. Using tongs, flip shishitos and continue to cook until blistered on second side, about 3 minutes. Transfer to serving platter and sprinkle with spice mixture. Serve with lime wedges.

shishito peppers with fennel pollen, aleppo, and lemon

If you can't find fennel pollen, you can substitute an equal amount of toasted, cracked fennel seeds.

Substitute Aleppo pepper for Espelette pepper, fennel pollen for paprika, and lemon zest and wedges for lime zest and wedges.

shishito peppers with mint, poppy seeds, and orange

Substitute dried mint for Espelette pepper, poppy seeds for paprika, and orange zest and wedges for lime zest and wedges.

shishito peppers with mustard and bonito flakes

Omit Espelette pepper. Substitute dry mustard for paprika. Sprinkle 2 tablespoons bonito flakes over shishitos just before serving.

blue cheese log with pistachio dukkah and honey

serves 8 to 10

- 4 ounces (1 cup) soft, mild blue cheese
- 8 ounces cream cheese
- 1 small garlic clove, minced
- ½ teaspoon pepper
- ⅓ cup Pistachio Dukkah (page 158)
- 2 tablespoons honey

Besides being fun party food, cheese logs are a perfect way to show your pairing prowess. We mixed up the cheese in the logs and matched each of their flavor profiles to one of our homemade sprinkling blends. The coating gives the log lively, interesting flavor that cuts through the richness of the cheese but also provides a textured contrast to the creaminess.

1 Process blue cheese, cream cheese, garlic, and pepper in food processor until smooth, scraping down sides of bowl as needed, about 1 minute.

2 Lay 18 by 11-inch sheet of plastic wrap on counter with long side parallel to counter edge. Transfer cheese mixture to center of plastic and shape into approximate 9-inch log with long side parallel to counter edge. Fold plastic over log and roll up. Pinch plastic at ends of log and roll on counter to form tight cylinder. Tuck ends of plastic underneath and freeze until completely firm, 1½ to 2 hours.

3 Unwrap cheese log and let sit until outside is slightly tacky to the touch, about 10 minutes. Spread dukkah into even layer on large plate and roll cheese log in dukkah to coat evenly, pressing gently to adhere. (Garnished cheese log can be tightly wrapped in plastic and refrigerated for up to 2 days.) Transfer to serving platter and let sit at room temperature until softened, about 1 hour. Drizzle with honey and serve.

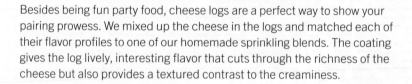

cheddar cheese log with everything bagel blend

Omit honey and decrease cream cheese to 6 ounces. Substitute 1½ cups shredded extra-sharp yellow cheddar cheese for blue cheese and ⅓ cup Everything Bagel Blend (page 159) for pistachio dukkah. Add ¼ cup mayonnaise, 1 tablespoon drained prepared horseradish, and 2 teaspoons Worcestershire sauce to food processor with cheddar.

goat cheese log with hazelnut-nigella dukkah

Substitute 1½ cups goat cheese for blue cheese and decrease cream cheese to 6 ounces. Substitute ⅓ cup Hazelnut-Nigella Dukkah (page 158) for pistachio dukkah, and extra-virgin olive oil for honey.

feta cheese log with advieh and olive oil

Substitute feta cheese for blue cheese, ¼ cup Advieh (page 156) for pistachio dukkah, and extra-virgin olive oil for honey. Add ¼ cup extra-virgin olive oil to food processor with feta.

fluke crudo with furikake

serves 4 to 6

12 ounces skinless sushi-grade
   fluke fillets

1½ tablespoons extra-virgin olive oil

1 tablespoon lemon juice

1 tablespoon soy sauce

2 teaspoons Furikake (page 159)

why this recipe works At its simplest, crudo is nothing more than raw seafood dressed with olive oil, salt, and acid (such as lemon juice or good-quality vinegar). Once you have the freshest of seafood covered, it's just about contrasting the raw fish with the right garnish; we added flavor and texture to our recipe by finishing the dish with the Japanese seaweed—sesame seed spice blend known as *furikake*. The sprinkled furikake created a beautiful presentation, ensured that each bite packed an umami-rich punch, and added nice crunch against the fish. Freshness is key when serving fish raw. Speak with your fishmonger to make sure you are purchasing high-quality, sushi-grade fish. If fluke is not available, you can substitute other sushi-grade fish such as sea bass or tuna. Inspect the fillets for bones and remove before slicing. Freeze the fish for about 15 minutes to make slicing easier. We prefer to use our homemade Furikake (page 159), but you can substitute store-bought furikake.

1 Using sharp knife, cut fluke lengthwise into 2- to 3-inch-wide strips. Working with 1 strip at a time, slice fluke crosswise on bias into ⅛-inch-thick slices. Arrange fluke attractively on individual chilled plates.

2 Whisk oil, lemon juice, and soy sauce together in small bowl. Drizzle sauce over fluke and sprinkle with furikake. Serve immediately.

slicing fluke for crudo

1 Cut fluke lengthwise into 2- to 3-inch-wide strips.

2 Slice each strip on bias into ⅛-inch-thick slices.

soba noodles with pork, scallions, and shichimi togarashi

serves 4 to 6

3 tablespoons vegetable oil

1½ pounds pork tenderloin, trimmed and sliced thin crosswise

10 ounces shiitake mushrooms, stemmed and quartered

6 garlic cloves, minced

1 tablespoon grated fresh ginger

6 ounces (3 cups) bean sprouts

½ cup soy sauce

¼ cup mirin

¼ cup rice vinegar

8 ounces dried soba noodles

1 tablespoon salt

4 scallions, sliced thin

¼ cup Shichimi Togarashi (page 158)

why this recipe works Soba noodle dishes are a bit smoky from the buckwheat noodles, but balanced in flavor from the salty, sweet, earthy, and aromatic ingredients that usually make their surrounding broth or sauce. But the noodles' flavor is still delicate and can benefit from something pungent to heighten them at the end, which is why they are often served with peppery, aromatic *shichimi togarashi* sprinkled on top. Quick-cooking pork tenderloin stir-fried in minutes and gave the noodles rich flavor. For a sweet-savory sauce, we experimented with countless combinations of ingredients and aromatics before settling on a blend of soy sauce, mirin, and rice vinegar spiked with plenty of garlic and ginger. And then, of course, we added the finishing sprinkle that brought the dish together and enlivened it further. For this dish, avoid the darker colored soba noodles made from 100 percent buckwheat as they take twice the amount of time to cook as the lighter colored soba, which are made with part buckwheat and part regular wheat. We prefer to use our homemade Shichimi Togarashi (page 158), but you can substitute store-bought shichimi togarashi.

1 Heat 1 tablespoon oil in 12-inch nonstick skillet over high heat until just smoking. Add pork in single layer and cook, without moving, for 1 minute. Stir and continue to cook until pork is lightly browned around edges and little pink remains, about 3 minutes; transfer to bowl.

2 Add remaining 2 tablespoons oil to now-empty skillet and heat over medium-high heat until just smoking. Add mushrooms and cook until browned, about 4 minutes. Push mushrooms to sides of skillet. Add garlic and ginger to center and cook, mashing mixture into skillet, until fragrant, about 30 seconds. Stir mixture into mushrooms. Stir in bean sprouts, soy sauce, mirin, rice vinegar, and pork along with any accumulated juices. Cook until pork is just heated through, about 1 minute. Remove from heat and cover to keep warm.

3 Meanwhile, bring 4 quarts water to boil in large pot. Add noodles and salt and cook, stirring often, until al dente, about 4 minutes. Reserve ½ cup cooking water, then drain noodles and return to pot. Stir in pork-mushroom mixture and scallions and adjust consistency with reserved cooking water as needed. Sprinkle individual portions with shichimi togarashi. Serve.

sautéed spinach with yogurt and pistachio dukkah

serves 4

½ cup plain yogurt

1½ teaspoons lemon zest plus 1 teaspoon juice

3 tablespoons extra-virgin olive oil

20 ounces curly-leaf spinach, stemmed

2 garlic cloves, minced

Salt and pepper

¼ cup Pistachio Dukkah (page 158)

why this recipe works Earthy, tender spinach and creamy, tangy yogurt are a perfect match found throughout the eastern Mediterranean region. Still don't think you're a spinach eater? Try spicing this dish up even further with a sprinkle of nutty pistachio-studded *dukkah*. It solves both of the common sautéed spinach problems: lack of texture and one-note flavor. We found that we greatly preferred the hearty flavor and texture of curly-leaf spinach to baby spinach, which wilted down to mush. We cooked the spinach in olive oil and, once it was cooked, used tongs to squeeze the excess moisture out of the leaves. Lightly toasted minced garlic, cooked after the spinach in the same pan, added a sweet nuttiness. We emphasized the yogurt's tanginess with lemon zest and juice, and drizzled it over our garlicky spinach before sprinkling on the dukkah. Two pounds of flat-leaf spinach (about three bunches) can be substituted for the curly-leaf spinach. We prefer to use our homemade Pistachio Dukkah (page 158), but you can use store-bought dukkah.

1 Combine yogurt and lemon zest and juice in bowl; set aside. Heat 1 tablespoon oil in Dutch oven over high heat until shimmering. Add spinach, 1 handful at a time, stirring and tossing each handful to wilt slightly before adding more. Cook spinach, stirring constantly, until uniformly wilted, about 1 minute. Transfer spinach to colander and squeeze between tongs to release excess liquid.

2 Wipe pot dry with paper towels. Add remaining 2 tablespoons oil and garlic to now-empty pot and cook over medium heat until fragrant, about 30 seconds. Add spinach and toss to coat, gently separating leaves to evenly coat with garlic oil. Off heat, season with salt and pepper to taste. Transfer spinach to serving platter, drizzle with yogurt sauce, and sprinkle with dukkah. Serve.

roasted fennel with rye crumble

serves 4 to 6

6 tablespoons unsalted butter, melted

1 tablespoon lemon juice

¼ teaspoon dried thyme

Salt and pepper

2 fennel bulbs, stalks discarded, bulbs halved and cut into 1-inch wedges

3 ounces rye bread, cut into 1-inch pieces (3 cups)

1 ounce Parmesan cheese, grated (½ cup)

1 teaspoon caraway seeds

why this recipe works These subtly caramelized wedges of perfectly roasted fennel make an elegant tableside presentation, especially when capped with something a little indulgent and a little surprising: a hearty rye bread crumble starring a generous amount of earthy caraway seeds and nutty Parmesan. To start, we cut the fennel bulbs into 1-inch-thick wedges through the core before tossing them in a mixture of butter, lemon juice, and thyme and placing them in a baking dish. Covering the dish with aluminum foil for the first half-hour of roasting ensured that the edges didn't dry out. With the fennel in the oven, we used the time to make a simple crumb topping in the food processor. Once the fennel wedges were nearly tender, we uncovered the dish, sprinkled the topping evenly over the top, and baked until the crumble was crisped and deep golden brown and the fennel perfectly tender in this wonderfully aromatic dish. Don't core the fennel bulb before cutting it into wedges; the core will help hold the layers of fennel together during cooking.

1 Adjust oven rack to middle position and heat oven to 425 degrees. Whisk 3 tablespoons melted butter, lemon juice, thyme, 1 teaspoon salt, and ¼ teaspoon pepper together in large bowl. Add fennel and toss to coat. Arrange fennel cut side down in single layer in 13 by 9-inch baking dish. Cover with aluminum foil and bake until fennel is nearly tender, 25 to 30 minutes.

2 Meanwhile, pulse bread, Parmesan, caraway seeds, ¼ teaspoon salt, ⅛ teaspoon pepper, and remaining 3 tablespoons melted butter in food processor to coarse crumbs, about 20 pulses.

3 Remove foil from dish and sprinkle fennel with bread-crumb mixture. Continue to bake, uncovered, until fennel is tender and topping is browned and crisp, 15 to 20 minutes. Let cool for 5 minutes before serving.

DOLLOP AND DRIZZLE IT

Our finishing spice blends alone can make a cooked dish special. But you can also mix spices into a host of ingredients—sauces, mayonnaises, dressings—to make composing dishes more fun. Follow our suggestions, or find your own ways to make dishes saucy. All of these sauces make about 1 cup.

› spiced sauces

cider-caraway vinaigrette

If using for salad, you will need about 1 tablespoon of vinaigrette per 2 cups of greens. You will need a 2-cup Mason jar with a tight-fitting lid for this recipe.

- 1 **tablespoon mayonnaise**
- 1 **tablespoon molasses**
- 1 **tablespoon Dijon mustard**
- 2 **teaspoons caraway seeds, toasted and cracked**
  Salt and pepper
- ¼ **cup apple cider vinegar**
- ½ **cup extra-virgin olive oil**
- ¼ **cup vegetable oil**

1 Combine mayonnaise, molasses, mustard, caraway seeds, and ½ teaspoon salt in 2-cup Mason jar. Stir with fork until mixture is milky in appearance and no lumps remain. Add vinegar, seal jar, and shake until smooth, about 10 seconds.

2 Add ¼ cup olive oil, seal jar, and shake vigorously until combined, about 10 seconds. Repeat, adding remaining ¼ cup olive oil and vegetable oil in separate additions and shaking vigorously until combined after adding each. Vinaigrette should be glossy and lightly thickened after all oil has been added, with no surface pools of oil. Season with salt and pepper to taste. (Vinaigrette can be refrigerated for up to 1 week; shake briefly to recombine before using.)

› how to use Pair with any green, dress a bread salad, drizzle over roasted root vegetables, serve with roast beef or pork.

world's easiest vinaigrette method

What's the secret to the world's easiest vinaigrette dressing? Hint: Shake things up. For a simple vinaigrette to toss with salad or finish dishes, we wanted the ability to skip the classical step of slowly whisking in oil to emulsify. A lidded jar lets us shake all the ingredients until blended, and mayonnaise, molasses, and Dijon mustard provide emulsifying power to keep the dressing smooth even after shaking; the latter two ingredients also contribute great flavor.

› spiced sauces

chermoula

Chermoula is a traditional Moroccan marinade and sauce that pairs bright cilantro and lemon with earthy, fragrant cumin, paprika, and cayenne, plus a hefty amount of garlic for a big punch.

- 1½ cups fresh cilantro leaves
- 5 garlic cloves, minced
- 1 teaspoon ground cumin
- 1 teaspoon paprika
- ¼ teaspoon cayenne pepper
  Salt and pepper
- ¼ cup lemon juice (2 lemons)
- ½ cup extra-virgin olive oil

1 Pulse cilantro, garlic, cumin, paprika, cayenne, and ¼ teaspoon salt in food processor until coarsely chopped, about 10 pulses, scraping down sides of bowl as needed. Add lemon juice and pulse briefly to combine.

2 Transfer mixture to bowl and slowly whisk in oil until incorporated. Cover and let sit at room temperature until flavors meld, about 1 hour. Season with salt and pepper to taste. (Chermoula can be refrigerated for up to 2 days; bring to room temperature and whisk to recombine before using.)

› **how to use** Drizzle over roasted cauliflower, serve with firm white fish, dress carrot salads, top tagines or other stews, use as a marinade for lamb or swordfish kebabs.

za'atar yogurt sauce

We prefer to use our homemade Za'atar, but you can substitute store-bought za'atar; different za'atar blends include varying salt amounts.

- 1 cup plain whole-milk yogurt
- 1 tablespoon Za'atar (page 156)
- 1 garlic clove, minced
- 1 teaspoon grated lemon zest plus 1 tablespoon juice
  Salt and pepper

Whisk yogurt, za'atar, garlic, and lemon zest and juice together in bowl and season with salt and pepper to taste. Cover and refrigerate so flavors meld, about 30 minutes. (Sauce can be refrigerated for up to 4 days.)

› **how to use** Serve with falafel, use as marinade for chicken pieces for kebabs, drizzle over sautéed greens, dollop on flatbreads.

wasabi mayonnaise

Adding uniquely spicy wasabi powder to mayonnaise with a dash of soy makes a punchy condiment to add flavor to mild ingredients.

- 1 cup mayonnaise
- 3 tablespoons wasabi powder
- 2 teaspoons soy sauce
- 1 teaspoon water

Whisk all ingredients together in bowl. (Mayonnaise can be refrigerated for up to 4 days.)

› **how to use** Drizzle over sushi rolls; spread on a turkey sandwich; lightly dollop on seared scallops; use as a sauce for tempura, or a dip for fries or kale chips.

saffron aïoli

Regular garlic-flavored mayonnaise is great, but add aromatic saffron and the condiment takes on a subtle floral complexity. Remove any green germ (or stem) in the garlic before mincing as it's hot and bitter. The egg yolks in this are not cooked; if you prefer, ¼ cup Egg Beaters may be substituted.

- 1 teaspoon boiling water, plus extra as needed
- ⅛ teaspoon saffron threads, crumbled
- 2 large egg yolks
- 4 teaspoons lemon juice
- 1 garlic clove, minced
- ¼ teaspoon Dijon mustard
- ⅛ teaspoon sugar
- Salt and white pepper
- ½ cup vegetable oil
- ¼ cup extra-virgin olive oil

1 Combine boiling water and saffron in small bowl and let steep for 10 minutes.

2 Process saffron mixture, egg yolks, lemon juice, garlic, mustard, sugar, and ¼ teaspoon salt in blender until combined, about 10 seconds, scraping down sides of blender jar as needed. With blender running, slowly add oils and process until aïoli is emulsified, about 2 minutes. Adjust consistency with extra cold water as needed. Season with salt and pepper to taste. Cover and refrigerate until flavors meld, at least 2 hours or up to 3 days.

› **how to use** Dollop on paella or seafood stew, spoon over steamed asparagus; serve with fish, spread on a vegetable sandwich, use as a dip for fries.

creamy cajun-spiced dip

We prefer to use our homemade Cajun Rub, but you can substitute store-bought Cajun seasoning or Old Bay seasoning.

- ½ cup plain Greek yogurt
- ¼ cup mayonnaise
- 1 tablespoon Dijon mustard
- 1 tablespoon Cajun-Style Rub (page 74)
- Salt and pepper

Combine yogurt, mayonnaise, mustard, and Cajun rub in bowl and season with salt and pepper to taste. (Dip can be refrigerated for up to 4 days.)

› **how to use** Spread on po' boys or other sandwiches; use as a dip for potato wedges, sweet potato fries, onion rings, fried seafood, or chicken tenders; dollop on pan-seared white fish or bluefish fillets.

fattoush

serves 4 to 6

- 2 (8-inch) pita breads
- 7 tablespoons extra-virgin olive oil
- Salt and pepper
- 3 tablespoons lemon juice
- 4 teaspoons ground sumac, plus extra for sprinkling
- ¼ teaspoon minced garlic
- 1 pound ripe tomatoes, cored and cut into ¾-inch pieces
- 1 English cucumber, peeled and sliced ⅛ inch thick
- 1 cup arugula, chopped coarse
- ½ cup chopped fresh cilantro
- ½ cup chopped fresh mint
- 4 scallions, sliced thin

why this recipe works *Fattoush* is an eastern Mediterranean salad that combines fresh produce and herbs, toasted pita bread, and bright, tangy sumac. Sumac is a commonly used spice across the region—where it's often used on its own as a finishing spice—and it traditionally lends its citrusy punch to this salad. We opted to use an ample amount of sumac in the dressing to intensify the flavor, and also used it as a garnish for the finished salad. To prevent the bread from becoming soggy, many recipes call for eliminating excess moisture by seeding and salting the cucumbers and tomatoes. We skipped these steps in order to preserve the crisp texture of the cucumber and the flavorful seeds and juice of the tomatoes. Instead, we made the pita pieces moisture-repellent by brushing their craggy sides with plenty of olive oil before baking them. The oil prevented the pita from absorbing moisture from the salad and becoming soggy while still allowing them to pick up flavor from the lemony dressing. The success of this recipe depends on ripe, in-season tomatoes.

1 Adjust oven rack to middle position and heat oven to 375 degrees. Using kitchen shears, cut around perimeter of each pita and separate into 2 thin rounds. Cut each round in half. Place pitas smooth side down on wire rack set in rimmed baking sheet. Brush 3 tablespoons oil on surface of pitas. (Pitas do not need to be uniformly coated; oil will spread during baking.) Season with salt and pepper to taste. Bake until pitas are crisp and light golden brown, 10 to 14 minutes. Let cool completely.

2 Whisk lemon juice, sumac, garlic, and ¼ teaspoon salt together in large bowl and let stand for 10 minutes. Whisking constantly, slowly drizzle in remaining ¼ cup oil. Add tomatoes, cucumber, arugula, cilantro, mint, and scallions. Break pitas into ½-inch pieces and add to bowl; gently toss to coat. Season with salt and pepper to taste. Serve, sprinkling individual portions with extra sumac.

wasabi tuna salad

¾ cup Wasabi Mayonnaise
(page 180)

1 red bell pepper, stemmed,
seeded, and chopped fine

4 scallions, sliced thin

1 tablespoon pickled ginger,
chopped

¼ teaspoon grated lime zest plus
2 teaspoons juice

Salt

3 (5-ounce) cans solid white tuna
in water, drained and flaked

why this recipe works Wasabi, or Japanese horseradish, is the fiery, green, nose-clearing condiment that is traditionally served with sushi. Fresh wasabi is grown only in Asia and is rarely found in U.S. grocery stores. Far more common is wasabi powder, which, when mixed with water to form a paste, achieves an approximation of the fresh root ground to a paste. We found that adding some to mayonnaise with a dash of soy sauce created a dressing that was perfect for punching up milder ingredients. We combined this pungent condiment with the arguably tired lunch staple, tuna salad. Substituting wasabi mayo for the regular kind, thinly sliced scallions for red onions, and a crunchy red bell pepper for celery gave us a satisfying and slightly surprising twist on an American classic. To add some aromatic warmth, we incorporated a little sweet pickled ginger and fragrant lime zest. Our favorite brand of canned tuna is Wild Planet Wild Albacore Tuna. If you can't find it, use canned solid white albacore tuna packed in water. Serve in a wrap, sandwich, or lettuce cup.

Stir wasabi mayonnaise, bell pepper, scallions, pickled ginger, lime zest and juice, and ¼ teaspoon salt together in bowl until combined. Gently fold in tuna and season with salt to taste. Serve. (Salad can be refrigerated for up to 24 hours.)

polenta fries with saffron aïoli

serves 4

4 cups water

Salt and pepper

1 cup instant polenta

½ teaspoon dried oregano

1 teaspoon grated lemon zest

½ cup vegetable oil

Coarse finishing salt

1 cup Saffron Aïoli (page 181)

why this recipe works Fries—no matter the variety—require a dipping sauce, and this recipe pairs fry and sauce perfectly. For a fresh take on how to use polenta, we found that if we cooked polenta and then chilled it until firm, we could slice it into thin sticks that would become crisp when fried—and irresistible when dipped into a rich, heady sauce like our Saffron Aïoli, which complemented the corn flavor without overwhelming it. We began our testing of polenta fries using instant polenta so we could minimize time on the stove. Stirring oregano and lemon zest into the fully cooked polenta lent an aromatic backbone to our fries and helped to brighten the flavor. We then poured our flavored polenta into a straight-sided 13 by 9-inch baking pan to set up in the refrigerator for easy slicing. Once our fries were cut, we looked at methods for cooking them. Deep frying resulted in fries that clumped together and stuck to the bottom of the pot, but pan frying resulted in perfectly crisp fries with a tender and fluffy interior. We seasoned the fries lightly with salt as they came out of the pan. Do not substitute coarse-ground cornmeal or traditional polenta. You can use your preferred coarse finishing salt in this recipe; for more information on finishing salts, see pages 22–23.

1 Line 13 by 9-inch baking pan with parchment paper and grease parchment. Bring water to boil in large saucepan and add 1 teaspoon salt. Slowly add polenta in steady stream while stirring constantly with wooden spoon. Reduce heat to low and cook, uncovered, stirring often, until polenta is soft and smooth, 3 to 5 minutes.

2 Off heat, stir in oregano and lemon zest and season with salt and pepper to taste. Pour polenta into prepared pan. Refrigerate, uncovered, until firm and sliceable, about 1 hour. (Polenta can be covered and refrigerated for up to 24 hours.)

3 Gently flip chilled polenta out onto cutting board and discard parchment. Cut polenta in half lengthwise, then slice each half crosswise into sixteen ¾-inch-wide fries. (You will have 32 fries total.)

4 Adjust oven rack to middle position and heat oven to 200 degrees. Set wire rack in rimmed baking sheet. Heat oil in 12-inch nonstick skillet over medium heat until shimmering and edge of polenta sizzles when dipped in oil. Fry half of polenta until crisp and beginning to brown, 6 to 7 minutes per side. Transfer to prepared rack, season with finishing salt to taste, and keep warm in oven. Repeat with remaining polenta. Serve warm with saffron aïoli.

crispy pan-fried chicken cutlets with garlic-curry sauce

serves 4

garlic-curry sauce

⅓ cup mayonnaise

¼ cup plain yogurt

2 tablespoons ketchup

2 teaspoons Mild Curry Powder (page 118)

1 teaspoon lemon juice

¼ teaspoon minced garlic

chicken

2 cups panko bread crumbs

2 large eggs

Salt

4 (6- to 8-ounce) boneless, skinless chicken breasts, trimmed, halved horizontally, and pounded ¼ inch thick

½ cup vegetable oil

why this recipe works At its heart, Japanese chicken *katsu* is essentially a classic breaded chicken cutlet—crispy, delicious, but, in our opinion, even better when sliced and served over rice with a tangy sauce. Here, we chose something creamy and garlicky with heady curry spice. But no matter how good the sauce, we wouldn't settle for a soggy, greasy, unevenly browned coating for the chicken. Our first improvement was to swap out the usual bread crumbs in favor of drier, crunchier panko. To streamline the traditional multistep breading process, we ditched the flour and found that we got a more delicate crust. To make sure the frying oil was at just the right temperature, we added a pinch of panko to the skillet with the oil and waited for the crumbs to turn golden brown before adding the cutlets. Letting the cutlets rest on a wire rack ensured that they weren't greasy and retained their crunch. Be sure to remove any tenderloins from the breasts before halving them; reserve them for another use. To make the breasts easier to slice, freeze them for 15 minutes. If you are working with 8-ounce breasts, the skillet will initially be crowded; the cutlets will shrink slightly as they cook. We prefer to use our homemade Mild Curry Powder (page 118), but you can substitute store-bought curry powder. Mild curry powder is also known as sweet curry powder in the grocery store.

1 **for the garlic-curry sauce** Whisk all ingredients together in bowl; refrigerate until ready to serve.

2 **for the chicken** Place panko in large zipper-lock bag and lightly crush with rolling pin. Transfer to shallow dish. Whisk eggs and 1 teaspoon salt in second shallow dish until well combined. Working with 1 cutlet at a time, dredge in egg mixture, allowing excess to drip off, then coat with panko, pressing gently to adhere. Transfer cutlets to rimmed baking sheet.

3 Adjust oven rack to middle position and heat oven to 200 degrees. Set wire rack in second rimmed baking sheet. Heat ¼ cup oil and small pinch panko in 12-inch skillet over medium-high heat. When panko has turned golden brown, place 4 cutlets in skillet. Cook, without moving cutlets, until deep golden brown on first side, 2 to 3 minutes. Using tongs, carefully flip cutlets and cook until deep golden brown on second side, 2 to 3 minutes. Transfer cutlets to prepared rack, season with salt, and keep warm in oven. Wipe skillet clean with paper towels. Repeat with remaining ¼ cup oil and remaining 4 cutlets. Serve immediately with garlic-curry sauce.

pan-seared flank steak with sage-shallot compound butter

serves 4 to 6

steak

- 1 (1½- to 1¾-pound) flank steak, trimmed
- 1 teaspoon salt
- 1 teaspoon sugar
- ½ teaspoon pepper
- 2 tablespoons vegetable oil

compound butter

- 4 tablespoons unsalted butter, softened
- 1 large shallot, minced
- ½ teaspoon dried sage
- ¼ teaspoon salt
- ⅛ teaspoon pepper

why this recipe works Flank steak is nice and meaty, but it's quite lean and could use some enriching. Compound butter (simply softened butter combined with flavorful ingredients) is a quick, rich, elegant way to add finishing flavor. Here we turn to herbaceous dried sage to up the elegance, along with some softened shallot, salt, and pepper to back it up. For a cooking method that produces a juicy, well-browned flank steak cooked to medium throughout, we cut the flank steak into four portions that fit neatly in a 12-inch skillet and sprinkle them with salt for seasoning and sugar for browning. Then we bake the steaks in a very low oven until they reach 120 degrees. To develop a flavorful crust, we then sear them in a hot skillet, flipping them several times to even out the contraction of the muscle fibers on each side to prevent buckling. After lavishing the lean steaks with compound butter, we slice them thin against the grain for maximum tenderness and dot them with even more butter for finishing flavor. Open the oven as infrequently as possible in step 1. If the meat is not yet up to temperature, wait at least 5 minutes before taking its temperature again.

1 **for the steak** Adjust oven rack to middle position and heat oven to 225 degrees. Pat steak dry with paper towels. Cut steak in half lengthwise. Cut each piece in half crosswise to create 4 steaks. Combine salt, sugar, and pepper in small bowl. Sprinkle steaks with salt mixture, pressing gently to adhere. Place steaks on wire rack set in rimmed baking sheet and transfer sheet to oven. Roast until meat registers 120 degrees, 30 to 40 minutes.

2 **for the compound butter** Meanwhile, microwave 1 tablespoon butter, shallot, sage, salt, and pepper in bowl, stirring occasionally, until shallot is softened and mixture is fragrant, about 2 minutes. Let cool completely, about 10 minutes. Using fork, mash remaining 3 tablespoons butter into shallot mixture until well combined; set aside. (Butter can be refrigerated for up to 1 week or frozen for up to 1 month; let soften at room temperature before using.)

3 Heat oil in 12-inch skillet over medium-high heat until just smoking. Sear steaks, flipping every 1 minute, until brown crust forms on both sides, 4 minutes total. (Do not move steaks between flips.) Return steaks to wire rack and let rest for 10 minutes. Transfer steaks to cutting board with grain running from left to right. Spread 1½ teaspoons compound butter on top of each steak. Slice steak as thin as possible against grain. Transfer sliced steak to warm platter and dot with remaining butter. Serve.

pan-roasted pork tenderloin with cider-caraway vinaigrette

serves 4 to 6

2 (12- to 16-ounce) pork tenderloins, trimmed

Salt and pepper

1 tablespoon vegetable oil

½ cup Cider-Caraway Vinaigrette (page 178)

why this recipe works In the test kitchen, we know how to boost flavor in quick-cooking, convenient, lean pork tenderloin—sear on the stovetop for a colorful crust and then transfer to the oven to finish cooking through. But while a browned crust adds flavor, we wanted even more appeal to lift our tenderloins out of the ordinary. Enter: our homemade cider-caraway vinaigrette, which paired perfectly with the pork. The tang of the vinegar enlivened the sweet meat; the apple notes naturally meshed with the pork; and the pungent, aromatic caraway seeds complemented both the pork and apple—and packed a punch. These simple pork tenderloins plus the easy vinaigrette were delicious, and the way to flavor took very little work. If the pork is enhanced (injected with a salt solution), do not season with salt in step 1.

1 Adjust oven rack to middle position and heat oven to 400 degrees. Pat tenderloins dry with paper towels and season with salt and pepper. Heat oil in 12-inch ovensafe skillet over medium-high heat until just smoking. Brown tenderloins on all sides, about 10 minutes. Transfer skillet to oven and roast until pork registers 145 degrees, 10 to 15 minutes.

2 Transfer tenderloins to carving board, tent with aluminum foil, and let rest for 20 minutes. Slice tenderloins into ½-inch-thick slices and transfer to serving platter. Drizzle with vinaigrette and serve.

grilled lamb kofte with za'atar yogurt sauce

serves 4 to 6

½ cup pine nuts

4 garlic cloves, peeled

1½ teaspoons smoked hot paprika

1 teaspoon salt

1 teaspoon ground cumin

½ teaspoon pepper

¼ teaspoon ground coriander

¼ teaspoon ground cloves

⅛ teaspoon ground nutmeg

⅛ teaspoon ground cinnamon

1½ pounds ground lamb

½ cup grated onion, drained

⅓ cup minced fresh parsley

⅓ cup minced fresh mint

1½ teaspoons unflavored gelatin

1 (13 by 9-inch) disposable aluminum roasting pan (if using charcoal)

1 cup Za'atar Yogurt Sauce (page 180)

why this recipe works In the Middle East, kebabs called *kofte* feature ground meat (not chunks) mixed with lots of spices and fresh herbs that is formed around metal skewers and quickly grilled. We like them dressed with a za'atar yogurt sauce; the kebabs' spices and extreme savor are contrasted with welcome herbal freshness and tang from the za'atar while the creaminess from the also-tart yogurt cuts through the richness. For the kofte, the biggest challenge was getting the patties' sausagelike texture right. We found that adding a small amount of powdered gelatin to the ground lamb helped the meat firm up and hold fast to the skewer. Ground pine nuts added to the meat prevented toughness and contributed their own pleasant texture and a boost in richness. A concentrated charcoal fire setup mimicked the intense heat of a kofte grill. Serve with rice pilaf, or make sandwiches with warm pita bread, sliced red onion, tomatoes, and fresh mint; just make sure to drizzle with the spiced sauce. You will need eight 12-inch metal skewers for this recipe.

1 Process pine nuts, garlic, paprika, salt, cumin, pepper, coriander, cloves, nutmeg, and cinnamon in food processor until coarse paste forms, 30 to 45 seconds. Transfer mixture to large bowl. Add lamb, onion, parsley, mint, and gelatin and knead with your hands until thoroughly combined and mixture feels slightly sticky, about 2 minutes. Divide mixture into 8 equal portions. Shape each portion into 5-inch-long cylinder about 1 inch in diameter. Using eight 12-inch metal skewers, thread 1 cylinder onto each skewer, pressing gently to adhere. Transfer kebabs to lightly greased baking sheet, cover with plastic wrap, and refrigerate for at least 1 hour or up to 24 hours.

2A **for a charcoal grill** Using skewer, poke 12 holes in bottom of disposable pan. Open bottom vent completely and place pan in center of grill. Light large chimney starter two-thirds filled with charcoal briquettes (4 quarts). When top coals are partially covered with ash, pour into disposable pan. Set cooking grate in place, cover, and open lid vent completely. Heat grill until hot, about 5 minutes.

2B **for a gas grill** Turn all burners to high, cover, and heat grill until hot, about 15 minutes. Leave all burners on high.

3 Clean and oil cooking grate. Place kebabs on grill (directly over coals if using charcoal) at 45-degree angle to bars. Cook (covered if using gas) until browned and meat easily releases from grill, 4 to 7 minutes. Flip kebabs and continue to cook until meat is browned on second side and registers 160 degrees, about 6 minutes. Transfer kebabs to serving platter and serve, passing yogurt sauce separately.

crab cakes with cajun-spiced dip

serves 4

1 pound jumbo lump crabmeat, picked over for shells and pressed dry between paper towels

4 scallions, green parts only, minced

1 tablespoon chopped fresh parsley, cilantro, dill, or basil

¼ cup mayonnaise

2–4 tablespoons bread crumbs

1½ teaspoons Cajun-Style Rub (page 74)

Salt and pepper

1 large egg, lightly beaten

¼ cup all-purpose flour

¼ cup vegetable oil

1 cup Creamy Cajun-Spiced Dip (page 181)

why this recipe works To improve upon the often lackluster ordinary crab cake, we wanted cakes with a crisp brown exterior and a creamy, well-seasoned filling bursting with sweet crab flavor—and, of course, a zesty dipping sauce. As Cajun spice is a common seasoning for crab, we traded the traditional rémoulade sauce for our Creamy Cajun-Spiced Dip, using additional Cajun blend in the cakes themselves to kick up their flavor. Fresh crabmeat provided the best taste and texture and was worth its high price tag. After experimenting with different binders, we settled on fine dry bread crumbs; their mild flavor kept the crabmeat front and center. Beyond the spice, some herbs were the only other additions we found necessary to keep the cakes fresh. The amount of bread crumbs you need will depend on the crabmeat's juiciness. Start with the smallest amount and add more after adding the egg only if the cakes won't hold together. Use fresh or pasteurized crabmeat (usually sold next to the fresh seafood) rather than the canned crabmeat (packed in tuna fish–like cans) found in the supermarket aisles. We prefer to use our homemade Cajun-Style Rub (page 74), but you can substitute store-bought Cajun seasoning or Old Bay seasoning.

1 Gently mix crabmeat, scallions, parsley, mayonnaise, 2 tablespoons bread crumbs, and Cajun rub in bowl, being careful not to break up crab lumps. Season with salt and pepper to taste. Carefully fold in egg with rubber spatula until mixture just clings together. If cakes don't bind, add more bread crumbs, 1 tablespoon at a time, until they do.

2 Divide crab mixture into 4 portions and shape into ½-inch-thick round cakes. Transfer cakes to large plate, cover, and refrigerate until firm, at least 30 minutes.

3 Spread flour in shallow dish. Lightly dredge crab cakes in flour. Heat oil in 12-inch nonstick skillet over medium-high heat until shimmering. Add crab cakes and cook until crisp and well browned on both sides, 8 to 10 minutes. Serve with dip.

grilled eggplant with chermoula

serves 4 to 6

6 tablespoons extra-virgin olive oil

5 garlic cloves, minced

⅛ teaspoon red pepper flakes

2 pounds eggplant, sliced into
  ¼-inch-thick rounds

  Salt and pepper

1 cup Chermoula (page 180)

why this recipe works On its own, grilled eggplant is great—meaty and deep in flavor. But it's even better when bathed in fragrant chermoula. The North African condiment's zestiness gives the rich vegetable welcome dimension. Unfortunately, grilled eggplant can easily turn out leathery or spongy. After a series of tests, we found that ¼-inch-thick rounds worked best; the interiors became tender by the time the exteriors were nicely grill-marked. Since it was necessary to brush the rounds with olive oil so they didn't stick to the grill, we infused that oil with minced garlic and red pepper flakes to add even more flavor. And we saved the browned and crisped minced garlic used to make the garlic oil to sprinkle on top with the chermoula. It is important to slice the eggplant thin so that the slices will cook through by the time the exterior is browned.

1 Combine oil, garlic, and pepper flakes in bowl. Microwave until garlic is golden brown and crisp, about 2 minutes. Strain garlic oil through fine-mesh strainer into small bowl. Reserve garlic oil and garlic separately.

2A for a charcoal grill Open bottom vent completely. Light large chimney starter filled with charcoal briquettes (6 quarts). When top coals are partially covered with ash, pour evenly over grill. Set cooking grate in place, cover, and open lid vent completely. Heat grill until hot, about 5 minutes.

2B for a gas grill Turn all burners to high, cover, and heat grill until hot, about 15 minutes. Turn all burners to medium-high.

3 Clean and oil cooking grate. Brush eggplant with garlic oil and season with salt and pepper. Place half of eggplant on grill and cook (covered if using gas) until browned and tender, about 4 minutes per side; transfer to serving platter. Repeat with remaining eggplant; transfer to platter. Drizzle chermoula over eggplant and sprinkle with garlic. Serve.

let it steep

spice-infused oils, pickles, and preserves

Steeping is about flavor transportation. If it's an infused oil, steeping opens up the complexities of the spice within; if it's a pickle, the warm brine transports spice flavor to the very center of the vegetable. Then, you can add layers of complexity to other recipes when you incorporate these transformed products. Discover how and where to use these infusions— like pairing mango chutney with scallops for intriguing sweetness and warmth, or brightening burgers, sandwiches, and salads with homemade pickled vegetables. Or, sometimes, the infusion will be the dish itself, like mustardy beer and brats or saffron-infused tapas.

INFUSE IT

While a spice "infusion" might seem abstract or difficult, in this book, we're talking about condiments—flavored oils or spice pastes, chutneys, and pickles. And they couldn't be easier: Let the ingredients do the work of releasing flavor themselves. We teach you everything you need to know about infusing and what spice-infused products you can make.

infusing versus steeping

It's easy to use "steeping" and "infusing" interchangeably in writing—but on a more technical level, you *infuse* flavor into something by *steeping* an ingredient. Steeping means soaking an ingredient in a liquid of choice (we steep in oil, vinegar, or water) for a certain amount of time to extract its soluble (more on this at right) flavors. Often this involves heat—at some level below the boiling point as steeping benefits from slow extraction. Flavor molecules dissolve to a greater extent in a warm solvent (such as fat or oil) than a cold one. As we learned from the concepts of toasting and—especially applicable here—blooming in chapter three, heat coaxes flavor out of spices and allows their complexity to blossom.

why infuse?

Infusing liquid or fat with flavor from spices brings out interesting, complex flavors. These flavors don't develop when the spice is simply stirred in. In fact, even blooming isn't always enough to do this. It's all about time. The longer a spice or seasoning steeps, the more flavor is extracted and imparted to the liquid, often until the spice is completely spent. Spiced oils are a favorite example; we tasted fennel in a new way once we steeped seeds in warm oil. Its flavor became less pungent and more floral than we could imagine.

DIY infusions are a great way to harness the flavors of spices for easy additions later on. Steep chiles in vinegar for a shelf-stable condiment that's ready to go whenever you crave something with a splash of pungent heat.

When seasonings are allowed to steep, flavors meld extremely effectively. Instead of a spice standing out in bold contrast to other ingredients, it blends in to encourage flavors that are amazingly complex but also balanced. There are a bunch of spices in our Chipotle Ketchup (page 216), but none overpowers the others because their brash properties mellow with time and their complexities bloom: Peppercorns provide straightforward heat; cloves, cinnamon, and allspice offer round warmth that complements the sweetness. Mustard seeds counterbalance with pungency that underscores the vinegar kick. And, of course, the chipotle chile adds sultry, smoky heat. The simmer time lets the flavors blend.

flavor compounds in spices

The flavors in the spices we steep in liquid fall into two categories: those that are water-soluble and those that are fat-soluble. These terms are pretty explicit: Water-soluble flavor compounds are those that can transfer to water, and fat-soluble compounds are those that can transfer to fat (usually oil). When infused in their respective appropriate liquids, the flavor molecules are released from a solid state into solution form, where they mix and interact, thereby producing even more complex flavors. The list of fat-soluble spices is more robust than that of water-soluble ones: Many of the grassy, fruity, nutty, spicy, and funky aromas in spices—so some of the best-tasting elements—dissolve much more readily in oil than in water. That's why we often need more spice in water infusions.

our infusions

Technically tea is an infusion, but the recipes we've developed are condiments—those you drizzle, spread, or sprinkle on foods to liven them up. And they're all fresher-tasting and much more economical than versions in specialty stores. We reference these recipes through-out the chapter.

› spice-infused oils

Beyond use as a cooking medium, oil provides fat and flavor. And olive oil already has a fruitiness that can benefit dishes. But oil's flavor is only improved when you infuse it with awoken spice. For our simply spiced oils—those that are an infusion of just one to two spices—we kept things fast and easy: We heated the spices in the oils over medium-low heat for a few minutes to extract their flavor (the process is efficient; the main flavor compounds in most spices are fat-soluble), and then let the oils steep off heat for an additional 4 hours; this off-heat steeping was perfect for ensuring maximum flavor transfer, as any more heated steeping made the spice taste harsh.

Sichuan Chili Oil is a bit more complex: The hallmark of Sichuan chili oil is a balance between *la*—the concentrated heat from dried chiles—and *ma*—the numbing effect of Sichuan peppercorns. It's common to bloom the aromatics (ginger, bay leaves, star anise, and cardamom) in vegetable oil until darkened—that way you know their flavor has been extracted enough to build a pungent base. Then we poured this hot flavored oil over the chili powder, which helped build a deep, savory toasted chili flavor without burning the chili powder. As harissa also includes dried spices, we turn to the microwave to steep to prevent burning there and create rich warmth. All of these infused oils make about 1 cup, except for Sichuan Chili Oil which makes 1½ cups. They can be stored in an airtight container in the refrigerator for up to 3 months; except for Harissa. The flavors will continue to deepen over time. Bring the oils to room temperature before serving.

---

rosemary oil

You can strain the finished oil through a fine-mesh strainer just before serving, if desired.

- **1 cup extra-virgin olive oil**
- **2 tablespoons dried rosemary**

Heat oil and rosemary in small saucepan over medium-low heat until fragrant and starting to bubble, 2 to 3 minutes. Off heat, let sit until flavors meld, about 4 hours.

› **how to use** Drizzle on grilled meats, mashed potatoes, or white beans; use as a dip for ciabatta or focaccia; substitute for the oil in vinaigrettes; finish soups.

fennel oil

You can strain the finished oil through a fine-mesh strainer just before serving, if desired.

- **1 cup extra-virgin olive oil**
- **3 tablespoons fennel seeds, cracked**

Heat oil and fennel in small saucepan over medium-low heat until fragrant and starting to bubble, 2 to 3 minutes. Off heat, let sit until flavors meld, about 4 hours.

› **how to use** Serve with a log of goat cheese or chunks of feta; drizzle on pizza; finish seared white fish; toss with roasted vegetables; finish vegetable stews.

chipotle-coriander oil

You can strain the finished oil through a fine-mesh strainer just before serving, if desired.

- **1 cup vegetable oil**
- **3 tablespoons coriander seeds, cracked**
- **1 teaspoon chipotle chile powder**

Heat oil, coriander, and chile powder in small saucepan over medium-low heat until fragrant and starting to bubble, 2 to 3 minutes. Off heat, let sit until flavors meld, about 4 hours.

› **how to use** Top hummus or other dips; drizzle on steak tacos or grilled corn; use as a dip for pita; poach fish or shrimp; whisk into Southwestern salad dressings.

sichuan chili oil

Asian chili powder is similar to hot red pepper flakes but is milder and more finely ground. A Sichuan chili powder is preferred, but Korean red pepper flakes, called gochugaru, are a good alternative.

- ½ cup **Asian chili powder**
- 2 tablespoons **sesame seeds**
- 2 tablespoons **Sichuan peppercorns, coarsely ground**
- ½ teaspoon **salt**
- 1 cup **vegetable oil**
- 1 **(1-inch) piece ginger, unpeeled, sliced into ¼-inch rounds and smashed**
- 3 **star anise pods**
- 5 **cardamom pods, crushed**
- 2 **bay leaves**

1 Combine chili powder, sesame seeds, half of peppercorns, and salt in bowl. Cook oil, ginger, star anise, cardamom, bay leaves, and remaining peppercorns in small saucepan over low heat, stirring occasionally, until spices have darkened and mixture is very fragrant, 25 to 30 minutes.

2 Strain mixture through fine-mesh strainer into bowl with chili powder mixture (mixture may bubble slightly); discard solids in strainer. Stir well to combine. Let sit at room temperature until flavors meld, about 12 hours.

> **how to use** Toss with fresh Asian noodles; serve with rice dishes; drizzle over steamed or blanched vegetables; use as a dip for dumplings.

harissa

Making harissa involves steeping spices in oil, but the product is more of a chile sauce or paste. If you can't find Aleppo pepper, you can substitute 1½ teaspoons paprika and 1½ teaspoons finely chopped red pepper flakes.

- ¾ cup **extra-virgin olive oil**
- 12 **garlic cloves, minced**
- ¼ cup **paprika**
- 2 tablespoons **ground coriander**
- 2 tablespoons **ground dried Aleppo pepper**
- 2 teaspoons **ground cumin**
- 1½ teaspoons **caraway seeds**
- 1 teaspoon **salt**

Combine all ingredients in bowl and microwave until bubbling and very fragrant, about 1 minute, stirring halfway through microwaving. Let cool completely before serving. (Harissa can be refrigerated for up to 4 days. Bring to room temperature before serving.)

> **how to use** Rub on meats before cooking; use as a condiment for falafel and gyros; stir into soups; fold into scrambled eggs; toss with potatoes or vegetables before roasting.

bruschetta with ricotta, roasted red peppers, and rosemary oil

serves 8

10 ounces (1¼ cups) whole-milk ricotta cheese

½ teaspoon grated lemon zest plus ½ teaspoon juice

¼ teaspoon salt

⅛ teaspoon pepper

1 cup jarred roasted red peppers, patted dry and cut into ¼-inch pieces

¼ cup pitted kalamata olives, chopped

2 tablespoons Rosemary Oil (page 204), plus extra for drizzling

1 (18-inch) baguette, sliced ¾ inch thick on bias

1 garlic clove, peeled

2 tablespoons chopped fresh parsley

why this recipe works This antipasto is a delicious study in contrasts—crunchy, hot toasts smothered with creamy, cool ricotta that's seasoned with just salt, pepper, and lemon zest and then topped with a zippy mix of roasted red peppers and kalamata olives. That might seem like a lot of flavor, but it's one of our infused staples, Rosemary Oil, that really brought the snack together with a distinctly Italian flavor and earthy richness. Tossing the peppers and olives with the oil gave them a beautiful gloss, and a finishing drizzle over the toasts easily upped the sophistication. The layer of ricotta prevented any of the topping from seeping through and turning the toasts soggy. Paying attention to detail, we rubbed garlic onto our freshly toasted bread and finished with a sprinkling of parsley. Toast the bread just before assembling the bruschetta. We prefer the rich flavor of whole-milk ricotta; however, part-skim ricotta can be substituted. Do not use fat-free ricotta.

1 Adjust oven rack 4 inches from broiler element and heat broiler. Combine ricotta, lemon zest, salt, and pepper in bowl. Combine red peppers, olives, rosemary oil, and lemon juice in second bowl.

2 Arrange bread in single layer on rimmed baking sheet and broil until bread is deep golden and toasted, 1 to 2 minutes per side.

3 Lightly rub 1 side of each toast with garlic (you will not use all of garlic). Spread ricotta mixture evenly on toasts, top with red pepper mixture, sprinkle with parsley, and drizzle with extra rosemary oil. Serve immediately.

marinated green and black olives

serves 8

- 1 cup brine-cured green olives with pits, rinsed and patted dry
- 1 cup brine-cured black olives with pits, rinsed and patted dry
- ¾ cup extra-virgin olive oil
- 1 shallot, minced
- 1 garlic clove, minced
- 2 teaspoons grated lemon zest
- ½ teaspoon dried thyme
- ½ teaspoon dried oregano
- ½ teaspoon red pepper flakes
- ½ teaspoon salt

why this recipe works After bathing in an oil-and-spice mixture for 4 hours, simple-to-make homemade marinated olives taste worlds better than ones you find at the store deli bar. Because we infuse them with spices for just long enough, they're perfumed with balanced flavor, not just floating in a slimy, harsh oil-and-vinegar concoction. For the spice-infused marinade, we found that dried thyme and oregano gave us a robust herbal flavor, and a dash of red pepper flakes brought everything into focus with a touch of heat. Shallot and garlic offered fresh aromatic flavor, and some lemon zest provided a subtle citrus note. This infusion complemented the brininess of the olives for a superlative snack. Olives with pits have better flavor than pitted ones, and tasters preferred brine-cured olives to salt-cured for their subtler flavors. A combination of black and green olives boosted visual appeal. Make sure to bring the mixture to room temperature before serving or the oil will look cloudy and congealed.

Toss all ingredients in bowl, cover with plastic wrap, and refrigerate until flavors meld, about 4 hours. Let olives sit at room temperature for 30 minutes before serving. (Olives can be refrigerated for up to 4 days.)

marinated cauliflower and chickpeas with saffron

serves 6 to 8

- ½ head cauliflower (1 pound), cored and cut into 1-inch florets
- Salt and pepper
- ¼ cup hot water
- ⅛ teaspoon saffron threads, crumbled
- ⅓ cup extra-virgin olive oil
- 5 garlic cloves, peeled and smashed
- 1½ teaspoons sugar
- 1½ teaspoons smoked paprika
- 1 small sprig fresh rosemary
- 2 tablespoons sherry vinegar
- 1 cup canned chickpeas, rinsed
- ½ lemon, sliced thin
- 1 tablespoon minced fresh parsley

why this recipe works The small portions of tapas demand big flavor in every bite, so we set out to flavor creamy chickpeas and earthy cauliflower with a bold, Spanish-inspired marinade. First, we blanched the cauliflower, softening it so that it would readily absorb the spice-infused dressing. We established the marinade's base by steeping saffron in hot water to coax out more of its distinct, complex flavors. Heating smashed garlic cloves in olive oil infused the oil with flavor while also taming the garlic's harsh edge. Along with the saffron, smoked paprika and a sprig of rosemary gave the marinade a vibrant brick-red hue and earthy, aromatic flavor. Thin slices of lemon lent bright citrus flavor and made for a pretty presentation. We stirred together our marinade, adding the saffron and flavor-enhancing sherry vinegar (a go-to ingredient in Spanish cuisine) off the heat. Canned chickpeas were a time-savvy choice, promising reliably tender beans without the wait. We combined our marinade with the chickpeas and cauliflower and rested the mixture in the refrigerator, allowing the flavors to meld and deepen. The chickpeas and cauliflower emerged with a golden hue, brimming with deep, complex flavor. Use a small sprig of rosemary, or its flavor will be overpowering. The garlic will soften over time. This dish can be served cold or at room temperature.

1 Bring 2 quarts water to boil in large saucepan. Add cauliflower and 1 tablespoon salt and cook until florets begin to soften, about 3 minutes. Drain florets and transfer to paper towel–lined baking sheet.

2 Combine the hot water and saffron in bowl; set aside. Heat oil and garlic in small saucepan over medium-low heat until fragrant and beginning to sizzle but not brown, 4 to 6 minutes. Stir in sugar, paprika, and rosemary and cook until fragrant, about 30 seconds. Off heat, stir in saffron mixture, vinegar, 1½ teaspoons salt, and ¼ teaspoon pepper.

3 Combine florets, saffron mixture, chickpeas, and lemon in large bowl. Cover and refrigerate, stirring occasionally, until flavors meld, about 4 hours. (Cauliflower mixture can be refrigerated for up to 3 days.) To serve, discard rosemary sprig, transfer cauliflower and chickpeas to serving bowl with slotted spoon, and sprinkle with parsley.

one-pan chicken with couscous, carrots, and harissa

serves 4 to 6

- 8 (5- to 7-ounce) bone-in chicken thighs, trimmed

- Salt and pepper

- 1 teaspoon vegetable oil

- 1 pound carrots, peeled and cut into 2-inch lengths, thin pieces halved lengthwise, thick pieces quartered lengthwise

- 1 onion, chopped

- 1 (15-ounce) can chickpeas, rinsed

- ¾ cup water

- 2 tablespoons Harissa (page 205), plus extra for serving

- 1 cup couscous

- ⅓ cup minced fresh parsley

- 2 tablespoons lemon juice

why this recipe works When a weeknight dinner includes the "one-pan" moniker, it might evoke thoughts of dull flavors or tired pairings. But all it took was a stir-in of spicy harissa for this skillet supper to quickly squash those notions. Couscous cooks in a fraction of the time required for most grains and rice, so we centered the dish on this starch. Other ingredients common to North African cuisine, creamy chickpeas and sweet carrots, accompanied the ultrarich and savory bronzed-skinned chicken thighs. And of course, our powerful harissa deeply and easily flavored it all without us having to turn to a litany of spices, garlic, and oil. Searing the thighs first added a load of tasty fond to the pan; then, we quickly braised them while the couscous cooked in the same pan. Finishing with lemon juice and fresh parsley brightened up this savory dish, which we served with more of the seductive spice paste. We prefer to use our homemade Harissa (page 205), but you can substitute store-bought harissa. You will need a 12-inch ovensafe skillet with a lid for this recipe. The couscous mixture will appear dry in step 3; do not add extra liquid as the chicken will release juices as it cooks.

---

1 Adjust oven rack to middle position and heat oven to 450 degrees. Pat chicken dry with paper towels and season with salt and pepper. Heat oil in 12-inch ovensafe skillet over medium-high heat until just smoking. Add half of chicken, skin side down, and cook until skin is crisped and golden, 7 to 9 minutes. Flip chicken and continue to cook until browned on second side, 7 to 9 minutes longer; transfer skin side up to plate. Repeat with remaining chicken; transfer to plate.

2 Pour off all but 1 tablespoon fat from skillet. Add carrots, onion, 1 teaspoon salt, and ½ teaspoon pepper and cook over medium heat until onions are softened, about 5 minutes. Stir in chickpeas, water, and harissa, scraping up any browned bits, and bring to boil.

3 Stir in couscous, scraping down any that sticks to sides of skillet. Nestle chicken into skillet skin side up along with any accumulated juices. Cover, transfer skillet to oven, and bake until chicken registers 175 degrees, 15 to 20 minutes.

4 Using pot holders, remove skillet from oven and transfer chicken to serving platter. Being careful of hot skillet handle, add parsley and lemon juice to couscous mixture and fluff with fork to combine. Season with salt and pepper to taste. Serve, passing extra harissa separately.

grilled shrimp skewers with sichuan chili oil and napa cabbage slaw

serves 4

Salt and pepper

2 tablespoons sugar

1½ pounds jumbo shrimp (16 to 20 per pound), peeled and deveined

¼ cup vegetable oil

¼ cup Sichuan Chili Oil (page 205)

2 tablespoons white wine vinegar

1 small head napa cabbage (1½ pounds), cored and sliced thin

4 scallions, sliced thin on bias

1 cup fresh cilantro leaves

¼ cup salted dry-roasted peanuts, chopped

Shrimp skewers are one of the quickest-cooking grilled entrées, and one of the most crowd-pleasing. That might make them seem a bit boring. They're not—grill char is a magical flavor tool—and served with one of four infused oils and sides, they're the quickest route to your new favorite seasonal dinner. You will need four 12-inch metal skewers for this recipe.

1   Dissolve 2 tablespoons salt and sugar in 1 quart cold water in large container. Submerge shrimp in brine, cover, and refrigerate for 15 minutes. Remove shrimp from brine and pat dry with paper towels. Thread shrimp tightly onto four 12-inch metal skewers, alternating direction of heads and tails. Brush both sides of shrimp with 1 tablespoon vegetable oil and season with pepper.

2A for a charcoal grill Open bottom vent completely. Light large chimney starter mounded with charcoal briquettes (7 quarts). When top coals are partially covered with ash, pour evenly over grill. Set cooking grate in place, cover, and open lid vent completely. Heat grill until hot, about 5 minutes.

2B for a gas grill Turn all burners to high, cover, and heat grill until hot, about 15 minutes. Leave all burners on high.

3   Clean and oil cooking grate. Place skewers on grill and cook (covered if using gas) until lightly charred, about 2½ minutes. Flip skewers and cook until shrimp are opaque throughout, 2 to 3 minutes. Using tongs, slide shrimp off skewers onto serving platter and drizzle with chili oil.

4   Meanwhile, whisk remaining 3 tablespoons vegetable oil, vinegar, and ½ teaspoon salt together in large bowl. Add cabbage, scallions, and cilantro and toss to coat. Season with salt and pepper to taste. Sprinkle with peanuts and serve with shrimp.

grilled shrimp skewers with harissa and carrot salad

Substitute extra-virgin olive oil for vegetable oil; Harissa (page 205) for chili oil; 1½ pounds carrots, peeled and shredded, for cabbage; chopped mint for cilantro; and toasted pistachios for peanuts.

grilled shrimp skewers with fennel oil and zucchini ribbon salad

Substitute extra-virgin olive oil for vegetable oil, Fennel Oil (page 204) for chili oil, 3 tablespoons lemon juice for vinegar, 1½ pounds zucchini, sliced lengthwise into thin ribbons for cabbage, ½ cup chopped parsley for cilantro, and toasted pine nuts for peanuts. Sprinkle 2 ounces shaved Parmesan over salad.

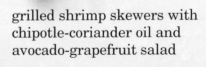

grilled shrimp skewers with chipotle-coriander oil and avocado-grapefruit salad

Substitute extra-virgin olive oil for vegetable oil, Chipotle-Coriander Oil (page 204) for chili oil, 2 sliced avocados for cabbage, and roasted pepitas for peanuts. Reduce vinegar to 1 teaspoon. Add 3 red grapefruits, peel and pith removed, halved and sliced ¼ inch thick, to salad.

› sandwich starters

Ketchup and mustard are so essential to our snack food, and they're both infusions. Stock special homemade versions—chipotle ketchup instead of the cloying standard and Dijon, the Cadillac of mustards—and you'll use them with intention. Ketchup requires heat; we cook a sachet of aromatics and spices with the tomato mixture to extract their flavor (as in tea), and reduce the mixture to thicken the ketchup to a dipable consistency. Dijon similarly calls for cooking spices in liquid—water, vinegar, and wine, reduced to tame its alcohol burn—so the flavors meld, but for a shorter time. And we softened the mustard seeds, as well as the other spices, overnight in the liquid before combining, which also aids flavor transfer. Both condiments make about 2 cups.

chipotle ketchup

The thick puree has a hard time passing through the strainer in step 4 without assistance; we find that pressing the back of a ladle into the strainer is the simplest way to extract as much ketchup as possible.

- 2 **bay leaves**
- 1 **teaspoon black peppercorns**
- 1 **teaspoon yellow mustard seeds**
- 1 **teaspoon whole cloves**
- 1 **cinnamon stick, broken in half**
- ¼ **teaspoon allspice berries**
- 1 **tablespoon vegetable oil**
- 1 **onion, chopped**
- 1 **(6-ounce) can tomato paste**
- 3 **garlic cloves, minced**
- 2 **tablespoons minced canned chipotle chile in adobo sauce**
- 3¾ **pounds tomatoes, cored and chopped coarse**
- ¾ **cup cider vinegar**
- ⅓ **cup packed dark brown sugar**
- 1½ **teaspoons salt**

1 Bundle bay leaves, peppercorns, mustard seeds, cloves, cinnamon stick, and allspice in cheesecloth and tie with kitchen twine to secure; set aside.

2 Heat oil in Dutch oven over medium heat until shimmering. Add onion and cook until softened, 5 to 7 minutes. Stir in tomato paste and garlic and cook, scraping bottom of pot, until fragrant, about 1 minute.

3 Transfer mixture to blender, add chipotle and half of tomatoes, and process until smooth, about 30 seconds; transfer to bowl. Process remaining tomatoes in blender until smooth, about 30 seconds; transfer to bowl with puree.

4 Working in batches, strain puree through fine-mesh strainer set over now-empty pot, pressing firmly on solids with ladle to extract as much tomato pulp as possible; discard solids. Stir in vinegar, sugar, salt, and spice sachet and bring mixture to simmer over medium heat. Cook, stirring occasionally and scraping bottom of pot, until mixture has thickened, darkened in color, and reduced to about 2 cups, 30 minutes to 1 hour. (Ketchup will continue to thicken as it cools.)

5 Discard spice sachet and let ketchup cool slightly. Transfer ketchup to airtight container and refrigerate until chilled, about 1 hour. (Ketchup can be refrigerated for up to 2 months.)

dijon mustard

Through our testing we found the mustard required some aging time before serving in order to develop a more balanced flavor. Five days was the minimum amount of time before we thought the mustard was sufficiently matured. Different brands of mustard powder have different flavors; we prefer using Colman's mustard powder in this recipe.

1⅓ cups water
¾ cup white wine vinegar
½ cup yellow mustard seeds
3 tablespoons dry mustard
4 teaspoons onion powder
1 tablespoon salt
¾ teaspoon garlic powder
¼ teaspoon ground cinnamon
⅛ teaspoon ground turmeric
1⅓ cups dry white wine

1 Combine water, vinegar, mustard seeds, dry mustard, onion powder, salt, garlic powder, cinnamon, and turmeric in bowl. Cover with plastic wrap and let sit at room temperature for at least 8 hours or up to 24 hours.

2 Bring wine to simmer in small saucepan over medium-high heat and cook until reduced to ⅔ cup, 10 to 15 minutes.

3 Process reduced wine and mustard seed mixture in blender until smooth, about 2 minutes, scraping down sides of blender jar as needed. Transfer mixture to now-empty saucepan and cook over medium-low heat, stirring often, until mixture has thickened slightly, 5 to 8 minutes. Strain mustard through fine-mesh strainer set over bowl, pressing firmly on solids with ladle to extract as much mustard as possible; discard solids. Let mustard cool slightly, then transfer to airtight container and refrigerate until flavors mature, at least 5 days or up to 6 months. (Mustard's flavor will continue to deepen over time.)

southwestern burgers with chipotle ketchup

serves 4

2 pounds sirloin steak tips, trimmed and cut into ½-inch pieces

4 tablespoons unsalted butter, melted and cooled

Salt and pepper

1 teaspoon vegetable oil

4 slices pepper Jack cheese (4 ounces)

4 large hamburger buns, toasted

1 avocado, halved, pitted, and sliced thin

Bibb lettuce leaves

¼ cup Chipotle Ketchup (page 216)

why this recipe works People have their preferred burger condiment—mustard, ketchup, or mayo. But one taste of our home-made Chipotle Ketchup on your burger, and we have a feeling you'll fall squarely in the ketchup camp. The punchy condiment, which ably stands up to the assertive richness of the meat, also creates a burger with the intriguing taste of the Southwest. Pepper Jack cheese and sliced avocado contribute to the Southwestern-inspired stack. A perfectly dressed burger is worthy only with a perfect patty, so we ground the meat for it ourselves from sirloin steak tips. A little melted butter in the mix improved juiciness. The stovetop provided intense heat for searing, and then the oven's ambient heat allowed a gentle, even finish. Sirloin steak tips are often sold as flap meat. Do not overwork the meat or the burgers will be dense. For the best flavor, season the burgers aggressively just before cooking. We prefer to cook these burgers to medium-rare, but if you prefer them more or less done, see our guidelines on page 280. For some extra kick, serve these burgers with pickled jalapeños and sliced red onion.

---

1 Arrange beef in single layer on rimmed baking sheet and freeze until very firm and starting to harden around edges but still pliable, about 35 minutes.

2 Working in 4 batches, pulse beef in food processor until finely ground into 1/16-inch pieces, about 20 pulses, stopping to redistribute meat as needed. Return the ground beef to sheet and spread evenly, discarding any long strands of gristle and large chunks of fat.

3 Adjust oven rack to middle position and heat oven to 300 degrees. Drizzle beef with melted butter, sprinkle with 1 teaspoon pepper, and gently toss with fork to combine. Divide beef into 4 lightly packed balls, then gently flatten into ¾-inch-thick burgers. Cover and refrigerate until ready to cook. (Patties can be refrigerated for up to 24 hours.)

4 Season patties with salt and pepper. Heat oil in 12-inch skillet over high heat until just smoking. Cook patties, without moving them, until browned on first side, about 2 minutes. Flip patties and continue to cook for 2 minutes. Transfer to clean rimmed baking sheet, top with pepper Jack, and cook until burgers register 120 to 125 degrees (for medium-rare), 3 to 5 minutes. Transfer burgers to serving platter, tent with aluminum foil, and let rest for 5 minutes. Serve burgers on buns, with avocado, lettuce, and chipotle ketchup.

wisconsin brats and beer

serves 8 to 12

2 large onions, sliced into
½-inch-thick rounds
(do not separate rings)

3 tablespoons vegetable oil

Pepper

3 cups mild lager, such as
Budweiser

⅔ cup Dijon Mustard (page 217)

1 teaspoon sugar

1 teaspoon caraway seeds

1 (13 by 9-inch) disposable
aluminum roasting pan

2 pounds bratwurst
(8 to 12 sausages)

8–12 (6-inch) Italian sub rolls

why this recipe works Most (especially Midwesterners) would agree that sturdy rolls topped with meaty, beer-soaked bratwurst and savory-sweet grilled onions are the perfect tailgating dish or fall snack. But fewer might stop to notice that spices are what make this dish much more than just sausages and onions floating in hot beer. Zesty mustard not only gives the otherwise very rich dish brightness and heat, but it also provides the beer bath with lots of body. Another addition, caraway seeds, contributes a savory-sweet anise-like element. We started by mixing up a beer-based marinade flavored with these and let the links sit in it while we prepared the grill. We then grilled the onions and added them in with the sausages so both could braise in this marinade (in a disposable aluminum pan) on the grill and become infused with its flavor. After the braise, we threw the sausages directly onto the grate for a final crisping to give them a great sear. We prefer to use our home-made Dijon Mustard (page 217), but you can substitute store-bought Dijon. You'll need a 13 by 9-inch disposable aluminum roasting pan for this recipe.

1 Brush onions with oil and season with pepper; set aside. Combine beer, mustard, sugar, caraway, and 1 teaspoon pepper in disposable pan, then add sausages in single layer.

2A **for a charcoal grill** Open bottom vent completely. Light large chimney starter filled with charcoal briquettes (6 quarts). When top coals are partially covered with ash, pour evenly over grill. Set cooking grate in place, cover, and open lid vent completely. Heat grill until hot, about 5 minutes.

2B **for a gas grill** Turn all burners to high, cover, and heat grill until hot, about 15 minutes. Leave all burners on high.

3 Clean and oil cooking grate. Place onions on grill and cook, flipping as needed, until lightly charred on both sides, 6 to 10 minutes. Transfer onions to disposable pan with beer and sausage. Place pan in center of grill, cover, and cook for 15 minutes.

4 Move disposable pan to 1 side of grill. Transfer sausages to cooking grate and cook until browned on all sides, about 5 minutes. Transfer sausages to serving platter and tent with aluminum foil. Continue to cook onion mixture, uncovered, in disposable pan until slightly thickened, about 5 minutes. Serve sausages and onions on rolls.

› spice-infused brines

Bright, tangy condiments made from brines are most effective at saving food from dullness. A brine itself can be a condiment, as in the hot pepper vinegar that adds bright heat to savory foods with a splash. In the case of the pickles, the condiment is made from a heated brine, which infuses cucumbers with flavor. Whether for the vinegar condiment or the quick pickle, vinegar for a brine usually requires a boil with spices to pick up flavor. And because vinegar is mainly water, some spices need to be used in larger quantity than they would if they were infusing oil for their impact to be felt. Both of these recipes make about 2 cups.

hot pepper vinegar

You will need a 1-pint Mason jar with a tight-fitting lid for this recipe. Heating the jar with warm water and then draining it before adding the hot brine ensures that the jar won't crack from an abrupt temperature change.

- ½ ounce (about 20) dried arbol chiles
- 2 cups distilled white vinegar
- 4 teaspoons sugar
- 1 teaspoon salt
- ½ teaspoon black peppercorns

1 Prick chiles with fork and set aside. Combine vinegar, sugar, salt, and peppercorns in small saucepan and bring to boil over medium-high heat.

2 Fill one 1-pint Mason jar with hot tap water to warm. Drain jar, then pack with chiles. Using ladle, pour hot brine over chiles to cover. Let cool to room temperature, about 30 minutes. Cover and refrigerate until flavors meld, about 24 hours. (Vinegar can be refrigerated for up to 3 months; flavor will continue to deepen over time.)

quick pickle chips

For guaranteed crunch, choose the freshest, firmest pickling cucumbers available; we like Kirby cucumbers. You will need a 1-pint Mason jar with a tight-fitting lid for this recipe. Heating the jar with warm water and then draining it before adding the hot brine ensures that the jar won't crack from an abrupt temperature change.

- ¾ cup seasoned rice vinegar
- ¼ cup water
- 1 garlic clove, peeled and halved
- ¼ teaspoon ground turmeric
- ⅛ teaspoon black peppercorns
- ⅛ teaspoon yellow mustard seeds
- 8 ounces pickling cucumbers, trimmed, sliced ¼ inch thick crosswise
- 2 sprigs fresh dill

1 Bring vinegar, water, garlic, turmeric, peppercorns, and mustard seeds to boil in medium saucepan over medium-high heat.

2 Fill one 1-pint Mason jar with hot tap water to warm. Drain jar, then pack with cucumbers and dill sprigs. Using ladle, pour hot brine over cucumbers to cover. Let cool to room temperature, about 30 minutes. Cover and refrigerate until chilled and flavors meld, about 3 hours. (Pickles can be refrigerated for up to 6 weeks.)

chicken salad with pickled fennel, watercress, and macadamia nuts

serves 4 to 6

¾ cup seasoned rice vinegar

¼ cup water

1 garlic clove, peeled and smashed

1 (3-inch) strip orange zest

¼ teaspoon fennel seeds

⅛ teaspoon black peppercorns

⅛ teaspoon mustard seeds

1 fennel bulb, stalks discarded, 2 tablespoons fronds minced and bulb halved, cored, and sliced thin

Salt and pepper

4 (6- to 8-ounce) boneless, skinless chicken breasts, trimmed

2 tablespoons extra-virgin olive oil

10 ounces (10 cups) watercress, torn into bite-size pieces

½ cup macadamia nuts or cashews, toasted and chopped

why this recipe works Pickling is a perfect technique to imbue fresh, crunchy vegetables with complexity and nuance, tenderize raw textures, and introduce punchy flavor—and it's not just for cucumbers. We loved the way a quick stint in a spiced, hot brine rounded out the fresh, vegetal flavor of fennel with the more floral notes of fennel seeds. The base of our quick pickle brine was sweet and mellow rice vinegar, which we balanced and punched up with mustard seed and black peppercorns, added savor and aroma with garlic, and highlighted the floral notes with complementary orange zest. Pickling doesn't have to take a long time; here 30 minutes is sufficient, and we prepared our light meal while the pickles were steeping. We gently poached some chicken breasts for a vibrant salad and then made further use of the flavorful pickling liquid by incorporating it into our vinaigrette. Then it was just a matter of tossing spicy watercress, macadamia nuts, and the pickled fennel with our perfectly cooked chicken. Not wanting to waste anything, we used some of the fennel fronds to add another fresh element. If your fennel comes without fronds, they can be omitted.

1 Combine vinegar, water, garlic, orange zest, fennel seeds, peppercorns, and mustard seeds in 2-cup liquid measuring cup and microwave until boiling, about 5 minutes. Stir in sliced fennel bulb until completely submerged and let cool completely, about 30 minutes. (Pickled fennel can be refrigerated for up to 6 weeks.)

2 Meanwhile, dissolve 2 tablespoons salt in 6 cups cold water in Dutch oven. Cover chicken with plastic wrap and pound to even 1-inch thickness. Submerge chicken in water and heat over medium heat until water registers 170 degrees. Turn off heat, cover, and let sit until chicken registers 160 degrees, 13 to 16 minutes.

3 Transfer chicken to paper towel–lined baking sheet and refrigerate until chicken is cool, about 30 minutes. Transfer chicken to cutting board and shred into bite-sized pieces using 2 forks.

4 Drain fennel, reserving ⅓ cup brine; discard solids. Whisk reserved brine, oil, and ¼ teaspoon salt in large bowl. Add chicken, pickled fennel, watercress, and fennel fronds and toss to combine. Season with salt and pepper to taste. Sprinkle with macadamia nuts and serve.

quick collard greens with hot pepper vinegar

serves 4 to 6

Salt and pepper

2½ pounds collard greens, stemmed

4 slices thick-cut bacon, cut into ½-inch pieces

2 garlic cloves, minced

¼ cup Hot Pepper Vinegar (page 223), plus extra for serving

why this recipe works Porky braised collard greens are a staple of the South, and while the silky cooked greens are already deeply flavored, a splash of hot pepper vinegar—simply chile-infused vinegar that's made in a quick boil—gives the deep, rich greens a clarifying heat and a refreshing finish. Our quick version of the typically long-cooked collards blanches the leaves in salt water to tenderize them and remove their bitterness in minutes. To get rid of the excess moisture, we squeezed them dry and then formed them into a log that we chopped into thin slices that needed only a quick sauté. We rendered the flavorful fat from a few slices of bacon and used that as our sautéing fat (we also kept the crispy little nuggets of bacon) since these quick greens didn't have time to cook with a ham hock. We finished off with some aromatic garlic and then deglazed the pan with our intense pepper vinegar for brightness and heat. You can substitute mustard or turnip greens for the collards; reduce their boiling time to 2 minutes.

1 Bring 4 quarts water to boil in large pot. Stir in 1 tablespoon salt, then add collard greens, 1 handful at a time. Cook until tender, about 5 minutes. Drain collards in colander and rinse with cold water until greens are cool, about 1 minute. Drain, pressing greens with rubber spatula to release excess liquid.

2 Place greens on clean kitchen towel and compress into 10-inch log. Roll up towel tightly and squeeze over sink to release excess liquid. Remove greens from towel and cut crosswise into ¼-inch slices.

3 Cook bacon in 12-inch nonstick skillet over medium heat until crisp, 6 to 8 minutes. Increase heat to medium-high, stir in greens, and cook, stirring frequently, until lightly browned, 3 to 4 minutes. Stir in garlic and cook until greens are spotty brown, 1 to 2 minutes. Stir in vinegar and cook until liquid evaporates, about 30 seconds. Season with salt and pepper to taste. Serve, passing extra vinegar separately.

flank steak tacos with cumin and corn relish

serves 4 to 6

⅓ cup cider vinegar

1 tablespoon sugar

1 tablespoon water

½ teaspoon cumin seeds

½ teaspoon ground coriander

Salt and pepper

1 shallot, minced

1 poblano chile, stemmed, seeded, and cut into ¼-inch pieces

1 Fresno or jalapeño chile, stemmed, seeded, and minced

1 ear corn, kernels cut from cob

1 (1½- to 2-pound) flank steak, trimmed and cut with grain into 4 equal pieces

2 tablespoons vegetable oil

12 (6-inch) corn tortillas, warmed

why this recipe works These tacos are a clear example of how just one great spiced-infused condiment can make the meal—and make it easier. As lovers of tacos know, the key to a great one is its cornucopia of flavors, textures, and temperatures: Long-braised and intensely spiced meat, tangy pickles, crunchy vegetables, complex sauces, and warmed corn tortillas. This also means a lot of time and effort for the cook. We found we could get all the tang, crunch, and complexity we wanted in our taco simply by making a sweet-sour fresh corn salsa that is deeply flavored thanks to the judicious incorporation of a couple spices. We made a powerful brine of vinegar, cumin, and coriander for simmering some bright chiles. Corn kernels, added to the warm brine, became infused with its flavor as the mixture cooled. Then, for the beef, it was simply a matter of searing quick-cooking, tender flank steak. Just one spiced-infused condiment and some beefy flank steak and we had the liveliest of tacos to enjoy. Warm tortillas by stacking them on a plate, covering them with a damp dish towel, and microwaving for 60 to 90 seconds. If fresh corn is unavailable, you can substitute ¾ cup thawed frozen corn. We prefer to cook this steak to medium-rare, but if you prefer it more or less done, see our guidelines on page 280.

1 Bring vinegar, sugar, water, cumin seeds, coriander, and ½ teaspoon salt to boil in small saucepan over medium-high heat. Stir in shallot, poblano, and Fresno and cook until softened, about 5 minutes. Off heat, stir in corn and transfer to serving bowl. Let relish cool completely, about 30 minutes. Cover and refrigerate until chilled and flavors meld, about 1 hour. (Relish can be refrigerated for up to 1 month; flavor will continue to deepen over time.)

2 Pat steaks dry with paper towels and season with salt and pepper. Heat oil in 12-inch skillet over medium-high heat until just smoking. Cook steaks until well browned and meat registers 120 to 125 degrees (for medium-rare), 2 to 5 minutes per side. Transfer steaks to cutting board, tent with aluminum foil, and let rest for 5 minutes. Slice steaks thin against grain. Serve with tortillas and relish.

seared scallops with mango chutney and mint

serves 4

- 1 shallot, minced
- 3 tablespoons vegetable oil
- 1 teaspoon grated fresh ginger
- ½ teaspoon ground coriander
- ¼ teaspoon dry mustard
- ¼ teaspoon ground turmeric
- ⅛ teaspoon cayenne pepper
- 1 ripe but firm mango, peeled, pitted, and cut into ½-inch pieces (1½ cups)
- 2 tablespoons white wine vinegar
- 1 tablespoon dried currants
- 1 tablespoon packed light brown sugar
- Salt and pepper
- 2 tablespoons coarsely chopped mint
- 1½ pounds large sea scallops, tendons removed

why this recipe works If your experience with fruit chutneys is confined to the generic, sticky-sweet confected jars of the stuff, be assured that homemade versions are an altogether different class of conserve. They marry fresh-tasting fruits with bloomed Indian spices in a sweet-savory, tart-spicy profile and so can either add intrigue to simple dishes or complement and enliven more complex ones. Here we do the former; we particularly liked the pairing of mango chutney with sweet scallops that developed a nutty sear from a ripping hot pan. The clean-tasting seafood benefited from the spiced addition. We started by blooming spices in oil, their warmth soon offset by the luscious fruit of just-ripe mango. Some white wine vinegar in the infusing medium provided the pucker, and brown sugar and dried currants balanced it out with sweetness. A little shallot brought some fresh allium flavor and savor; not wanting to overpower the dish with its rawness, we moderated the shallot's bite by letting it soak in water while the chutney simmered away. A finishing sprinkle of mint made all the flavors come alive. We recommend buying "dry" scallops, which don't have chemical additives and taste better than "wet." Dry scallops will look ivory or pinkish; wet scallops are bright white.

1 Combine shallot and 2 cups water in bowl; set aside. Heat 1 tablespoon oil in small saucepan over medium heat until shimmering. Add ginger, coriander, mustard, turmeric, and cayenne and cook until fragrant, about 30 seconds. Stir in mango, ¼ cup water, vinegar, currants, sugar, and ¼ teaspoon salt. Bring to simmer and cook, stirring occasionally, until mixture is thickened and reduced to about 1 cup, 10 to 15 minutes. Drain shallot and stir into chutney. Let chutney cool to room temperature, about 30 minutes. Stir in mint and season with salt and pepper to taste.

2 Place scallops on rimmed baking sheet lined with clean kitchen towels. Place second clean kitchen towel on top of scallops and press gently on towel to blot liquid. Let scallops sit at room temperature, covered with towel, for 10 minutes.

3 Pat scallops dry and season with salt and pepper. Heat remaining 2 tablespoons oil in 12-inch skillet over high heat until just smoking. Add half of scallops in single layer and cook, without moving, until well browned on first side, about 1½ minutes. Flip scallops and continue to cook until sides are firm and centers are opaque, about 1½ minutes. Transfer scallops to plate and tent with aluminum foil. Repeat with remaining scallops; transfer to plate. Serve scallops with chutney.

go beyond vanilla

bringing sophisticated flavor to baked goods and desserts

When you hear "spiced," you might think of appetizers or lunch or dinner dishes like the ones found in this book so far. But you can make baked goods (sweet or savory) or your last course more interesting by looking beyond vanilla to flavor them (although vanilla is full of aroma itself!). Sure, this means turning to baking-spice classics like warm cinnamon, but it also means infusing custards with tea or making sweet buns with saffron and turmeric. Check out the homemade blends, infusions, and distillations we use to spice up our sweets, followed by the breakfast treats, breads, and desserts we developed to use them.

SWEETEN IT

Some spices are expected pairings with sweets: The round warmth of cinnamon, for example, adds depth to breakfast treats, cakes, cookies, fruit pies, and more. Throughout this chapter, we'll push your taste buds. Spices with floral qualities such as vanilla bean, dried lavender or rose, and saffron also taste lovely with desserts. Even the bite of black pepper or the earthiness of turmeric have a place in your baked goods.

› sweet spice blends

Spice up desserts in this chapter and more with these spice (and spice-sugar) blend ideas. The sugar mixes make about 1 cup and the spice blend makes about ½ cup. All can be stored in an airtight container at room temperature for up to 1 month.

vanilla sugar

- 2 vanilla beans
- 1 cup (7 ounces) sugar

Cut vanilla beans in half lengthwise. Using tip of paring knife or spoon, scrape out seeds. Using fingers, rub vanilla seeds and 2 tablespoons sugar in bowl until combined. Whisk in remaining sugar. Transfer sugar mixture and spent vanilla bean pods to airtight container and let sit until flavors meld, about 2 days.

› **how to use** Roll molasses or peanut butter drop cookie dough in sugar, sprinkle over pound cake batter or pie crust before baking, sweeten coffee or tea, toss with pears before roasting, sugar rim of cocktail glass, toss with fruit for fruit salad.

strawberry—black pepper sugar
You can find freeze-dried strawberries in the baking or natural foods aisle of most well-stocked supermarkets.

- 1¼ cups (1 ounce) freeze-dried strawberries
- ¾ cup (5¼ ounces) sugar
- 1 teaspoon pepper

Working in batches, process strawberries in spice grinder until finely ground, about 30 seconds. Transfer to small bowl and whisk in sugar and pepper.

› **how to use** Sprinkle over yogurt, shake over crème brûlée or other custards before torching, coat strips of puff pastry before twisting and baking into straws, roll logs of shortbread dough in sugar before slicing and baking, sprinkle over muffin batter before baking, toss with stone fruit before roasting, sprinkle on buttered toast.

pumpkin pie spice

- 6 (3-inch) cinnamon sticks, broken into pieces
- 2¾ teaspoons allspice berries
- 2 tablespoons ground ginger
- 1 tablespoon ground nutmeg

Working in batches, process cinnamon sticks and allspice in spice grinder until finely ground, about 30 seconds. Transfer to small bowl and whisk in ginger and nutmeg.

› **how to use** Stir into oatmeal or applesauce; toss with apples before sautéing, baking, or roasting; substitute for cinnamon in cinnamon rolls; add to drinks like coffee, mulled cider, or a hot toddy; flavor cream cheese frosting.

INFUSE AND DISTILL IT

Extract is an infusion that we make by steeping an ingredient in alcohol. (Yes, the same concept as in chapter five—this time on the sweeter side.) Making vanilla extract at home—if you buy the beans in bulk and use inexpensive vodka—will save you about $1 per ounce, and homemade vanilla has a more full-bodied taste. Rose water, a widely used ingredient in Middle Eastern and Indian cooking, is, as its name suggests, water touched with the flavor of roses. Traditionally, fresh rose petals are heated and the resulting vapors condensed to a liquid state and collected. This distillation produces a crystal clear hydrosol— a mixture of water and volatile essential oils. We were able to replicate this process at home for a delicate product—and a fun science experiment.

› spice extracts

Homemade vanilla extract and rose water are fresh-tasting— and deceptively easy. You'll impress when you divulge you've made your own for baking. Both make about 1 cup.

vanilla extract

Plan ahead; the extract needs to steep for at least 6 weeks before using. You will need a 1-pint Mason jar with a tight-fitting lid for this recipe. Heating the jar with warm water and then draining it before adding the hot brine ensures that the jar won't crack from the abrupt temperature change.

8 **vanilla beans**
1 **cup vodka**

1 Cut vanilla beans in half lengthwise. Using tip of paring knife or spoon, scrape out seeds and transfer to small saucepan. Cut vanilla bean pods into 1-inch pieces and add to saucepan. Add vodka, cover, and cook over medium-low heat until mixture is hot and steaming, about 2 minutes. (Do not open lid while pot is over flame or alcohol will ignite.)

2 Fill one 1-pint Mason jar with hot tap water to warm. Drain jar, then pour vanilla mixture into jar and let cool completely. Cover and let sit in dark place until flavors meld, at least 6 weeks or up to 10 weeks, shaking jar occasionally.

3 Line fine-mesh strainer with double layer of coffee filters and set over 2-cup liquid measuring cup. Strain extract through filters, then transfer to clean Mason jar with lid; discard solids. (Vanilla extract can be stored at room temperature for up to 3 months.)

maximum extraction

Vanilla extract tastes and smells a bit boozy; that's because alcohol enables maximum extraction of flavor from the beans. We use vodka (rather than rum or bourbon) for pure flavor. Scraping out the seeds helps speed extraction, as does heating the vodka.

distilling— in a dutch oven

To make small-batch rose water a reality using easy to obtain dried rose petals rather than fresh, we started by grinding the petals to make extraction more effective. We simmered these petals in water, placed a bowl in the pot, and inverted the lid. We added ice to the top of the lid. The rapid cooling of vapors produced condensation at the surface of the lid, which collected in the bowl.

rose water

This rose water is milder but more nuanced than store-bought rose water; plan to use about 3 times as much called for in recipes outside this book. Be sure to use food-grade dried rose buds, which you can find at spice shops and specialty markets. The ice bag helps the rose water steam condense on the underside of the lid and collect in the bowl. You will need a round Dutch oven and a heavy nonreactive heatproof bowl that will fit inside the pot.

2½ **ounces (4 cups) dried rose buds**
  4 **cups water**

1 Process rose buds in food processor until coarsely ground, about 1 minute; transfer to Dutch oven with water. Nestle nonreactive heatproof bowl into pot and cover pot with inverted lid. Fill 1-gallon zipper-lock freezer bag with ice; seal bag and place on lid. Cook over low heat, removing lid as little as possible, until about ¾ cup rose water collects in bowl, about 30 minutes. (Refill zipper-lock bag with ice as needed.)

2 Remove pot from heat and let sit, still covered, for 10 minutes. Carefully remove bowl from pot and transfer rose water to airtight container; discard solids. (Rose water can be refrigerated for up to 3 months.)

> how to use Flavor pound cake, custards, and rice pudding; add to simple syrup for cocktails or for soaking baked goods; stir into lemonade; add to frostings.

blueberry streusel muffins

makes 12 muffins

streusel

1¼ cups (6¼ ounces) all-purpose flour

⅓ cup packed (2⅓ ounces) dark brown sugar

⅓ cup (2⅓ ounces) granulated sugar

½ teaspoon ground cinnamon

   Pinch salt

7 tablespoons unsalted butter, melted

muffins

1 large egg

1 cup (7 ounces) granulated sugar

4 tablespoons unsalted butter, melted and cooled slightly

1 teaspoon vanilla extract

1 teaspoon grated lemon zest

½ cup buttermilk

2 cups (10 ounces) all-purpose flour

1 tablespoon baking powder

½ teaspoon salt

1½ cups frozen blueberries

why this recipe works Blueberry muffins are homey and comforting, but their ubiquity can make them a bit boring. We found just one addition turned blueberry muffins into the most sought-after choice in the breakfast bread basket: a cinnamon-spiced streusel topping. A crown of chewy streusel nuggets was a nice foil to a muffin base bursting with juicy berries (frozen, as fresh berries made our muffins soggy), and the warm spice rounded out the tartness of the fruit. Replacing the sour cream in our standard recipe with buttermilk created muffins with a sturdy-but-light texture that was able to support the weight of our streusel, which we broke into both cobbly chunks and smaller pea-size pieces for textural contrast. To prevent a streaky batter, leave the blueberries in the freezer until the last possible moment.

***

1 **for the streusel** Combine flour, brown sugar, granulated sugar, cinnamon, and salt in bowl. Drizzle with melted butter and toss with fork until evenly moistened and mixture forms large chunks with some pea-size pieces throughout; set aside.

2 **for the muffins** Adjust oven rack to middle position and heat oven to 375 degrees. Generously spray 12-cup muffin tin, including top, with baking spray with flour. Vigorously whisk egg, sugar, melted butter, vanilla, and lemon zest in large bowl until thick and combined. Add buttermilk and whisk until combined.

3 Set aside 1 tablespoon flour. Whisk remaining flour, baking powder, and salt together in separate bowl, then stir into egg mixture until just combined. Toss blueberries with reserved flour and fold into batter until just combined.

4 Divide batter evenly among prepared muffin cups and sprinkle evenly with streusel. Bake until light golden brown and toothpick inserted in center comes out with few moist crumbs attached, 23 to 27 minutes, rotating muffin tin halfway through baking. Let muffins cool in muffin tin on wire rack for 10 minutes. Remove muffins from muffin tin and let cool completely, about 1 hour. Serve.

pumpkin spice muffins

makes 12 muffins

streusel

- ½ cup (2½ ounces) all-purpose flour
- 5 tablespoons (2¼ ounces) sugar
- 1 teaspoon Pumpkin Pie Spice (page 234)
- Pinch salt
- 4 tablespoons unsalted butter, melted

muffins

- 1 cup canned unsweetened pumpkin puree
- 8 tablespoons unsalted butter, melted
- 2 large eggs
- ¼ cup milk
- 2 teaspoons vanilla extract
- 2½ cups (12½ ounces) all-purpose flour
- 2 cups (14 ounces) sugar
- 1 tablespoon Pumpkin Pie Spice (page 234)
- 2 teaspoons baking powder
- ¾ teaspoon salt

why this recipe works Pumpkin pie spice has become more than a baking ingredient—it's a part of popular culture. Originally intended for easily seasoning its namesake pie at the holidays, pumpkin pie spice deserves its place elsewhere—when it makes sense. (Packaged pumpkin spice kale chips? No thanks.) We give suggestions for a host of uses for homemade Pumpkin Pie Spice (see page 234), but here we use the spice blend sensibly in a pumpkin baked good. Pumpkin muffins become less vegetal and more multidimensional and full-flavored with a slight tingle from these sweet spices. To get the most out of our pumpkin pie spice, we added the spice mix not only to the muffin batter but also to the sweet, crunchy streusel topping; the spice in the batter gave the muffins a warm, subtle fragrance and the spice in the topping a more direct hit. Our favorite canned pumpkin puree is made by Libby's. We prefer our homemade Pumpkin Pie Spice (page 234), but you can substitute store-bought pumpkin pie spice.

1 **for the streusel** Combine flour, sugar, pumpkin pie spice, and salt in bowl. Drizzle with melted butter and toss with fork until evenly moistened and mixture forms large chunks with some pea-size pieces throughout; set aside.

2 **for the muffins** Adjust oven rack to middle position and heat oven to 375 degrees. Generously spray 12-cup muffin tin, including top, with baking spray with flour. Whisk pumpkin, melted butter, eggs, milk, and vanilla together in large bowl until combined. Whisk flour, sugar, pumpkin pie spice, baking powder, and salt together in separate bowl, then stir into pumpkin mixture until just combined.

3 Divide batter evenly among prepared muffin cups (batter should completely fill cups) and sprinkle evenly with streusel. Bake until golden brown and toothpick inserted in center comes out with few moist crumbs attached, 22 to 25 minutes, rotating muffin tin halfway through baking. Let muffins cool in muffin tin on wire rack for 10 minutes. Remove muffins from muffin tin and let cool completely, about 1 hour. Serve.

vanilla sugar doughnuts

**makes about
16 doughnuts**

3 cups (15 ounces) all-purpose
flour

2¼ teaspoons instant or
rapid-rise yeast

½ teaspoon salt

⅔ cup whole milk,
room temperature

2 large eggs

6 tablespoons (2⅔ ounces)
granulated sugar

6 tablespoons unsalted butter,
cut into 6 pieces and
softened

2 quarts peanut or vegetable oil

½ cup Vanilla Sugar (page 234)

Our yeasted doughnuts are light, fluffy, slightly chewy—and so good that
they're delicious rolled in just sugar. But they're even better when you
introduce one of our three spiced sugars or a glaze with our homemade
Rose Water. A quick toss or glaze and your kitchen is a trendy doughnut
shop. Be sure to use a small bowl to better coat the doughnuts in sugar.

1 Whisk flour, yeast, and salt
together in bowl of stand mixer.
Whisk milk, eggs, and sugar in
2-cup liquid measuring cup until
sugar has dissolved. Using dough
hook on low speed, slowly add milk
mixture to flour mixture and mix
until no dry flour remains, about
2 minutes, scraping down bowl as
needed. Increase speed to medium
and knead until dough begins to
form rough ball, 8 to 10 minutes.

2 Fit stand mixer with paddle.
With mixer running on medium
speed, add butter, 1 tablespoon at
a time, and knead until butter is
fully incorporated and dough is no
longer shiny, about 2 minutes.

3 Transfer dough to lightly
floured counter and knead by hand
to form smooth, round ball, about
30 seconds. Place seam side down
in lightly greased large bowl or
container, cover tightly with plastic
wrap, and let rise until nearly doubled in size, 2 to 2½ hours. (Unrisen
dough can be refrigerated for at
least 8 hours or up to 16 hours; let
sit at room temperature for 1 hour
before rolling in step 4.)

4 Set wire rack in rimmed baking
sheet. Line second sheet with
parchment paper and dust lightly
with flour. Press down on dough
to deflate, then transfer to lightly
floured counter. Press and roll dough
into 12-inch round, about ½ inch
thick. Cut dough using 2½- or
3-inch doughnut cutter, gathering
scraps and rerolling them as
needed. Place doughnut rings and
holes on floured sheet, cover loosely
with greased plastic, and let rise
until puffy, 30 to 45 minutes.

5 Add oil to large Dutch oven
until it measures about 1½ inches
deep and heat over medium-high
heat to 375 degrees. Gently drop
4 dough rings and 4 dough holes
into hot oil and fry until golden
brown, 1 to 2 minutes, flipping halfway through frying. Using wire
skimmer or slotted spoon, transfer
doughnuts and doughnut holes to
prepared wire rack.

6 Place vanilla sugar in small
bowl. Let doughnuts and doughnut
holes cool for 10 minutes, then toss
in vanilla sugar, pressing to adhere.
Serve warm or at room temperature.

rose water–glazed doughnuts

If using store-bought rose water, reduce amount to 1 teaspoon and supplement with 2 teaspoons of water.

Omit vanilla sugar. Whisk 2 cups confectioners' sugar, ¼ cup milk, 1 tablespoon Rose Water (page 237), and pinch salt in bowl until smooth. Dip 1 side of each doughnut and hole into glaze, let excess drip off, and return to wire rack. Let glaze set, about 15 minutes.

pumpkin spice sugar doughnuts

Omit vanilla sugar. Whisk ½ cup sugar and 1 tablespoon Pumpkin Pie Spice (page 234) until combined. Use sugar mixture to coat doughnuts in step 6.

strawberry–black pepper sugar doughnuts

Substitute Strawberry–Black Pepper Sugar (page 234) for vanilla sugar.

st. lucia buns

makes 16 buns

¼ cup boiling water

¼ teaspoon saffron threads, crumbled

⅛ teaspoon ground turmeric

3½ cups (17½ ounces) all-purpose flour

2 teaspoons instant or rapid-rise yeast

¾ cup whole milk, room temperature

6 tablespoons unsalted butter, melted

⅓ cup (2⅓ ounces) granulated sugar

2 large eggs (1 at room temperature, 1 lightly beaten with 1 tablespoon water and pinch salt)

1 teaspoon salt

⅓ cup currants

1 large egg, lightly beaten with 1 tablespoon water and pinch salt

¼ cup pearled sugar (optional)

why this recipe works Sunny yellow from their saffron flavoring, *Lussebullar*—also known as St. Lucia buns—are a staple of St. Lucia Day, which in Sweden is a festival of light that ushers in the holiday season. Saffron was revered in times past by royalty, but many modern commercial bakeries now rely on artificial food dye for their St. Lucia buns. We wanted to re-create the classic dough. We found through testing that we needed just a small amount of saffron—¼ teaspoon—to give these sweet treats balanced flavor, but this left the color a little lacking. We knew we didn't want to tint our buns with food coloring, so we turned to another yellow spice, turmeric, whose flavor went undetected. Steeping the saffron and turmeric in boiling water for 15 minutes helped release the full potential of the saffron's water-soluble flavor compounds. One-third cup each of sugar and currants (the customary mix-in) gave these buns just enough sweetness. While the dough can be shaped into a variety of traditional forms, we stuck with the most popular "S," or "cat's tail," shape. Brushing the buns with egg wash and giving each an optional sprinkling of pearled sugar created a glossy and festive finish. For an accurate measurement of boiling water, bring a full kettle of water to a boil and then measure out the desired amount. If the dough becomes too soft to work with at any point, refrigerate it until it's firm enough to easily handle.

1 Combine boiling water, saffron, and turmeric in small bowl and let steep for 15 minutes.

2 Whisk flour and yeast together in bowl of stand mixer. Whisk milk, melted butter, granulated sugar, egg, and saffron mixture in 4-cup liquid measuring cup until sugar has dissolved. Using dough hook on low speed, slowly add milk mixture to flour mixture and mix until cohesive dough starts to form and no dry flour remains, about 2 minutes, scraping down bowl as needed. Cover bowl and let dough sit for 10 minutes.

3 Add salt to dough and knead on medium-low speed until dough is smooth and elastic and clears sides of bowl but sticks to bottom, about 8 minutes. Reduce speed to low, slowly add currants, and mix until incorporated, about 2 minutes.

4 Transfer dough to lightly floured counter and knead by hand to form smooth, round ball, about 30 seconds. Place dough seam side down in lightly greased large bowl or container, cover tightly with greased plastic wrap, and let rise until increased in size by about half, 1½ to 2 hours.

5 Line 2 rimmed baking sheets with parchment paper. Press down on dough to deflate, then transfer to clean counter. Press and roll dough into 16 by 6-inch rectangle, with long side parallel to counter edge. Using pizza cutter or chef's knife, cut rectangle vertically into 16 (6 by 1-inch) strips and cover loosely with greased plastic.

6 Working with 1 dough strip at a time (keep remaining pieces covered), stretch and roll into 16-inch rope. (If dough resists stretching, let it relax for 5 to 10 minutes before trying to stretch it again.) Coil ends of rope in opposite directions to form tight S shape. Arrange buns on prepared sheets, spaced about 2½ inches apart. Cover loosely with greased plastic and let rise until puffy, 30 minutes to 1 hour.

7 Adjust oven racks to upper-middle and lower-middle positions and heat oven to 350 degrees. Gently brush buns with egg mixture and sprinkle with pearled sugar, if using. Bake until golden brown, 15 to 20 minutes, switching and rotating sheets halfway through baking. Transfer rolls to wire rack and let cool completely, about 1 hour, before serving.

spiced granola with walnuts and dried apple

makes about 9 cups

⅓ cup maple syrup

⅓ cup packed (2⅓ ounces) light brown sugar

4¾ teaspoons Pumpkin Pie Spice (page 234)

4 teaspoons vanilla extract

½ teaspoon salt

½ teaspoon pepper

½ cup vegetable oil

5 cups old-fashioned rolled oats

2 cups walnuts, chopped coarse

2 cups dried apples, chopped

why this recipe works Warm-spiced oats, toasty nuts, and dried apples are go-to breakfast ingredients when the air gets nippy. Whether topping yogurt, served with milk, or eaten out of hand, granola is the perfect vehicle for these flavors, but store-bought versions are often stale and too sweet (and expensive), and DIY recipes tend to turn out loose and gravelly mixes, with the delicious spices and mix-ins falling to the bottom of the container. We wanted granola with evenly distributed flavor and big, crisp clusters. We found granola shortcomings derive from the slow baking and frequent stirring, which prevent the ingredients from sticking together. Instead, we firmly packed the granola mixture into a rimmed baking sheet before baking. Once it was baked, we could break it into crunchy clumps of any size. We stirred a generous amount of pumpkin pie spice and vanilla extract into the maple syrup–brown sugar mix so they coated all the clusters, and their flavor carried. The pie spice allowed us to get the full flavor from a few spices in just one dash. Walnuts and dried apples completed the fall feel. Do not use quick-cooking oats. We prefer to use our homemade Pumpkin Pie Spice (page 234), but you can substitute store-bought pumpkin pie spice.

1 Adjust oven rack to upper-middle position and heat oven to 325 degrees. Whisk maple syrup, sugar, pumpkin pie spice, vanilla, salt, and pepper together in large bowl, then whisk in oil. Fold in oats and walnuts until thoroughly coated.

2 Transfer oat mixture to parchment paper–lined rimmed baking sheet and spread into thin, even layer about ⅜ inch thick. Using stiff metal spatula, compress oat mixture until very compact. Bake until lightly browned, 40 to 45 minutes, rotating sheet halfway through baking.

3 Let granola cool completely in sheet on wire rack, about 1 hour. Break cooled granola into pieces of desired size. Stir in apples and serve. (Granola can be stored at room temperature for up to 2 weeks.)

tropical granola with dried mango and ginger

Omit pumpkin pie spice and add 1½ teaspoons ground ginger and ¾ teaspoon freshly grated nutmeg. Reduce vanilla extract to 2 teaspoons. Substitute coarsely chopped macadamias for walnuts, 1½ cups unsweetened shredded coconut for 1 cup of oats, and chopped dried mango for apples.

southern cheese straws

makes about 48 cheese straws

8 ounces extra-sharp cheddar cheese, shredded (2 cups)

1½ cups (7½ ounces) all-purpose flour

8 tablespoons unsalted butter, cut into 8 pieces and chilled

¾ teaspoon salt

¾ teaspoon paprika

½ teaspoon baking powder

¼ teaspoon cayenne pepper

3 tablespoons ice water

why this recipe works These delicate, crumbly, cheesy, buttery spiced crackers are popular in the South but should be required snacking everywhere. And while they're mostly about the cheese, the crackers would have one-note richness without the added pizazz of some back-up spices: sweet, peppery paprika and cayenne. These give the cracker interest, back up the extra-sharp cheddar's bold flavor, and add pleasant heat. To make a version that mimicked cheese straws' signature decorative stripes without using a cookie press, we rolled out the dough into a square and made lines with the tines of a fork before cutting the dough into strips and baking. Using a food processor to buzz the grated cheese, chilled butter, flour, and baking powder together resulted in crackers with a short, extra-tender texture. A variation pairs nutty Parmesan and black pepper for a slightly more refined straw with the perfect salt and pepper balance.

1 Adjust oven rack to middle position and heat oven to 350 degrees. Line rimmed baking sheet with parchment paper. Process cheddar, flour, butter, salt, paprika, baking powder, and cayenne in food processor until mixture resembles wet sand, about 20 seconds. Add ice water and process until dough ball starts to form, about 25 seconds.

2 Transfer dough to lightly floured counter and knead by hand to form smooth, round ball, about 30 seconds. Using your hands, pat dough into rough 4-inch square. Roll dough into 10-inch square, about ¼ inch thick, flouring counter and dough as needed to prevent sticking.

3 Position dough so 1 side is parallel to counter edge. Using rounded side of fork, drag tines across entire surface of dough to make decorative lines. Using pizza cutter or chef's knife, trim away and discard outer ½ inch of dough to make neat square. Cut dough into 3 equal pieces perpendicular to lines. Working with 1 section of dough at a time, cut into ½-inch-wide strips in direction of lines.

4 Evenly space cheese straws on prepared sheet, about ½ inch apart. Bake until edges of straws are light golden brown, 35 to 40 minutes, rotating sheet halfway through baking. Let straws cool completely on sheet. Serve. (Straws can be stored at room temperature for up to 1 week.)

parmesan–black pepper cheese straws

Reduce extra-sharp cheddar to 6 ounces (1½ cups). Add 1 cup grated Parmesan to food processor with flour in step 1. Substitute 1 teaspoon pepper for cayenne.

everything bagel bread

makes 1 loaf

- 3 cups (16½ ounces) bread flour
- 2¼ teaspoons instant or rapid-rise yeast
- ¼ cup light corn syrup
- 2¼ teaspoons salt
- 1½ teaspoons baking soda
- ¼ cup Everything Bagel Blend (page 159)
- 1 large egg, lightly beaten

why this recipe works We won't discriminate against any bagel in the test kitchen, but the "everything" bagel has, well, everything, with its aromatic seasoning and seedy crunch. In fact, the flavor, density, and chew of everything bagels make us want to use them in a number of bready applications—except they don't fit in some toasters, and they don't lend themselves well to sandwich making. Enter: bagel bread, a sliceable (and toastable) loaf. We sprinkled the surface of the loaf pan as well as the high-protein bagel bread dough with our home-made Everything Bagel Blend so there was plenty of seasoning. We even boiled the risen, not-yet-baked loaf in a solution of water, baking soda, and corn syrup, just like with real bagels; this achieved a lovely brown crust and gently set exterior so that when the dough continued to rise in the oven, it had a tight, chewy crumb. Making slashes across the top of the dough allowed steam to escape as it baked and expanded. The resulting loaf delivered bagel-like bliss. We prefer our homemade Everything Bagel Blend (page 159), but you can substitute store-bought everything bagel topping if you wish. The test kitchen's preferred loaf pan measures 8½ by 4½ inches; if you use a 9 by 5-inch pan, start checking for doneness 5 minutes early.

1 Spray 8½ by 4½-inch loaf pan with vegetable oil spray. Whisk flour and yeast together in bowl of stand mixer. Whisk 1¼ cups room temperature water and 2 tablespoons corn syrup in 4-cup liquid measuring cup until syrup has dissolved. Using dough hook on low speed, slowly add water mixture to flour mixture and mix until cohesive dough starts to form and no dry flour remains, about 2 minutes, scraping down bowl as needed. Cover bowl and let dough sit for 10 minutes.

2 Add salt to dough and knead on medium speed until dough is smooth and elastic, about 10 minutes. Transfer dough to clean counter and form into round ball by pinching and pulling edges under so top is smooth. Flip dough smooth side down.

3 Pat dough into 6-inch square and position parallel to counter edge. Fold top edge of dough down to midline, pressing to seal. Fold bottom edge of dough up to meet first seam at midline and press to seal. Fold dough in half so top and bottom edges meet; pinch together to seal. Flip dough seam side down and roll into 8-inch log.

4 Transfer to prepared pan, seam side down, and cover loosely with greased plastic wrap. Let sit in warm place until dough rises to lip of pan, about 1 hour.

5   Adjust oven rack to middle position and heat oven to 350 degrees. Line large plate with clean dish towel. Bring 2 quarts water to boil in Dutch oven. Once boiling, add baking soda and remaining 2 tablespoons corn syrup.

6   Gently tip dough out of pan onto counter. Lift dough, gently lower into boiling water, and cook for 45 seconds per side. Using wire skimmer or 2 slotted spoons, transfer dough to prepared plate. Fold dish towel over dough gently to wick away excess moisture on top. Let sit until cool enough to handle, about 2 minutes.

7   Respray now-empty pan with oil spray. Add 2 tablespoons bagel blend to pan and shake until bottom and sides of pan are evenly coated. Transfer dough to prepared pan, seam side down, pushing it in at edges to fit if necessary.

8   Using paring knife, make six ¼-inch-deep slashes crosswise along surface of dough, about 1 inch apart. Brush dough with egg, then sprinkle with remaining 2 tablespoons bagel blend. Bake until golden brown and loaf registers at least 200 degrees, about 45 minutes. Let bread cool completely in pan, about 2 hours. Remove from pan, slice, and serve, toasted if desired.

za'atar finger bread

serves 6 to 8

3½ cups (19¼ ounces) bread flour

2½ teaspoons instant or rapid-rise yeast

2½ teaspoons sugar

1⅓ cups ice water

½ cup plus 2 tablespoons extra-virgin olive oil

2 teaspoons salt

⅓ cup Za'atar (page 156)

Coarse finishing salt

why this recipe works Inspired by *mana'eesh*, a round Arabic flatbread almost completely covered with a thick coating of zesty, herbal za'atar, we set out to develop a recipe for a finger-licking-good snack bread to eat alone or to dip in a yogurt sauce. To showcase the za'atar, we started by kneading together a simple dough; stretching it across a baking sheet; and slathering it with the oil-moistened za'atar. The top was a delight, but the bottom of the bread paled in comparison—it was blond and limp. Coating the pan with a generous amount of olive oil essentially fried the bottom of the flatbread as it baked, and shifting the oven rack to the lower-middle position created a crisp, golden base. We prefer to use our homemade Za'atar (page 156), but you can use store-bought za'atar; different za'atar blends include varying salt amounts. You can use your preferred coarse finishing salt in this recipe; for more information on finishing salts, see pages 22–23. Plan ahead; you will need to refrigerate the dough for at least 24 hours or up to 3 days before baking.

1   Pulse flour, yeast, and sugar in food processor until combined, about 5 pulses. With processor running, slowly add ice water and process until dough is just combined and no dry flour remains, about 10 seconds. Let dough rest for 10 minutes.

2   Add 2 tablespoons oil and salt to dough and process until dough forms satiny, sticky ball that clears sides of bowl, 30 to 60 seconds. Transfer dough to lightly floured counter and knead by hand to form smooth, round ball, about 30 seconds. Place seam side down in lightly greased large bowl or container, cover tightly with plastic wrap, and refrigerate for at least 24 hours or up to 3 days.

3   Remove dough from refrigerator and let sit at room temperature for 1 hour. Coat rimmed baking sheet with 2 tablespoons oil. Gently press down on dough to deflate any large gas pockets. Transfer dough to prepared sheet and, using your fingertips, press out to uniform thickness, taking care not to tear dough. (Dough may not fit snugly into corners.) Cover loosely with greased plastic and let dough rest for 1 hour.

4   Adjust oven rack to lower-middle position and heat oven to 375 degrees. Using your fingertips, gently press dough into corners of sheet and dimple entire surface. Combine remaining 6 tablespoons oil and za'atar in bowl. Using back of spoon, spread oil mixture in even layer over entire surface of dough to edge. Bake until bottom crust is evenly browned and edges are crisp, 20 to 25 minutes, rotating sheet halfway through baking. Let bread cool in sheet for 10 minutes, then transfer to cutting board with metal spatula. Sprinkle with finishing salt to taste, tear into large pieces, and serve warm.

molasses spice cookies

makes 24 cookies

2¼ cups (11¼ ounces) all-purpose
    flour

 1 teaspoon baking soda

1½ teaspoons ground cinnamon

1½ teaspoons ground ginger

 ½ teaspoon ground cloves

 ¼ teaspoon ground allspice

 ¼ teaspoon salt

 ¼ teaspoon pepper

12 tablespoons unsalted butter,
    softened

 ⅓ cup packed (2⅓ ounces) dark
    brown sugar

 ⅓ cup (2⅓ ounces) granulated sugar

 1 large egg yolk

 1 teaspoon vanilla extract

 ½ cup molasses

 ½ cup Vanilla Sugar (page 234)

why this recipe works The best molasses spice cookies combine a homespun crinkled appearance with a chewy texture and a gently spiced, deep molasses flavor. Molasses is an assertive sweetener so we needed a powerful yet balanced team of spices to complement it. Cinnamon, ginger, cloves, allspice, and black pepper provided warmth and just enough bite, and a spoonful of vanilla smoothed out any rough edges. A roll in granulated sugar is a given for molasses cookies for a crackly exterior, and we thought this was a nice place to use our Vanilla Sugar (page 234), which complemented the spices within without overshadowing them. When rolling the balls of dough, we found that dipping our hands in water prevented the dough from sticking to them and also helped the sugar adhere to the dough balls. For the best texture and appearance, be sure to bake the cookies one sheet at a time and pull them from the oven when they still look substantially underdone. (They will continue to bake and harden as they cool, with the insides remaining soft and moist.) Do not use blackstrap molasses here as it is too bitter.

1 Adjust oven rack to middle position and heat oven to 375 degrees. Line 2 rimmed baking sheets with parchment paper. Whisk flour, baking soda, cinnamon, ginger, cloves, allspice, salt, and pepper together in bowl.

2 Using stand mixer fitted with paddle, beat butter, brown sugar, and granulated sugar on medium speed until pale and fluffy, about 3 minutes. Reduce speed to medium-low, add egg yolk and vanilla, and beat until combined, about 30 seconds. Beat in molasses until incorporated, about 30 seconds, scraping down bowl as needed. Reduce speed to low and slowly add flour mixture until combined, about 30 seconds (dough will be soft). Give dough final stir by hand to ensure that no flour pockets remain.

3 Place vanilla sugar in small bowl. Working with 2 tablespoons dough at a time, roll into balls with your dampened hands, then roll in vanilla sugar to coat. Space dough balls 2 inches apart on prepared sheets. (Dough balls can be frozen for up to 1 month; bake frozen dough balls in 300 degree oven for 30 to 35 minutes.)

4 Bake cookies, 1 sheet at a time, until edges are set but centers are still soft, puffy, and cracked (cookies will look raw between cracks and seem underdone), 10 to 12 minutes, rotating sheet halfway through baking. Let cookies cool on sheet for 10 minutes. Serve warm or transfer to wire rack and let cool completely.

anise biscotti

makes 30 cookies

Vegetable oil spray

1¼ cups whole almonds, lightly toasted

1¾ cups (8¾ ounces) all-purpose flour

2 teaspoons baking powder

1½ teaspoons anise seeds

¼ teaspoon salt

2 large eggs, plus 1 large white beaten with pinch salt

1 cup (7 ounces) sugar

4 tablespoons unsalted butter, melted and cooled

1½ teaspoons anise-flavored liqueur (such as ouzo or anisette)

½ teaspoon vanilla extract

why this recipe works Biscotti, twice-baked cookies that are perfect alongside coffee or a glass of vin santo, come in a few classic flavor variations, but we love the aromatic, licorice-y flavor of anise versions. Their herbal notes offset the deep nuttiness of the almonds for an intriguing sweet treat. We made the dough in the food processor; mixing the anise seeds with the flour broke them down a bit. A small splash of anise liqueur backed up the seeds' flavor. The almonds will continue to toast during baking, so toast them just until they're fragrant.

1 Adjust oven rack to middle position and heat oven to 325 degrees. Using ruler and pencil, draw two 8 by 3-inch rectangles, spaced 4 inches apart, on piece of parchment paper. Spray baking sheet with oil spray and place parchment on it, marked side down.

2 Pulse 1 cup almonds in food processor until coarsely chopped, 8 to 10 pulses; transfer to small bowl and set aside. Process remaining ¼ cup almonds in now-empty food processor until finely ground, about 45 seconds. Add flour, baking powder, anise seeds, and salt and process to combine, about 15 seconds. Transfer flour mixture to second bowl. Process 2 eggs in now-empty food processor until lightened in color and almost doubled in volume, about 3 minutes. With processor running, slowly add sugar until thoroughly combined, about 15 seconds. Add melted butter, anise liqueur, and vanilla and process until combined, about 10 seconds. Transfer egg mixture to large bowl. Sprinkle half of flour mixture over egg mixture and, using spatula, gently fold until just combined. Add remaining flour mixture and chopped almonds and gently fold until just combined.

3 Divide dough in half. Using floured hands, form each half into 8 by 3-inch rectangle, using lines on parchment as guide. Spray each loaf lightly with oil spray. Using rubber spatula lightly coated with oil spray, smooth tops and sides of loaves. Gently brush tops of loaves with beaten egg white.

4 Bake until loaves are golden and just beginning to crack on top, 25 to 30 minutes, rotating sheet halfway through baking. Let loaves cool on sheet for 30 minutes, then transfer to cutting board. Using serrated knife, slice each loaf on slight bias into ½-inch-thick pieces.

5 Set wire rack in rimmed baking sheet. Space slices, cut side down, about ¼ inch apart on prepared rack. Bake until crisp and golden brown on both sides, about 35 minutes, flipping slices halfway through baking. Let cool completely before serving. (Biscotti can be stored at room temperature for up to 1 month.)

pistachio baklava with cardamom and rose water

makes 32 to 40 pieces

sugar syrup

1¾ cups (12¼ ounces) sugar

½ cup plus 1 tablespoon water

1 tablespoon lemon juice

10 black peppercorns

⅛ teaspoon salt

3 tablespoons Rose Water (page 237)

nut filling

2¾ cups (12 ounces) shelled pistachios

2 tablespoons sugar

1 teaspoon ground cardamom

⅛ teaspoon salt

pastry

5 tablespoons extra-virgin olive oil

1 pound (14 by 9-inch) phyllo, thawed

why this recipe works Many know the flavors of Greek-style baklava, with its honey, nuts (often walnuts or a combination), and warm baking spices. It's delicious, but there are equally intriguing variations baked across the Middle East. We love the enchanting combination of a rose water–kissed syrup soaking phyllo diamonds with a cardamom-spiced pistachio filling. The pastries are a floral, earthy, sweet treat. It's also an example of how a simple stir-in of rose water can pleasantly perfume and instantly elevate a dish. Letting the baklava sit overnight before serving dramatically improved its flavor. A straight-sided traditional metal baking pan works best for making baklava. Phyllo dough is also available in larger 18 by 14-inch sheets; if using, cut them in half to make 14 by 9-inch sheets. Do not thaw the phyllo in the microwave; let it sit in the refrigerator overnight or on the counter for 4 to 5 hours. While working with the phyllo, cover the sheets with plastic wrap and then a damp dish towel to prevent drying. Use the nicest, most intact phyllo sheets for the bottom and top layers; use sheets with tears or ones that are smaller than the size of the pan in the middle layers, where their imperfections will go unnoticed. We prefer to use our home-made Rose Water, but you can use store-bought rose water; if using store-bought, reduce rose water to 1 tablespoon and increase water to ¾ cup.

1 **for the sugar syrup** Bring sugar, water, lemon juice, peppercorns, and salt to boil in small saucepan over medium-high heat and cook, stirring occasionally, until sugar has dissolved, about 5 minutes. Transfer syrup to 2-cup liquid measuring cup and let cool completely. Discard peppercorns, stir in rose water, and set aside.

2 **for the nut filling** Pulse pistachios in food processor until very finely chopped, about 15 pulses; transfer to bowl. Measure out 1 tablespoon pistachios and set aside for garnish. Add sugar, cardamom, and salt to nut mixture and toss well to combine.

3 **for the pastry** Adjust oven rack to lower-middle position and heat oven to 300 degrees. Lay 1 phyllo sheet in bottom of greased 13 by 9-inch baking pan and brush thoroughly with oil. Repeat with 7 more phyllo sheets, brushing each with oil (you should have total of 8 layers of phyllo).

4 Sprinkle about one-third of nut filling evenly over phyllo. Cover nut filling with 6 more phyllo sheets, brushing each with oil, then sprinkle with additional one-third of nut filling. Repeat with 6 phyllo sheets, oil, and remaining nut filling.

5 Cover nut filling with 8 more phyllo sheets, brushing each layer, except final layer, with oil. Working from center outward, use palms of your hands to compress layers and press out any air pockets. Spoon remaining oil (about 2 tablespoons) on top layer and brush to cover surface.

6 Using serrated knife with pointed tip, cut baklava into diamonds. Bake until golden and crisp, about 1½ hours, rotating pan halfway through baking. Immediately pour all but 2 tablespoons cooled syrup over cut lines (syrup will sizzle when it hits hot pan). Drizzle remaining 2 tablespoons syrup over surface. Garnish center of each piece with pinch reserved pistachios. Let baklava cool completely in pan, about 3 hours, then cover with aluminum foil and let sit at room temperature for 8 hours before serving.

lavender tea cakes

makes 12 tea cakes

cakes

- ⅔ cup (4⅔ ounces) plus 2 tablespoons granulated sugar
- 8 tablespoons unsalted butter, 6 tablespoons cut into 6 pieces and softened, 2 tablespoons melted
- 1 cup (5 ounces) all-purpose flour
- ½ teaspoon salt
- ½ teaspoon baking powder
- ¼ teaspoon baking soda
- 1½ teaspoons dried lavender
- ¼ cup buttermilk, room temperature
- 1 teaspoon vanilla extract
- 2 large eggs, room temperature

glaze

- 1 vanilla bean
- 1¾ cups (7 ounces) confectioners' sugar
- 2–4 tablespoons milk

why this recipe works With tender, buttery interiors and fine, crisp exteriors, these lavender-infused tea cakes are a sophisticated treat. The key with dried lavender is adding enough that it's present, but not so much that your pastry tastes like soap; just 1½ teaspoons in the cakes carried its flavor throughout. To keep the cakes from sticking and to ensure a crackly exterior, we brushed the muffin tin with butter and sugar. After baking, we inverted the cakes so that their flat bottoms became the tops. We then bathed each in a bright-white glaze dotted with complementary vanilla bean. For a darling touch, decorate the cakes with candied violets. Be sure to use food-grade dried lavender, which you can find at spice shops and specialty markets.

1 **for the cakes** Adjust oven rack to lower-middle position and heat oven to 325 degrees. Whisk 2 tablespoons sugar and melted butter together in bowl. Brush 12-cup muffin tin with butter-sugar mixture.

2 Whisk flour, salt, baking powder, and baking soda together in bowl; set aside. Process lavender in spice grinder until coarsely ground, about 15 seconds; transfer to small bowl and whisk in buttermilk and vanilla. Using stand mixer fitted with paddle, beat remaining 6 table-spoons butter and remaining ⅔ cup sugar on medium-high speed until pale and fluffy, about 3 minutes. Add eggs, one at a time, and beat until combined. Reduce speed to low and add flour mixture in 3 additions, alternating with buttermilk mixture in 2 additions, scraping down bowl as needed. Increase speed to medium-high and beat until completely smooth, about 30 seconds. Give dough final stir by hand to ensure that no flour pockets remain.

3 Divide batter evenly among prepared muffin cups and smooth tops. Bake until golden brown and toothpick inserted in center of cake comes out clean, about 15 minutes, rotating muffin tin halfway through baking.

4 Let cakes cool in muffin tin on wire rack for 10 minutes. Invert muffin tin over wire rack and gently tap pan several times to help cakes release. Let cakes cool on rack, bottom side up, until completely cool, about 30 minutes. (Unglazed cakes can be stored in airtight container at room temperature for up to 24 hours.)

5 **for the glaze** Cut vanilla bean in half lengthwise. Using tip of paring knife or spoon, scrape out seeds. Whisk vanilla seeds, sugar, and 2 tablespoons milk together in bowl until smooth. Gradually add remaining 2 tablespoons milk as needed, 1 teaspoon at a time, until glaze is thick but pourable. Spoon glaze over top of each cooled cake, letting some drip down sides. Let glaze set for 10 minutes before serving.

gingerbread layer cake

serves 12 to 16

cake

1¾ cups (8¾ ounces) all-purpose flour

¼ cup (¾ ounce) unsweetened cocoa powder

2 tablespoons ground ginger

1½ teaspoons baking powder

1 teaspoon ground cinnamon

¾ teaspoon salt

½ teaspoon white pepper

⅛ teaspoon cayenne pepper

1 cup brewed coffee

¾ cup molasses

½ teaspoon baking soda

1½ cups (10½ ounces) sugar

¾ cup vegetable oil

3 large eggs, lightly beaten

2 tablespoons finely grated fresh ginger

¼ cup chopped crystallized ginger (optional)

frosting

1½ cups (10½ ounces) sugar

¼ cup (1¼ ounces) all-purpose flour

3 tablespoons cornstarch

½ teaspoon salt

1½ cups milk

24 tablespoons (3 sticks) unsalted butter, softened

2 teaspoons vanilla extract

why this recipe works Good gingerbread is dark and moist, with an intriguing hint of bitterness and a peppery finish. Usually it's a rustic square cake or maybe even an attractive Bundt, but why not give such a rich-tasting cake centerpiece status? We wanted to transform homey gingerbread into a stately layer cake. We knew we'd be filling and adorning our cake with frosting, which is naturally sweet and rich, so we wanted the cake to pack a kick you don't get in classic layer cakes. Ginger-three-ways put the ginger in gingerbread with bright flavor from freshly grated knobs, round heat from a generous amount of ground, and texture and good looks from an adornment of crystallized ginger. Cayenne and multidimensional white pepper bolstered the heat, and cinnamon gave the cake warm round notes. Replacing some of the flour with cocoa powder, an unexpected ingredient in gingerbread, added depth to the color and the molasses flavor. Bonus: As cocoa powder is mostly gluten-free starch and fat, it increased the cake's tenderness. A cooked vanilla frosting formed an extremely lush, silky coating, and its simple flavor let the spicy cake shine. Use a 2-cup liquid measuring cup to portion the cake batter. Do not use blackstrap molasses here as it is too bitter.

1 **for the cake** Adjust oven rack to middle position and heat oven to 350 degrees. Grease and flour two 8-inch round cake pans and line pans with parchment paper. Whisk flour, cocoa, ground ginger, baking powder, cinnamon, salt, white pepper, and cayenne together in large bowl. Whisk coffee, molasses, and baking soda in second bowl until combined. Add sugar, oil, eggs, and fresh ginger to coffee mixture and whisk until smooth.

2 Whisk coffee mixture into flour mixture until smooth. Pour 1⅓ cups batter into each prepared pan. Bake until toothpick inserted in center of cake comes out clean, 12 to 14 minutes. Let cakes cool in pans on wire rack for 10 minutes. Remove cakes from pan, discarding parchment, and let cool completely on rack, about 2 hours.

3 Meanwhile, wipe pans clean with paper towels. Let pans cool completely, then regrease and reflour pans and line with fresh parchment. Repeat process with remaining batter.

4 **for the frosting** Whisk sugar, flour, cornstarch, and salt together in medium saucepan. Slowly whisk in milk until smooth. Cook over medium heat, whisking constantly and scraping corners of saucepan, until mixture boils and is very thick, 4 to 8 minutes. Transfer mixture to wide bowl and let cool completely, about 2 hours.

5 Using stand mixer fitted with paddle, beat butter on medium-high speed until pale and fluffy, about 5 minutes. Reduce speed to medium, add cooled milk mixture and vanilla, and mix until combined, scraping down sides of bowl as needed. Increase speed to medium-high and beat until frosting is light and fluffy, 3 to 5 minutes.

6 Line edges of cake platter with 4 strips of parchment to keep platter clean. Place 1 cake layer on platter. Spread ¾ cup frosting evenly over top, right to edge of cake. Repeat with 2 more cake layers, pressing lightly to adhere and spreading ¾ cup frosting evenly over each layer. Top with remaining cake layer and spread remaining frosting evenly over top and sides of cake. Garnish top of cake with crystallized ginger, if using. Refrigerate until frosting is set, about 30 minutes. Serve. (Cake can be refrigerated for up to 2 days; bring to room temperature before serving.)

pink peppercorn–pomegranate panna cotta

serves 6

- 2 cups heavy cream
- 3 tablespoons pink peppercorns, cracked
- 1 cup pomegranate juice
- 2 teaspoons unflavored gelatin
- 3 tablespoons sugar
- ⅛ teaspoon salt
- ½ cup pomegranate seeds
- Shaved white chocolate
- Coarse finishing salt

why this recipe works We use pink peppercorns in a number of savory applications, but these peppercorns (not true pepper) are by far the fruitiest and most floral of the varieties, so they take well to dessert. The clean dairy flavor of creamy panna cotta was a lovely canvas for the subtle pungency of pink pepper, which we used to infuse our cream base. To balance the spiciness and richness, we incorporated pomegranate juice into the base, which provided not only complementary fruitiness but also smashing color. A garnish of pomegranate seeds and shaved white chocolate was a rich adornment, while a touch of coarse finishing salt brought all the flavors to life. To serve unmolded, you'll need six 4- to 5-ounce ramekins. Panna cotta may also be chilled and served in wineglasses. If you'd like to make the panna cotta a day ahead, reduce the amount of gelatin by ½ teaspoon and chill the filled ramekins for at least 18 hours or up to 24 hours. You can use your preferred coarse finishing salt in this recipe; for more information on finishing salts, see pages 22–23.

1 Bring heavy cream and peppercorns to simmer in medium saucepan over medium heat. Transfer to bowl, cover, and let sit until flavors meld, about 10 minutes.

2 Meanwhile, pour pomegranate juice into clean medium saucepan. Sprinkle surface evenly with gelatin and let sit until gelatin softens, about 5 minutes. Fill large bowl halfway with ice and water. Set six 4-to 5-ounce ramekins on rimmed baking sheet.

3 Heat juice and gelatin mixture over high heat, stirring constantly, until gelatin is dissolved and mixture registers 135 degrees, 1 to 2 minutes. Off heat, whisk in sugar and salt until dissolved, about 1 minute. Stirring constantly, slowly add cream mixture. Transfer mixture to now-empty bowl and set over prepared ice water bath. Stir mixture often until slightly thickened and mixture registers 50 degrees, about 20 minutes. Strain mixture through fine-mesh strainer into 4-cup liquid measuring cup, then divide evenly among ramekins. Cover all ramekins on baking sheet with plastic wrap and refrigerate until panna cottas are just set (mixture should wobble when shaken gently), at least 4 hours or up to 12 hours.

4 To unmold, run paring knife around perimeter of each ramekin. (If shape of ramekin makes this difficult, quickly dip ramekin into hot water bath to loosen panna cotta.) Hold serving plate over top of each ramekin and invert; set plate on counter and gently shake ramekin to release panna cotta. Sprinkle with pomegranate seeds, white chocolate shavings, and finishing salt. Serve.

crème brûlée

serves 6

1 vanilla bean

3 cups heavy cream

½ cup (3½ ounces) granulated sugar

Pinch salt

9 large egg yolks

9 teaspoons turbinado sugar or Demerara sugar

why this recipe works Crème brûlée is one of those traditional last courses that sticks around for good reason: It's much about the contrast between the crisp sugar crust and the silky vanilla-scented custard underneath. A vanilla bean gives our classic crème brûlée luxuriance that we love. But we also wanted to play with other ways to flavor crème brûlée, as custard is one of the easiest dessert mediums to infuse with spice flavor. Dried tea leaves are a spice themselves, so for one variation we steeped Irish Breakfast tea bags in the cream for a custard with warm, distinctive flavor that complemented the deeply caramelized crust. Another variation let orange blossom water lend an elegant floral, citrus flavor that challenged the traditional. Separate the eggs and whisk the yolks after the cream has finished steeping; if left to sit, the surface of the yolks will dry and form a film. While we prefer turbinado or Demerara sugar for the caramelized sugar crust, regular granulated sugar will work, too, but use only 1 teaspoon for each ramekin. Once the sugar on top is brûléed, serve within 30 minutes or the sugar crust will soften. You will need six 4- to 5-ounce ramekins (or shallow fluted dishes) for this recipe.

1 Adjust oven rack to lower-middle position and heat oven to 300 degrees. Cut vanilla bean in half lengthwise. Using tip of paring knife or spoon, scrape out vanilla seeds. Combine vanilla bean pod and seeds, 2 cups cream, granulated sugar, and salt in medium saucepan. Bring mixture to boil over medium heat, stirring occasionally to dissolve sugar. Off heat, cover and let steep for 15 minutes.

2 Stir remaining 1 cup cream into cream mixture. Whisk egg yolks in large bowl until uniform. Whisk about 1 cup cream mixture into yolks, then repeat with 1 cup more cream mixture. Whisk in remaining cream mixture until thoroughly combined. Strain mixture through fine-mesh strainer into 8-cup liquid measuring cup, discarding solids.

3 Meanwhile, place dish towel in bottom of large baking dish or roasting pan. Set six 4- or 5-ounce ramekins (or shallow fluted dishes) on towel. Bring kettle of water to boil.

4 Divide cream mixture evenly among ramekins. Set baking dish on oven rack. Taking care not to splash water into ramekins, pour enough boiling water into dish to reach two-thirds up sides of ramekins. Bake until centers of custards are just barely set and register 170 to 175 degrees, 25 to 35 minutes depending on ramekin type, checking temperature 5 minutes early.

5   Transfer ramekins to wire rack and let custards cool completely, about 2 hours. Set ramekins on rimmed baking sheet, cover tightly with plastic wrap, and refrigerate until cold, about 4 hours.

6   Uncover ramekins and gently blot tops dry with paper towels. Sprinkle each with 1 to 1½ teaspoons turbinado sugar (depending on ramekin type). Tilt and tap each ramekin to distribute sugar evenly, then dump out excess sugar and wipe rims of ramekins clean. Caramelize sugar with torch until deep golden brown, continually sweeping flame about 2 inches above ramekin. Serve.

orange blossom crème brûlée

Add 2 teaspoons orange blossom water to strained custard before portioning into ramekins.

tea-infused crème brûlée

Substitute 10 Irish Breakfast tea bags, tied together, for vanilla bean; after steeping tea in cream, squeeze bags with tongs or press into fine-mesh strainer to extract all liquid. Whisk 1 teaspoon vanilla extract into yolks before adding cream mixture.

ginger-turmeric frozen yogurt

makes about 1 quart

- 1 quart plain whole-milk yogurt
- 1 teaspoon unflavored gelatin
- 1½ teaspoons grated fresh ginger
- 1 teaspoon ground ginger
- 1 teaspoon ground turmeric
- ¾ cup sugar
- 3 tablespoons Lyle's Golden Syrup
- ⅛ teaspoon salt

why this recipe works Combinations of ginger and turmeric have been on the scene lately for their reported health benefits, most notably in the warm drink golden milk. But we love the two simply because they taste great. To showcase them in a dessert on the cold side, we incorporated fresh and ground ginger as well as ground turmeric into a tangy frozen yogurt—like a frozen lassi. The key to dense creaminess was controlling the water in the base so that the number of large ice crystals that formed during freezing was minimized. We strained excess liquid from the yogurt and dissolved and heated a teaspoon of gelatin in a portion of it to prevent water molecules from joining and forming large crystals. We swapped in a few tablespoons of Lyle's Golden Syrup for some of the granulated sugar; the syrup is 50 percent invert sugar whose molecules are better at depressing freezing point, so more water in the frozen yogurt stayed in the liquid state rather than crystallizing. We prefer richer-tasting Lyle's Golden Syrup, but you can substitute light corn syrup. If you're using a canister-style ice cream maker, be sure to freeze the empty canister for at least 24 hours and preferably 48 hours before churning. For self-refrigerating ice cream makers, pre-chill the canister by running the machine for 5 to 10 minutes before pouring in the yogurt.

1   Line colander or fine-mesh strainer with triple layer of cheesecloth and place over large bowl or measuring cup. Place yogurt in colander, cover with plastic wrap (plastic should not touch yogurt), and refrigerate until 1¼ cups whey has drained from yogurt, at least 8 hours or up to 12 hours. (If more than 1¼ cups whey drains from yogurt, stir extra back into yogurt.)

2   Discard ¾ cup drained whey. Sprinkle gelatin over remaining ½ cup whey in bowl and let sit until gelatin softens, about 5 minutes. Microwave until mixture is bubbling around edges and gelatin dissolves, about 30 seconds. Stir fresh ginger, ground ginger, and ground turmeric into mixture and let cool for 5 minutes. Strain mixture through fine-mesh strainer set over large bowl, pressing on solids to extract all liquid; discard solids. Whisk drained yogurt, sugar, syrup, and salt into cooled whey-gelatin mixture until sugar is completely dissolved. Cover and refrigerate until yogurt mixture registers 40 degrees or less, about 3 hours.

3   Churn yogurt mixture in ice cream maker until mixture resembles thick soft-serve frozen yogurt and registers about 21 degrees, about 20 minutes. Transfer frozen yogurt to airtight container and freeze until firm, about 2 hours. Serve. (Frozen yogurt can be stored in freezer for up to 5 days.)

chocolate chai masala truffles

makes 64 truffles

ganache

- 12 ounces bittersweet chocolate, coarsely chopped (2 cups)
- ½ cup heavy cream
- 2 chai tea bags
- 2 tablespoons light corn syrup
- ½ teaspoon vanilla extract
- Pinch salt
- 1½ tablespoons unsalted butter, cut into 8 pieces and softened

coating

- 1 cup (3 ounces) Dutch-processed cocoa powder
- ¼ cup (1 ounce) confectioners' sugar
- 1 teaspoon ground cinnamon

why this recipe works In the chocolate world, truffles are the ultimate indulgence, pleasing chocolate lovers not only with their wallop of cocoa flavor but with their creamy and silky-smooth texture. Intense hits of chocolate are good enough on their own, but chocolate is so multidimensional in flavor, we thought it would it taste even better when complemented with spice. We found that chai tea gave the chocolate a warm punch that enlivened the palate. We steeped chai tea bags in warm cream, and then stirred the cream into melted chocolate for a smooth consistency. Using corn syrup rather than sugar secured the perfect texture, and butter gave us a supersilky ganache. Gradually cooling the ganache before rolling the truffles staved off grainy sugar crystals, and rolling each truffle in confectioners' sugar, cocoa powder, and cinnamon gave our simple treats a professional finish and accentuated their warm-spice flavor. In step 5, running your knife under hot water and wiping it dry makes cutting the ganache easier. We prefer truffles made with 60 percent bittersweet chocolate; our favorite brands are Ghirardelli and Callebaut. If giving the truffles as a gift, set them in 1½-inch candy cup liners in a gift box and keep chilled.

---

1 **for the ganache** Lightly coat 8-inch square baking pan with vegetable oil spray. Make parchment paper sling by folding 2 long sheets of parchment so each is 8 inches wide. Lay sheets of parchment in pan perpendicular to each other, with extra parchment hanging over edges of pan. Push parchment into corners and up sides of pan, smoothing parchment flush to pan.

2 Microwave chocolate in bowl at 50 percent power, stirring occasionally, until mostly melted and few small chocolate pieces remain, 2 to 3 minutes; set aside. Microwave cream in 1-cup measuring cup until warm to touch, about 30 seconds. Add tea bags and let steep for 5 minutes. Remove tea bags and microwave cream for 20 seconds. Stir corn syrup, vanilla, and salt into cream and pour mixture over chocolate. Cover bowl with plastic wrap and set aside for 3 minutes, then stir with wooden spoon to combine. Stir in butter, one piece at a time, until fully incorporated.

3 Using rubber spatula, transfer ganache to prepared pan and let sit at room temperature for 2 hours. Cover pan and transfer to refrigerator; chill for at least 2 hours or up to 2 days.

4 **for the coating** Sift cocoa, sugar, and cinnamon through a fine-mesh strainer into large bowl. Sift again into large cake pan and set aside.

5 Using parchment overhang, lift ganache from pan. Cut ganache into sixty-four 1-inch squares (8 rows by 8 rows). (If ganache cracks during slicing, let it sit at room temperature for 5 to 10 minutes to soften and then proceed.) Dust hands lightly with cocoa mixture to prevent ganache from sticking and roll each square into ball. Transfer balls to cake pan with cocoa mixture and roll to evenly coat. Lightly shake truffles in hand over pan to remove excess coating.

6 Transfer coated truffles to airtight container and repeat with all ganache squares. Cover container and refrigerate until firm, about 2 hours.) Let truffles sit at room temperature until softened slightly, 5 to 10 minutes, before serving. (Truffles can be refrigerated for up to 1 week.)

mexican chocolate truffles

Omit chai tea bags. Add 1 teaspoon ground cinnamon and ⅛ teaspoon cayenne pepper to chocolate mixture before microwaving in step 2. Reduce cinnamon in coating to ¼ teaspoon.

nutritional information for our recipes

To calculate the nutritional values of our recipes per serving, we used Edamam. When using this program, we entered all the ingredients, using weights for important ingredients such as most vegetables. We also used our preferred brands in these analyses. When the recipe called for seasoning with an unspecified amount of salt and pepper, we added ½ teaspoon of salt and ¼ teaspoon of pepper to the analysis. We did not include additional salt or pepper for food that's "seasoned to taste." If there is a range in the serving size, we used the highest number of servings to calculate the nutritional values.

	Calories	Total Fat (G)	Sat Fat (G)	Chol (MG)	Sodium (MG)	Total Carbs (G)	Fiber (G)	Sugar (G)	Protein (G)
SEASON SMARTER									
› Fresh Herb Salt	0	0	0	0	320	0	0	0	0
› Chili-Lime Salt	3	0	0	0	173	0	0	0	0
› Cumin-Sesame Salt	1	0	0	0	80	0	0	0	0
› Smoked Salt	0	0	0	0	320	0	0	0	0
› Sriracha Salt	0	0	0	0	361	0	0	0	0
Radish Baguette with Chive Butter and Salt	161	11	6	25	269	14	1	2	3
Wedge Salad with Creamy Black Pepper Dressing	280	27	6	22	227	7	2	4	5
Grilled Chicken Salad	603	40	10	169	788	7	2	3	53
Pan-Seared Steaks with Brandy–Pink Peppercorn Sauce	723	55	24	171	181	6	1	2	44
Seared Duck Breasts with Green Peppercorn Sauce	386	19	9	174	222	11	1	6	37
Peppercorn-Crusted Beef Tenderloin with Hollandaise Sauce	655	53	25	288	557	4	0	1	45
White Peppercorn–Crusted Beef Tenderloin with Hollandaise Sauce	669	53	25	288	482	4	1	1	45
Pink Peppercorn–Crusted Beef Tenderloin with Lime Hollandaise Sauce	666	53	25	288	483	4	1	1	45
Green Peppercorn–Crusted Beef Tenderloin with Sun-Dried Tomato Hollandaise Sauce	673	54	25	288	492	5	1	1	45
Thick-Cut Pork Chops with Smoked Salt	664	41	8	197	670	0	0	0	69
Pan-Roasted Fish Fillets with Herb Salt	173	5	0	73	302	1	0	1	30
Spaghetti with Pecorino Romano and Black Pepper	242	14	7	44	596	16	1	2	14
Grill-Roasted Pork Loin	341	20	6	112	453	2	0	0	39
Pan-Seared Salmon with Cilantro-Mint Chutney	606	42	8	125	638	7	2	2	49
Crispy Salt and Pepper Shrimp	312	22	2	143	784	11	0	2	16
Grilled Brined Carrots with Cilantro-Yogurt Sauce	157	7	2	5	523	20	6	10	7
Grilled Brined Asparagus with Cilantro-Yogurt Sauce	133	7	2	5	667	12	6	6	10

	Calories	Total Fat (G)	Sat Fat (G)	Chol (MG)	Sodium (MG)	Total Carbs (G)	Fiber (G)	Sugar (G)	Protein (G)
SEASON SMARTER (cont.)									
Grilled Brined Zucchini with Cilantro-Yogurt Sauce	113	7	2	5	481	8	3	6	7
Crispy-Skinned Chicken Breasts with Lemon-Rosemary Pan Sauce	724	47	13	199	472	10	1	4	62
Salt-Baked Whole Branzino	292	6	1	116	397	1	0	0	55
Salt-Crusted Fingerling Potatoes	116	0	0	0	352	26	3	1	3
Smashed Cucumber Salad (Pai Huang Gua)	61	3	0	0	488	9	1	4	2
Preserved Lemons	4	0	0	0	320	1	0	0	0
GIVE IT A RUB									
〉 Classic Steak Rub	5	0	0	0	1	1	0	0	0
〉 Herbes de Provence	3	0	0	0	1	0	0	0	0
〉 Barbecue Rub	8	0	0	0	29	2	0	1	0
〉 Cajun-Style Rub	3	0	0	0	201	1	0	0	0
〉 Five-Spice Powder	7	0	0	0	1	1	1	0	0
〉 Jerk Rub	8	0	0	0	1	2	0	1	0
〉 Southwestern Rub	8	0	0	0	30	1	1	0	0
Spice-Rubbed Pan-Seared Salmon	380	25	5	94	104	3	1	0	35
Spice-Rubbed Roasted Chicken Parts	916	70	16	255	791	4	2	0	64
Spice-Rubbed Steaks	351	24	9	118	363	2	1	0	30
Spice-Rubbed Roasted Pork Loin	331	16	3	121	412	3	1	0	41
Cumin-Coriander Rubbed Cornish Game Hens	853	60	17	553	1346	0	0	0	81
Oregano-Anise Rubbed Cornish Game Hens	853	60	27	553	1123	0	0	0	81
Peri Peri Grilled Chicken	856	61	16	255	883	8	2	3	66
Latin-Style Fried Chicken	1588	119	20	255	1196	55	2	1	70
Barbecue Roast Chicken with Potatoes	867	49	13	333	1192	32	4	3	74
Ras el Hanout Roast Chicken with Carrots	801	50	13	333	1270	17	5	8	72
Five-Spice Roast Chicken with Turnips	786	49	13	333	1283	13	4	7	72
Herbes de Provence Roast Chicken with Fennel	792	50	13	333	1243	15	7	7	72
Spice-Crusted Rib-Eye Steaks	614	49	20	154	544	1	1	0	42
Coffee-Chipotle Top Sirloin Roast	465	33	11	149	504	1	0	0	38
Herbes de Provence–Rubbed Pork Tenderloin with Vegetables	432	19	3	111	373	27	13	9	42
South Carolina Pulled Pork	489	29	10	141	625	13	1	11	41
Oven-Roasted Jerk Pork Ribs	1106	89	26	272	928	20	2	14	54
Anise-Rubbed Rack of Lamb with Sweet Mint-Almond Relish	917	84	32	158	778	6	1	4	32
Blackened Snapper with Rémoulade	441	32	4	74	682	2	1	1	35
Juniper and Fennel–Rubbed Roast Side of Salmon with Orange Beurre Blanc	459	36	15	117	277	3	1	2	28
Popcorn Shrimp	847	52	4	332	965	53	3	0	41

	Calories	Total Fat (G)	Sat Fat (G)	Chol (MG)	Sodium (MG)	Total Carbs (G)	Fiber (G)	Sugar (G)	Protein (G)
GIVE IT A RUB (cont.)									
Thick-Cut Steakhouse Oven Fries	292	11	1	0	250	46	5	2	5
Spice-Roasted Butternut Squash with Honey-Lemon Butter	314	17	4	15	741	44	7	12	3
Spice-Roasted Butternut Squash with Honey-Lime Butter	315	17	5	15	742	45	7	12	4
Spice-Roasted Butternut Squash with Honey-Orange Butter	314	17	4	15	741	44	7	12	3
Black Pepper Candied Bacon	261	23	8	37	377	7	0	6	7
Five-Spice and Sesame Candied Bacon	279	23	8	37	376	10	0	9	7
Chipotle Candied Bacon	270	23	8	37	382	9	0	9	7
Cinnamon-Ginger Spiced Nuts	317	23	2	0	144	24	6	15	10
Chili-Lime Spiced Nuts	317	23	2	0	148	23	6	15	10
Orange-Cardamom Spiced Nuts	318	23	2	0	148	24	6	15	10
TOAST AND BLOOM									
Everyday Chili Powder	2	0	0	0	1	0	0	0	0
Smoky Cocoa Chili Powder	4	0	0	0	7	1	0	0	0
Ras el Hanout	7	0	0	0	7	1	1	0	0
Garam Masala	6	0	0	0	1	1	1	0	0
Mild Curry Powder	7	0	0	0	1	1	0	0	0
Vindaloo Curry Powder	10	0	0	0	2	2	1	1	0
Vadouvan Curry Powder	5	0	0	0	1	1	0	0	0
Thai Panang Curry Paste	7	0	0	0	6	2	0	1	0
Black Bean Chili	297	7	1	0	138	46	12	7	16
Best Ground Beef Chili	308	17	6	62	450	18	5	3	21
Tex-Mex Cheese Enchiladas	526	35	14	65	640	33	4	3	22
Crispy Spiced Ground Beef Tacos	589	40	8	70	559	37	5	3	25
Roast Butterflied Leg of Lamb with Coriander, Fennel, and Black Pepper	551	39	15	154	454	6	2	2	43
Lamb Vindaloo	714	55	21	159	799	14	2	6	40
Thai Panang Curry with Shrimp	548	38	20	255	980	13	4	3	42
Classic Vegetable Curry with Potatoes and Cauliflower	454	16	5	0	685	66	18	18	18
Vindaloo Vegetable Curry with Okra and Tomatoes	534	14	1	0	581	84	21	21	25
Vadouvan Vegetable Curry with Sweet Potatoes and Green Beans	393	12	1	0	698	63	16	19	15
Panang Vegetable Curry with Eggplant and Red Bell Peppers	392	15	5	0	667	55	18	19	15
Hungarian Beef Stew	561	32	12	152	624	25	6	11	47
Spanish Shellfish Stew	563	22	3	178	797	24	5	6	53
Chicken Tagine with Fennel, Chickpeas, and Apricots	764	39	10	257	448	44	9	13	59
Tandoori Chicken with Raita	887	62	18	271	1148	10	1	6	68
Pomegranate-Braised Beef Short Ribs with Prunes and Sesame	714	5	1	0	264	31	1	17	40
Rigatoni with Spiced Beef Ragu	714	33	13	112	336	63	4	5	39

	Calories	Total Fat (G)	Sat Fat (G)	Chol (MG)	Sodium (MG)	Total Carbs (G)	Fiber (G)	Sugar (G)	Protein (G)
TOAST AND BLOOM (cont.)									
Sichuan Braised Tofu with Beef	394	28	5	28	395	16	3	5	22
Sautéed Radishes with Vadouvan Curry and Almonds	84	7	4	15	191	5	2	2	1
Shakshuka	325	22	6	333	912	18	4	9	16
FINISH WITH FLAIR									
⟩ Za'atar	8	0	0	0	0	1	1	0	0
⟩ Advieh	1	0	0	0	2	0	0	0	0
⟩ Pistachio Dukkah	15	1	0	0	7	1	0	0	1
⟩ Hazelnut-Nigella Dukkah	12	1	0	0	6	1	0	0	0
⟩ Shichimi Togarashi	5	0	0	0	0	1	0	0	0
⟩ Furikake	8	1	0	0	4	1	0	0	0
⟩ Everything Bagel Blend	9	1	0	0	80	1	0	0	0
Homemade Yogurt Cheese with Hazelnut-Nigella Dukkah	46	3	1	8	32	3	0	3	2
Parmesan–Black Pepper Popcorn	111	9	4	14	50	6	1	0	2
Hot-and-Sweet Popcorn	111	8	3	11	6	9	1	3	1
Spiced Roasted Chickpeas	424	13	2	0	72	61	12	11	20
Barbecue-Spiced Roasted Chickpeas	423	12	2	0	72	61	12	11	19
Spanish-Spiced Roasted Chickpeas	418	13	2	0	71	60	12	10	19
Smoky Shishito Peppers with Espelette and Lime	75	7	0	0	167	4	1	1	1
Shishito Peppers with Fennel Pollen, Aleppo, and Lemon	77	7	1	0	151	3	1	1	1
Shishito Peppers with Mint, Poppy Seeds, and Orange	77	7	1	0	167	3	1	1	1
Shishito Peppers with Mustard and Bonito Flakes	76	7	0	0	168	3	1	1	1
Blue Cheese Log with Pistachio Dukkah and Honey	155	13	7	33	223	6	1	4	5
Cheddar Cheese Log with Everything Bagel Blend	182	17	8	39	351	2	1	1	6
Goat Cheese Log with Hazelnut-Nigella Dukkah	148	14	6	27	149	2	1	1	5
Feta Cheese Log with Advieh and Olive Oil	182	18	7	35	189	2	0	1	3
Fluke Crudo with Furikake	74	5	1	26	316	0	0	0	7
Soba Noodles with Pork, Scallions, and Shichimi Togarashi	394	12	2	74	1132	38	3	3	33
Sautéed Spinach with Yogurt and Pistachio Dukkah	189	15	3	4	146	10	4	3	7
Roasted Fennel with Rye Crumble	184	13	8	34	265	13	3	4	4
⟩ Cider-Caraway Vinaigrette	104	11	1	0	40	1	0	1	0
⟩ Chermoula	64	7	1	0	31	1	0	0	0
⟩ Za'atar Yogurt Sauce	11	1	0	2	7	1	0	1	1
⟩ Wasabi Mayonnaise	106	11	2	6	120	0	0	0	0
⟩ Saffron Aïoli	98	11	1	18	32	0	0	0	0
⟩ Creamy Cajun-Spiced Dip	35	3	1	3	62	0	0	0	1

	Calories	Total Fat (G)	Sat Fat (G)	Chol (MG)	Sodium (MG)	Total Carbs (G)	Fiber (G)	Sugar (G)	Protein (G)
FINISH WITH FLAIR (cont.)									
Fattoush	213	17	2	0	174	16	3	4	3
Wasabi Tuna Salad	470	37	6	62	851	3	1	2	26
Polenta Fries with Saffron Aïoli	678	60	8	23	336	31	2	1	3
Crispy Pan-Fried Chicken Cutlets with Garlic-Curry Sauce	743	51	6	214	346	25	1	4	45
Pan-Seared Flank Steak with Sage-Shallot Compound Butter	308	22	9	97	322	3	0	1	24
Pan-Roasted Pork Tenderloin with Cider-Caraway Vinaigrette	295	21	3	74	113	1	0	1	23
Grilled Lamb Kofte with Za'atar Yogurt Sauce	442	36	13	88	447	7	2	3	23
Crab Cakes with Cajun-Spiced Dip	516	40	6	206	889	11	1	2	26
Grilled Eggplant with Chermoula	329	32	4	0	86	12	5	6	2
LET IT STEEP									
❯ Rosemary Oil	117	14	2	0	0	0	0	0	0
❯ Fennel Oil	121	14	2	0	1	1	0	0	0
❯ Chipotle-Coriander Oil	126	14	1	0	0	1	0	0	0
❯ Sichuan Chile Oil	96	10	1	0	77	2	1	0	1
❯ Harissa	100	11	2	0	37	2	1	0	1
Bruschetta with Ricotta, Roasted Red Peppers, and Rosemary Oil	209	10	4	18	292	22	1	3	8
Marinated Green and Black Olives	89	9	1	0	345	3	1	1	1
Marinated Cauliflower and Chickpeas with Saffron	195	11	2	0	24	20	4	5	6
One-Pan Chicken with Couscous, Carrots, and Harissa	815	37	10	256	193	63	10	10	61
Grilled Shrimp Skewers with Sichuan Chili Oil and Napa Cabbage Slaw	485	30	3	214	2139	25	8	7	32
Grilled Shrimp Skewers with Harissa and Carrot Salad	490	30	4	214	1122	31	8	16	27
Grilled Shrimp Skewers with Fennel Oil and Zucchini Ribbon Salad	534	39	7	224	1179	18	3	12	32
Grilled Shrimp Skewers with Chipotle-Coriander Oil and Avocado-Grapefruit Salad	676	48	6	214	1196	39	11	20	29
❯ Chipotle Ketchup	38	1	0	0	165	7	2	5	1
❯ Dijon Mustard	22	1	0	0	41	1	0	0	1
Southwestern Burger with Chipotle Ketchup	1053	66	29	282	683	53	6	10	62
Wisconsin Brats and Beer	546	29	8	56	1167	48	3	4	18
❯ Hot Pepper Vinegar	5	0	0	0	37	1	0	1	0
❯ Quick Pickle Chips	7	0	0	0	86	2	0	2	0
Chicken Salad with Pickled Fennel, Watercress, and Macadamia Nuts	364	24	5	73	572	13	3	10	26
Quick Collard Greens with Hot Pepper Vinegar	146	9	3	13	185	11	8	1	8
Flank Steak Tacos with Cumin Corn Relish	355	15	4	77	177	28	3	4	27
Seared Scallops with Mango Chutney and Mint	291	12	1	41	671	25	2	16	22

	Calories	Total Fat (G)	Sat Fat (G)	Chol (MG)	Sodium (MG)	Total Carbs (G)	Fiber (G)	Sugar (G)	Protein (G)
GO BEYOND VANILLA									
› Vanilla Sugar	17	0	0	0	0	4	0	4	0
› Strawberry–Black Pepper Sugar	14	0	0	0	0	4	0	3	0
› Pumpkin Pie Spice	3	0	0	0	0	1	0	0	0
› Vanilla Extract	7	0	0	0	0	0	0	0	0
› Rose Water	2	0	0	0	1	0	0	0	0
Blueberry Streusel Muffins	349	11	7	42	240	57	2	28	5
Pumpkin Spice Muffins	400	13	8	58	246	67	2	39	5
Vanilla Sugar Doughnuts	307	19	4	32	86	30	1	12	4
Rose Water–Glazed Doughnuts	342	20	4	33	88	39	1	20	4
Pumpkin Spice Sugar Doughnuts	307	19	4	32	86	30	1	12	4
Strawberry–Black Pepper Sugar Doughnuts	363	20	4	33	88	44	1	25	4
St. Lucia Buns	191	6	3	33	141	31	1	7	5
Spiced Granola with Walnuts and Dried Apple	213	10	1	0	75	30	3	13	4
Tropical Granola with Dried Mango and Ginger	247	22	6	0	70	13	3	10	2
Southern Cheese Straws	52	4	2	10	35	3	0	0	2
Parmesan–Black Pepper Cheese Straws	57	4	2	10	59	4	0	0	2
Everything Bagel Bread	108	1	0	10	146	23	1	4	3
Za'atar Finger Bread	299	18	3	0	209	31	2	1	4
Molasses Spice Cookies	161	6	4	21	82	25	1	15	2
Anise Biscotti	110	5	1	15	50	14	1	7	3
Pistachio Baklava with Cardamom and Rose Water	166	6	1	0	70	24	1	10	3
Lavender Tea Cakes	235	9	5	47	152	38	0	30	2
Gingerbread Layer Cake	538	30	12	78	286	67	1	50	4
Pink Peppercorn–Pomegranate Panna Cotta	410	30	18	109	346	33	4	28	4
Crème Brûlée	567	49	29	382	104	28	0	27	6
Orange Blossom Crème Brûlée	570	49	29	382	104	27	0	27	6
Tea-Infused Crème Brûlée	569	49	29	382	104	28	0	27	6
Ginger-Turmeric Frozen Yogurt	169	4	3	16	94	29	0	29	5
Chocolate Chai Masala Truffles	103	6	4	7	16	14	4	9	2
Mexican Chocolate Truffles	84	5	3	7	14	11	2	8	1

conversions and equivalents

Some say cooking is a science and an art. We would say geography has a hand in it, too. Flours and sugars manufactured in the United Kingdom and elsewhere will feel and taste different from those manufactured in the United States. So we cannot promise that a loaf of bread you bake in Canada or England will taste the same as a loaf baked in the States, but we can offer guidelines for converting weights and measures. We also recommend that you rely on your instincts when making our recipes. Refer to the visual cues provided. If the dough hasn't come together as described, you may need to add more flour—even if the recipe doesn't tell you to. You be the judge.

The recipes in this book were developed using standard U.S. measures following U.S. government guidelines. The charts below offer equivalents for U.S. and metric measures. All conversions are approximate and have been rounded up or down to the nearest whole number.

example

1 teaspoon = 4.9292 milliliters, rounded up to 5 milliliters
1 ounce = 28.3495 grams, rounded down to 28 grams

volume conversions

U.S.	METRIC
1 teaspoon	5 milliliters
2 teaspoons	10 milliliters
1 tablespoon	15 milliliters
2 tablespoons	30 milliliters
¼ cup	59 milliliters
⅓ cup	79 milliliters
½ cup	118 milliliters
¾ cup	177 milliliters
1 cup	237 milliliters
1¼ cups	296 milliliters
1½ cups	355 milliliters
2 cups (1 pint)	473 milliliters
2½ cups	591 milliliters
3 cups	710 milliliters
4 cups (1 quart)	0.946 liter
1.06 quarts	1 liter
4 quarts (1 gallon)	3.8 liters

weight conversions

OUNCES	GRAMS
½	14
¾	21
1	28
1½	43
2	57
2½	71
3	85
3½	99
4	113
4½	128
5	142
6	170
7	198
8	227
9	255
10	283
12	340
16 (1 pound)	454

conversions for common baking ingredients

Because measuring by weight is far more accurate than measuring by volume, and thus more likely to produce reliable results, in our recipes we provide ounce measures in addition to cup measures for many ingredients. Refer to the chart below to convert these measures into grams.

INGREDIENT	OUNCES	GRAMS
Flour		
1 cup all-purpose flour*	5	142
1 cup cake flour	4	113
1 cup whole-wheat flour	5½	156
Sugar		
1 cup granulated (white) sugar	7	198
1 cup packed brown sugar (light or dark)	7	198
1 cup confectioners' sugar	4	113
Cocoa Powder		
1 cup cocoa powder	3	85
Butter†		
4 tablespoons (½ stick or ¼ cup)	2	57
8 tablespoons (1 stick or ½ cup)	4	113
16 tablespoons (2 sticks or 1 cup)	8	227

* U.S. all-purpose flour, the most frequently used flour in this book, does not contain leaveners, as some European flours do. These leavened flours are called self-rising or self-raising. If you are using self-rising flour, take this into consideration before adding leaveners to a recipe.

† In the United States, butter is sold both salted and unsalted. We recommend unsalted butter. If you are using salted butter, take this into consideration before adding salt to a recipe.

oven temperature

FAHRENHEIT	CELSIUS	GAS MARK
225	105	¼
250	120	½
275	135	1
300	150	2
325	165	3
350	180	4
375	190	5
400	200	6
425	220	7
450	230	8
475	245	9

converting temperatures from an instant-read thermometer

We include doneness temperatures in many of the recipes in this book. We recommend an instant-read thermometer for the job. Refer to the table above to convert Fahrenheit degrees to Celsius. Or, for temperatures not represented in the chart, use this simple formula:

Subtract 32 degrees from the Fahrenheit reading, then divide the result by 1.8 to find the Celsius reading.

example
"Flip chicken, brush with remaining glaze, and cook until breast registers 160 degrees, 1 to 3 minutes."

to convert
160°F − 32 = 128°
128° ÷ 1.8 = 71.11°C, rounded down to 71°C

taking the temperature of meat and poultry

Since the temperature of beef and pork will continue to rise as the meat rests—an effect called carryover cooking—they should be removed from the oven, grill, or pan when they are 5 to 10 degrees below the desired serving temperature. Carryover cooking doesn't apply to poultry (it lacks the dense muscle structure of beef and pork and doesn't retain heat as well), so it should be cooked to the desired serving temperature. The following temperatures should be used to determine when to stop the cooking process.

INGREDIENT	TEMPERATURE
beef/lamb	
rare	115 to 120 degrees (120 to 125 degrees after resting)
medium-rare	120 to 125 degrees (125 to 130 degrees after resting)
medium	130 to 135 degrees (135 to 140 degrees after resting)
medium–well	140 to 145 degrees (145 to 150 degrees after resting)
well–done	150 to 155 degrees (155 to 160 degrees after resting)
pork	
chops and tenderloin	145 degrees (150 degrees after resting)
loin roasts	140 degrees (145 degrees after resting)
chicken	
white meat	160 degrees
dark meat	175 degrees

index

Note: Page number in *italics* indicate photographs. <u>Underlined</u> page numbers indicate recipe where spice blend is featured.

J

Jerk Rub, 74, *74*, <u>94</u>
Juniper (berries)
about, 14
and Fennel–Rubbed Roast Side of Salmon with Orange
Beurre Blanc, 100–101, *101*

K

Ketchup, Chipotle, 216, *216*, <u>218</u>
Kofte, Grilled Lamb, with Za'atar Yogurt Sauce, *194*, 195

L

Lamb
Kofte, Grilled, with Za'atar Yogurt Sauce, *194*, 195
Rack of, Anise-Rubbed, with Sweet Mint-Almond
Relish, 96, *97*
rack of, trimming and frenching, 97
Roast Butterflied Leg of, with Coriander, Fennel,
and Black Pepper, 128–29, *129*
salting, before cooking, 57
Vindaloo, 130, *131*
Latin-Style Fried Chicken, *82*, 83
Lavender
about, 14
Tea Cakes, 260, *261*
Lemon grass
Thai Panang Curry Paste, 119, *119*, <u>133</u>, <u>135</u>
Lemon(s)
Chermoula, *179*, 180, <u>198</u>
-Honey Butter, Spice-Roasted Butternut Squash with, 106
Preserved, 68–69, *69*
-Rosemary Pan Sauce, Crispy-Skinned Chicken Breasts
with, 58–59, *60*
Saffron Aïoli, *179*, 181, <u>186</u>
Za'atar Yogurt Sauce, *179*, 180, <u>195</u>
Lime
-Chili Salt, 24, *25*
-Chili Spiced Nuts, 110
-Cilantro Hollandaise Sauce, Pink Peppercorn–Crusted
Beef Tenderloin with, 39
-Honey Butter, Spice-Roasted Butternut Squash with,
106, *107*
Latin-Style Fried Chicken, *82*, 83
Liquid smoke
Smoked Salt, 24, *25*, <u>41</u>
Liquid spices. *See* Spice extracts

M

Macadamia Nuts
Pickled Fennel, and Watercress, Chicken Salad with,
224, *225*
Tropical Granola with Dried Mango and Ginger, 247
Makrut lime leaves
Thai Panang Curry Paste, 119, *119*, <u>133</u>, <u>135</u>
Maldon sea salt, 22, *22*
Mango
Chutney and Mint, Seared Scallops with, 230, *231*
Dried, and Ginger, Tropical Granola with, 247
Marinated Cauliflower and Chickpeas with Saffron,
210, *211*
Marinated Green and Black Olives, *208*, 209
Marjoram
Herbes de Provence, 73, *73*, <u>85</u>, <u>91</u>
Mayonnaise
Creamy Cajun-Spiced Dip, *179*, 181, <u>196</u>
Saffron Aïoli, *179*, 181, <u>186</u>
Wasabi, *179*, 180, <u>185</u>
Meat. *See* Beef; Lamb; Pork
Mexican Chocolate Truffles, 271
Mild Curry Powder, 118, *118*, <u>134</u>, <u>189</u>
Mint
-Almond Relish, Sweet, Anise-Rubbed Rack of Lamb
with, 96, *97*
-Cilantro Chutney, Pan-Seared Salmon with, *50*, 51
dried, sprinkling over finished dishes, 159
and Mango Chutney, Seared Scallops with, 230, *231*
Poppy Seeds, and Orange, Shishito Peppers with, 167
Molasses Spice Cookies, 254, *255*
Mortar and pestle, 19
Muffins
Blueberry Streusel, 238, *239*
Pumpkin Spice, *240*, 241
Mushrooms
Black Bean Chili, *120*, 121
Soba Noodles with Pork, Scallions, and Shichimi
Togarashi, 172, *173*
Mustard
about, 14
and Bonito Flakes, Shishito Peppers with, 167
Creamy Cajun-Spiced Dip, *179*, 181, <u>196</u>
Jerk Rub, 74, *74*, <u>94</u>
Saffron Aïoli, *179*, 181, <u>186</u>
South Carolina Pulled Pork, 92–93, *93*
Mustard seeds
Chipotle Ketchup, 216, *216*, <u>218</u>
Dijon Mustard, 217, *217*, <u>220</u>
Mild Curry Powder, 118, *118*, <u>134</u>, <u>189</u>
Quick Pickle Chips, *222*, 223
Vadouvan Curry Powder, 118, *118*, <u>135</u>, <u>150</u>

R

Radish Baguette with Chive Butter and Salt, *28*, 29
Radishes, Sautéed, with Vadouvan Curry and Almonds, 150, *151*
Raita, Tandoori Chicken with, *142*, 143
Ras el Hanout, <u>85</u>, 117, *117*, <u>144</u>
Ras el Hanout Roast Chicken with Carrots, 85
Rasp grater, 19
Red pepper flakes
    about, 16
    Classic Steak Rub, 73, *73*, <u>105</u>
    Southwestern Rub, 75, *75*
Relish, Cumin and Corn, Flank Steak Tacos with, *228*, 229
Relish, Sweet Mint-Almond, Anise-Rubbed Rack of Lamb with, 96, *97*
Rémoulade, Blackened Snapper with, *98*, 99
Ricotta, Roasted Red Peppers, and Rosemary Oil, Bruschetta with, *206*, 207
Rigatoni with Spiced Beef Ragu, *146*, 147
Roast Butterflied Leg of Lamb with Coriander, Fennel, and Black Pepper, 128–29, *129*
Roasted Fennel with Rye Crumble, 176, *177*
Roots and rhizomes, about, 3
Rose buds
    about, 16
    Advieh, 156, *157*, <u>169</u>
    Rose Water, *235*, 237, <u>243</u>, <u>258</u>
Rosemary
    Herbes de Provence, 73, *73*, <u>85</u>, <u>91</u>
    -Lemon Pan Sauce, Crispy-Skinned Chicken Breasts with, 58–59, *60*
    Oil, *203*, 204, <u>207</u>
    Spice-Crusted Rib-Eye Steaks, 86, *87*
Rubs. *See* Spice Rubs
Rye Crumble, Roasted Fennel with, 176, *177*

S

Saffron
    about, 16
    Aïoli, *179*, 181, <u>186</u>
    Marinated Cauliflower and Chickpeas with, 210, *211*
    St. Lucia Buns, 244–45, *245*
    test kitchen favorite, 16
Sage-Shallot Compound Butter, Pan-Seared Flank Steak with, *190*, 191
Salads
    Avocado-Grapefruit, and Chipotle-Coriander Oil, Grilled Shrimp Skewers with, 215
    Carrot, and Harissa, Grilled Shrimp Skewers with, 215

Salads *(cont.)*
    Chicken, with Pickled Fennel, Watercress, and Macadamia Nuts, 224, *225*
    Fattoush, *182*, 183
    Grilled Chicken, 32, *33*
    Smashed Cucumber (Pai Huang Gua), 66, *67*
    Wasabi Tuna, *184*, 185
    Wedge, with Creamy Black Pepper Dressing, 30, *31*
    Zucchini Ribbon, and Fennel Oil, Grilled Shrimp Skewers with, 215
Salmon
    Juniper and Fennel–Rubbed Roast Side of, with Orange Beurre Blanc, 100–101, *101*
    Pan-Seared, with Cilantro-Mint Chutney, *50*, 51
    Spice-Rubbed Pan-Seared, 76
Salt
    about, 3, 16–17
    applying to foods, 56–57
    -Baked Whole Branzino, *61*, 62–63
    for brines, 46–47
    -Crusted Fingerling Potatoes, *64*, 65
    kosher, about, 16
    measuring conversions, 16
    and Pepper Shrimp, Crispy, 52–53, *53*
    sea, about, 17
    table (common), about, 16
    see also Finishing salts; Flavored salts
Salt storage containers, 18
Sandwiches and burgers
    Radish Baguette with Chive Butter and Salt, *28*, 29
    Southwestern Burgers with Chipotle Ketchup, 218, *219*
Sandwich starters. *See* Ketchup; Mustard
Sauces
    Chermoula, *179*, 180, <u>198</u>
    Cider-Caraway Vinaigrette, 178, *179*, <u>192</u>
    Creamy Cajun-Spiced Dip, *179*, 181, <u>196</u>
    Saffron Aïoli, *179*, 181, <u>186</u>
    Wasabi Mayonnaise, *179*, 180, <u>185</u>
    Za'atar Yogurt, *179*, 180, <u>195</u>
Sausages. *See* Brats
Sautéed Radishes with Vadouvan Curry and Almonds, 150, *151*
Sautéed Spinach with Yogurt and Pistachio Dukkah, *174*, 175
Scallions
    Pork, and Shichimi Togarashi, Soba Noodles with, 172, *173*
    Sichuan Braised Tofu with Beef, *148*, 149
Scallops
    Seared, with Mango Chutney and Mint, 230, *231*
    Spanish Shellfish Stew, 138–39, *139*
Seared Duck Breasts with Green Peppercorn Sauce, *36*, 37
Seared Scallops with Mango Chutney and Mint, 230, *231*